Anu Gītā Explained

Analysis and Application

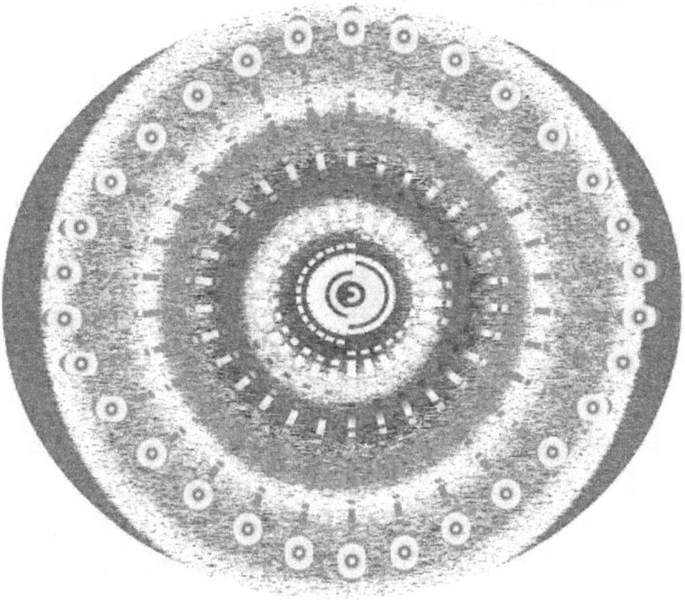

Michael Beloved

(Madhvācārya dās)

Original Sanskrit verse
–Electronic text Bhandarkar Oriental Research Institute (John Smith)
Devanagari script: Sanskrit 2003 Font
Transliteration: URW Palladio ITU font/ ITranslator
Word-for-Word typeset: Michael Beloved
Proof-reading Editors: Marcia Beloved, Dear Beloved
Shiva Art: Sir Paul Castagna
Illustrations: Author

Correspondence:
Michael Beloved
3703 Foster Ave
Brooklyn NY 11203
USA

Paul Castagna
204 N. Sophie St.
Bessemer MI 49911
USA

Email: axisnexus@gmail.com

ISBN:
978-0-9833817-9-2
LCCN:
2011914434

Sanskrit Text

ENGLISH

Transliteration Word-for-Word Meaning

TRANSLATION

Analysis

Application

Table of Contents

Scheme of Pronunciation

Consonants

Gutturals:	क	ख	ग	घ	ङ
	ka	kha	ga	gha	ṅa
Palatals:	च	छ	ज	झ	ञ
	ca	cha	ja	jha	ña
Cerebrals:	ट	ठ	ड	ढ	ण
	ṭa	ṭha	ḍa	ḍha	ṇa
Dentals:	त	थ	द	ध	न
	ta	tha	da	dha	na
Labials:	प	फ	ब	भ	म
	pa	pha	ba	bha	ma

Semivowels:

य	र	ल	व
ya	ra	la	va

Numbers:

०	१	२	३	४	५	६	७	८	९
0	1	2	3	4	5	6	7	8	9

Sibilants:	श	ष	स
	śa	ṣa	sa

Aspirate:	ह
	ha

Vowels:

अ	आ	इ	ई	उ	ऊ	ऋ	ॠ
a	ā	i	ī	u	ū	ṛ	ṝ
ए	औ	ओ	औ	ळ	ॡ	ं	ः
e	ai	o	au	lṛ	lṝ	ṁ	ḥ

Apostrophe ऽ

How to use this book:

Make a casual reading page for page without becoming stressed about the concepts and ideas. Read to become familiar with the language style and presentation. If you read something of particular interest make a mental note of it and read on to get through the entire book.

Make a second reading pausing at areas of interest, where you feel you can grasp the material. Here and there, you may not follow the meanings but read on nevertheless.

Make a third reading with intent to grasp the concepts and methods given.

Finally, make an indepth study of this information.

A note on the diacritical marks and pronounciation:

A name like Krishna is accepted in common English usage. Its English spelling has no diacritical marks.

Sanskrit letters with a ***dot*** *under them, should be pronounced while the tongue touches and is released curling slightly at the top of palate.*

The **s** *sound for* **ś** *carries an* **h** *with it and is said as the* **sh** *sound in* ***she****.*

The **s** *sound for* **ṣ** *carries an* **h** *with it and is said as the* **sh** *sound in* ***shun****.*

The **h** *sound for* **ḥ** *carries an echoing sound of the vowel before it, such that* ***oḥ*** *is actually* ***oho*** *and* ***aḥ*** *is actually* ***aha****.*

In many Sanskrit words the ***y*** *sound is said as an* ***i*** *sound, especially when the* ***y*** *sound preceeds an* ***ā****. For instance,* ***prāṇāyāma*** *should be* ***praa-nai-aa-muh****, rather than* ***praa-naa-yaa-muh****.*

The ***a*** *sound is more like* ***uh*** *in English, while the* ***ā*** *sound is like the* ***a*** *sound in* ***far****.*

The ***ṛ*** *sound is like the* ***ri*** *sound in* ***ridge****.*

The ***ph*** *sound is never reduced to an* ***f*** *sound as in English. The* ***p*** *sound is maintained.*

Whenever ***h*** *occurs after a consonant, its integrity is maintained as an air forced sound.*

If the ***h*** *sound occurs after a vowel and a consonant, one should let the consonant remain with the vowel which preceeds it and allow the* ***h*** *sound to carry with the vowel after it, such that Duryodhana is pronounced with the* ***d*** *consonant allied to the* ***o*** *before it and the* ***h*** *sound manages the* ***a*** *after it. Say* ***Dur-yod-ha-na*** *or* ***Dur-yod-han****. Do not say* ***Dur-yo-dha-na****. Separate the* ***d*** *and* ***h*** *sounds to make them distinct. In words where you have no choice and must combine the* ***d*** *and* ***h*** *sound, as in the word* ***dharma****. Make sure that the* ***h*** *sound is heard as an air sound pushed out from the throat. Dharma should never be mistaken for darma. But* ***adharma*** *should be* ***ad-har-ma****.*

The ***c*** *sound is* ***ch****, and the* ***ch*** *sound is* ***ch-h****.*

Introduction

Anu Gītā is extracted from the *Mahābhārata*. It is in the 14th Part which is Ashvamedha parva, beginning from chapter 16 through 19. Its importance springs mainly from the fact that Krishna declined to show Arjuna the Universal Form. In the *Bhagavad Gītā,* Arjuna requested the vision of the Universal Form. It was granted without hesitation. In fact it was granted so rapidly that Arjuna did not see it until he told Krishna that he would require the supernatural vision to perceive it.

The *Anu Gītā* is striking because the same Arjuna, the same friend of Krishna, asked in friendship again, that Krishna should reveal everything which was explained in the *Gītā,* since Arjuna admitted that he lost touch with that profound discourse. Krishna declined the request and instead repeated a discourse which was told to him by an ascetic from the celestial world.

The only way to deal with this issue is to read this discourse. If you read the *Bhagavad Gītā* and if you think you know what was essential to Krishna, then read this *Anu Gītā* and compare your insight about Krishna.

There is an analysis and application to each verse. These were inspired into the mind of the writer by Rishi Singh Gherwal* who is deceased. That information is vital to any advanced yogi, regarding how to know and transcend the course of transmigrations.

Published in service to my teachers, Rishi Singh Gherwal and Authur Beverford, who are both deceased

Chapter 1

Arjuna Forgot

the Bhagavad Gītā Experience*

yattu tadbhavatā proktaṁ tadā keśava sauhṛdāt
tatsarvaṁ puruṣavyāghra naṣṭaṁ me naṣṭacetasaḥ (1.6)

Indeed, O Keshava Krishna, what your noble self explained previously out of affection, know that all of it is forgotten by me. O tiger-like person, that is due to my having lost touch with that level of reality. (1.6)

**This chapter heading was introduced by the translator on the basis of the verse above. The Mahābhārata does not have a chapter heading.*

Verse 1

जनमेजय उवाच

सभायां वसतोस्तस्यां निहत्यारीन्महात्मनोः

केशवार्जुनयोः का नु कथा समभवद्द्विज

janamejaya uvāca
sabhāyāṁ vasatostasyāṁ nihatyārīnmahātmanoḥ
keśavārjunayoḥ kā nu kathā samabhavaddvija (1.1)

janamejaya – Janamejaya; uvāca – said; sabhāyāṁ - in the royal chambers; vasatostasyāṁ - sitting at leisure; nihaty = nihati (having eliminated, killed) + ārīnmah (enemy, opponent); ātmanoḥ - of the selves; keśavārjunayoḥ - between Keshava Krishna and Arjuna; kā – what; nu – really; kathā – discussion; samabhavad = samabhavat = from association, what transpired; dvija – O brahmin

Janamejaya said: O brahmin, while sitting at leisure in the state assembly-hall, after eliminating their opponents, what discussions transpired between Keshava Krishna and Arjuna?

Analysis:

Janamejaya was the great grandson of Arjuna, the famous warrior who heard the *Bhagavad Gītā* discourse on the Battlefield of Kurukshetra. Janamejaya took it upon himself to perform a religious sacrifice to avenge the death of his father who was King Parikshit. Parikshit was killed by a venomous serpent named Takshaka. Feeling that Takshaka had no justifiable reason to kill Parikshit, Janamejaya hired some ritual priests to do some damage to the race of snakes but his plan ended when a human relative of the reptiles, named Ashtika, appeared at the sacrificial place and asked for a favor, which was that the ceremony should be brought to an end.

This *Anu Gītā* is an extraction from the conversation between Janamejaya and a bard named Vaishampaiana. This described what happened after the battle of Kurukshetra took place and the Pandavas secured their ancestral kingdom and ruled without opposition from their rival cousins, the Kauravas.

Janamejaya was curious to know what lifestyle the Pandavas adopted after they deleted their opponents from the physical world. What sort of life were they living? How was their relationship with the most important person, who was Lord Krishna?

Application:

I came to narrate this conversation through Rishi Singh Gherwal, who is deceased. In the astral world he requested that I translate this from Sanskrit and write a commentary. He agreed to dictate into my mind much of what would be written as the analysis and application to these verses. Hence if you read this, you should know that it is by Rishi's instruction to me that this is possible.

What were Krishna and Arjuna discussing after things were normalized for the Pandavas? Was it the usual social intercourse or was it something which had spiritual content?

Verse 2

वैशंपायन उवाच

कृष्णेन सहितः पार्थः स्वराज्यं प्राप्य केवलम्

तस्यां सभायां रम्यायां विजहार मुदा युतः

vaiśaṁpāyana uvāca
kṛṣṇena sahitaḥ pārthaḥ svarājyaṁ prāpya kevalam
tasyāṁ sabhāyāṁ ramyāyāṁ vijahāra mudā yutaḥ (1.2)

vaiśaṁpāyana - Vaiśaṁpāyana; uvāca – said; kṛṣṇena – with Krishna; sahitaḥ - together with, pārthaḥ - the son of Pṛthā; svarājyaṁ - his own country; prāpya – having obtained; kevalam – alone, unrivalled; tasyāṁ - of them; sabhāyāṁ - in the assembly-hall; ramyāyāṁ - of luxurious; vijahāra – enjoying; mudā – with delight; yutaḥ - experiencing

Vaiśaṁpāyana said: Having autonomously secured his kingdom, the son of Pṛthā, in the company of Krishna, enjoyed with delight that luxurious assembly-hall.

Analysis:

Arjuna and his brothers secured the kingdom from their cousins. They did so by a battle confrontation which resulted in the death of their opponents and the killing of many of their friends. What should one do after such a battle? Can one live in peace and happiness after one's kinsmen are killed in a civil war?

Janamejaya was curious about the lifestyle of his forefathers after the battle, since even though he was born after the war, it had negative effects on him.

Application:

Material existence is so perverse, that even in the midst of blood and gore, a person can find enjoyment. Violence within and without the body is the single cause of rapid deterioration of the form, and yet a human being can enjoy violence. This illustrates the technicality of this situation.

Janamejaya wanted to hear of it, to perform an examination of the circumstances of Krishna, who laid claims as being God and Arjuna who was Krishna's best friend.

How did a person who claimed to be God proceed with life, after the death of millions in a battle. Did he enjoy the aftermath of war?

Verse 3

ततः कंचित्सभोद्देशं स्वर्गोद्देशसमं नृप

यदृच्छया तौ मुदितौ जग्मतुः स्वजनावृतौ

tataḥ kaṁcitsabhoddeśaṁ svargoddeśasamaṁ nṛpa
yadṛcchayā tau muditau jagmatuḥ svajanāvṛtau (1.3)

tataḥ - then, once; kaṁcit – while; sabhoddeśaṁ - area of a meeting place; svargod - like celestial world; deśasamaṁ (of the same place); nṛpa – O king; yadṛcchayā – it so happened; tau – of the two; muditau – two enjoying; jagmatuḥ - joined together; svajan – his own folk; āvṛtau – they went

Once, O King, it so happened, that while enjoying together, those two companions went with their folk to an area of that place which was like being in the celestial world.

Analysis:

Arjuna was enjoying but not Krishna. If Krishna is said to be enjoying, I admit that it was superficial only. By nature Krishna does not have the means to enjoy in the material world. He does not use the senses of a material body, the way a limited spirit would do. Vaishampaiana wanted to be clear that it appeared that both Krishna and Arjuna were on the same level of existence and were in fact having a good time together.

Their situation for all practical purposes looked wonderful. The beautiful spacious buildings, the lovely gardens, the opulent clothing, the lack of political rivals, all of this and more, reminded those who observed them of descriptions of life on the heavenly planets.

Application:

Is there a hidden backlash for enjoying life in the material world? Is there a flip side to heaven on earth? The time taken to enjoy this existence is history nevertheless. Is there a better use of circumstance? Is there something more sublime than to eke out enjoyment from the circumstances which are rolled out before us?

Verse 4

ततः प्रतीतः कृष्णेन सहितः पाण्डवोऽर्जुनः

निरीक्ष्य तां सभां रम्यामिदं वचनमब्रवीत्

tataḥ pratītaḥ kṛṣṇena sahitaḥ pāṇḍavo'rjunaḥ
nirīkṣya tāṁ sabhāṁ ramyāmidaṁ vacanamabravīt (1.4)

tataḥ - then; pratītaḥ - delightful; kṛṣṇena – with Krishna; sahitaḥ - being together; pāṇḍavo'rjunaḥ - Arjuna, the son of Pandu; nirīkṣya – viewing; tāṁ - to that; sabhāṁ - to the assembly-hall; ramyām – delightful; idaṁ - this; vacanam – words; abravīt – he said

Then being accompanied by Krishna, Arjuna, that son of Pandu, while viewing that delightful place, spoke these words:

Analysis:

There was something in the back of the mind of Arjuna. It was the discourse which Krishna lectured before the battle of Kurukshetra. The conversation served its immediate purpose which was to get Arjuna to do battle to establish right lifestyle as it was defined by Krishna. But Arjuna felt that something was lacking which was the application of that instruction in peacetime.

He wanted Krishna to again go over the details of the discourse but with application to non-emergency situations, to situations in which everything went well and one was not unnerved by material existence. Arjuna, though having so many achievements, was a bit unsettled because he lacked the technique of the application of yogic insight to the good times of material existence. Would Krishna be willing to give some hints about that?

Application:

The situation in the material world is such that one should not relax in the pursuit of spiritual purpose even when circumstances are to one's liking. With the progress of time nature never forgets to put an end to one's enjoyment. All healthy bodies will reach the end in one way or another. Thus even if the living entity forgets this, nature will be sure to remember.

Arjuna suspected that there was something amiss with the enjoyable circumstances which he and his brothers found themselves in after the battle. It would come to end. That was certain. But how? And when?

Verse 5

विदितं ते महाबाहो संग्रामे समुपस्थिते

माहात्म्यं देवकीमातस्तच्च ते रूपमैश्वरम्

viditaṁ te mahābāho saṁgrāme samupasthite
māhātmyaṁ devakīmātastacca te rūpamaiśvaram (1.5)

viditaṁ - knew, perceived; te - your; mahābāho - O superman; - saṁgrāme – in the battle; samupasthite – in commencing, before; māhātmyaṁ - infinite control; devakīmātas = devakīmātah – one whose mother is Devakī; tac = tat = that; ca – and; te – your; rūpam – form; aiśvaram – supernatural majestic form

O superman, person who is the son of Devakī, just before the battle, I perceived your infinite control and your supernatural majestic form.

Analysis:

On demand, Krishna displayed His colossal supernatural form which controlled all social situations in the material world. Arjuna saw it with supernatural eyes which were granted to him by Krishna's infusement of energy into Arjuna's subtle body. Even though it was such a rare apparition, Arjuna at this time after the battle, amidst the luxuries of the palace life, had that incidence tucked away in his memory as a faint impression of something that wonderful and awe-beholding.

Krishna, though essentially a spiritual being with supernatural reach into the material world, demonstrated even extraordinary material power. Thus Arjuna addressed Krishna as a superman, as mahābāho, the person with many arms who was capable of doing many things simultaneously.

Krishna was not just a spiritual and supernatural wonder but a physical one too. The display of the universal form was to give Arjuna some understanding about the translation of power from the supernatural plane into the physical existence.

What is the relationship between what occurs on the supernatural level and what happens in the physical reality? Is there a connection? Can something happen in the physical world which contradicts what is played by those beings who are on the supernatural level?

Application:

Arjuna was related to Krishna physically, but he found out before the battle that he was spiritually subordinate to Krishna and was required by the God, to serve as a disciplinarian in that life on earth. Still Arjuna addressed Krishna by their physical relationship, through Krishna's mother who was Devakī. She was married to Arjuna's maternal uncle, Vasudeva.

In material existence the connection from one physical body to another cannot be overlooked in entirety. A yogi has to learn to work with it and still make advancement. Physical relationship even between persons who are spiritually connected can be a bothersome feature. Too much reliance on it can cause one to neglect spiritual cultivation, a thing for which one may regret when one is confronted with the life hereafter.

Even though Arjuna was related to Krishna and was in fact a most dear friend of the Lord, still Arjuna regressed in Krishna consciousness after having the revelation of the forms of God.

Arjuna was embarrassed about losing touch with the Universal Form of Krishna as well as with the Four-handed Divine Form of the God. Thus he took this opportunity to request the supernatural and spiritual perception once again.

Arjuna planned to keep in touch with the vision by some means if it were revealed to him again.

Verse 6

यत्तु तद्भवता प्रोक्तं तदा केशव सौहृदात्

तत्सर्वं पुरुषव्याघ्र नष्टं मे नष्टचेतसः

yattu tadbhavatā proktaṁ tadā keśava sauhṛdāt
tatsarvaṁ puruṣavyāghra naṣṭaṁ me naṣṭacetasaḥ (1.6)

yat – what; tu – indeed; tadbhavatā = tat (that) + bhavatā(Your noble self); proktaṁ - explained; tadā – then; keśava - Keshava Krishna; sauhṛdāt – from friendship, from affection; tat – that; sarvaṁ - all; puruṣa – person; vyāghra – tiger; naṣṭaṁ - forgotten; me – by me; naṣṭacetasaḥ - lost awareness of, disconnected from that reality

Indeed, O Keshava Krishna, what your noble self explained previously out of affection, know that all of it is forgotten by me. O tiger-like person, that is due to my having lost touch with that level of reality.

Analysis:

This is a terrible admittance by Arjuna about losing touch with the supernatural and spiritual levels of existence. Previously, Krishna graciously gave Arjuna the vision on request but Arjuna admitted that he failed to maintain the infusion of energy which was given just before the battle.

Is this Arjuna's fault? Is this Krishna's doing? How is it possible that a divine limited being like Arjuna who supposedly transits with God from place to place, could lose touch with the supernatural and divine planes of existence. This is a shocking reality, that the limited beings are unable to hold the supernatural and divine formats if they are ever allowed access to these.

Application:

All sorts of religions all over the world promise that if the follower complies he or she will be rewarded with supernatural

and/or divine revelation and with transit to a spiritual location in the afterlife.

How then are we to understand this process if a person as great as Arjuna, who was a friend of the Supreme Being, lost track of the spiritual level of life? It is evident by Arjuna's confession that it is very difficult for a human being, even one who is very close to God, to maintain contact with the divine plane.

What would it take to maintain the insight to divine life, even to the concerns of God which trickle into this physical world for the support of righteous lifestyle as it was described by Krishna in **Bhagavad Gītā.**

Verse 7

मम कौतूहलं त्वस्ति तेष्वर्थेषु पुनः प्रभो

भवांश्च द्वारकां गन्ता नचिरादिव माधव

mama kautūhalaṁ tvasti teṣvartheṣu punaḥ prabho
bhavāṁśca dvārakāṁ gantā nacirādiva mādhava (1.7)

mama – me, my; kautūhalaṁ - eager, anxious, anxiety; tvasti = tu (but) + asti (it is);teṣvartheṣu = teṣu (in those) + artheṣu (in the value); punaḥ - again; prabho – sir, great person; bhavāṁśca = bhavān (you) = ca (and); dvārakāṁ - to Dvārakā; gantā – going; nacirādiva = nacirāt (soon) + iva (as if, since); mādhava - Mādhava

O great person, my anxiety is present for those valuable experiences to be bestowed again, since O Mādhava Krishna, you will soon be going to your city Dvārakā.

Analysis:

Arjuna assumed that Krishna would on the spur of the moment, again bestow the revelations of the Universal Form and of the four-handed divine body of God. It seemed that Krishna would do that, especially since they were physically related and were dear friends who stayed close to each other. Arjuna is a person of great value to Krishna as was expressed by Krishna in many verses of the *Bhagavad Gītā* where he described his endearing attention to Arjuna and his appreciation of Arjuna's piety and saintliness.

Application:

There are many devotees of Krishna all over in the world, especially in India. Many of them have not heard of the **Anu Gītā**. *And that might well be to their immediate benefit, since in this discourse the idea that hearing the* **Gītā** *from Krishna bestows upon the hearer, permanent insight, is contradicted. Always being in touch with Krishna, always being Krishna conscious and never forgetting what one imbibed about Krishna from an authority in the disciplic succession which stems from Krishna, remaining as a devotee of Krishna in all times and all places, should result in certain privileges in relation to Krishna, or so one may think.*

If what we hear in this text runs contrary to that, it means that many persons were misled either by an authority or by the hearer's fantasies.

At least Arjuna was in anxiety about losing touch with the supernatural and spiritual levels of existence. He pressed Krishna to again give the revelation so that Arjuna could again make the contact and perhaps maintain it from then onwards.

Verse 8

एवमुक्तस्ततः कृष्णः फल्गुनं प्रत्यभाषत

परिष्वज्य महातेजा वचनं वदतां वरः

evamuktastataḥ kṛṣṇaḥ phalgunaṁ pratyabhāṣata
pariṣvajya mahātejā vacanaṁ vadatāṁ varaḥ (1.8)

evam – thus; uktas = uktah = spoken to, requested of; tataḥ - then; kṛṣṇaḥ - Krishna; phalgunaṁ - Arjuna; pratyabhāṣata – replied, explained; pariṣvajya – embracing; mahātejā – person of vast energy; vacanaṁ - words, speech; vadatāṁ - of the speakers; varaḥ - the best

Then as requested, Krishna replied to Arjuna. After embracing him, Krishna, the person of vast energy, the best of the lecturers, said these words:

Analysis:

Everything is as usual, with Krishna embracing Arjuna in the same tight friendship as before.

Application:

One should be sure to pursue inquiries into spiritual life from a spiritual authority who is in the know and who has transcendental experiences which can light up the descriptions of the supernatural and spiritual worlds.

It does not matter if one is disappointed or if the authority is ignorant of the matter. One should persist in making inquiries again and again to one authority or another. One should also persist in meditation and out of body visitations to other dimensions, so that before the time of death of the physical body, one may become familiar with other systems of reality which might be available for migration.

There will be ups and downs, there will be progressions and digressions, and regardless the student yogi should persist in seeking out advanced souls and in transiting to other worlds. One should take nothing for granted. One should certainly not assume that one will go to a heavenly place after death because of a belief in such a place or because of confidence in its deity.

Verse 9

श्रावितस्त्वं मया गुह्यं ज्ञापितश्च सनातनम्

धर्मं स्वरूपिणं पार्थ सर्वलोकांश्च शाश्वतान्

śrāvitastvaṁ mayā guhyaṁ jñāpitaśca sanātanam
dharmaṁ svarūpiṇaṁ pārtha sarvalokāṁśca śāśvatān (1.9)

śrāvitas = śrāvitah = revealed, proclaimed; tvaṁ - you; mayā – by me; guhyaṁ - hidden reality; jñāpitaś = jñāpitah = what is known; ca – and; sanātanam – perpetual principle; dharmaṁ - righteous duty; svarūpiṇaṁ - of the actual format, form; pārtha – son of PÃhẠ sarvalokāṁś = sarvalokān = all dimensions; ca – and; śāśvatān – eternal reality

O son of Pṛthā, what was revealed to you by me is the unmanifest perpetual principle, the actual format of righteous duty, all the dimensions and the eternal reality.

Analysis:

Did Arjuna get more than his psyche could retain? Why did he lose touch with the unmanifest perpetual principle, the spiritual reality which is eternal and which transcends the material world? How did Arjuna lose the scope of the format of righteous duty as explained by Krishna when Krishna inducted Arjuna into the disciplic succession of yogically-trained rulers like Manu? Did Arjuna lose touch with the supernatural dimensions which he saw in the Universal Form of Krishna, and the spiritual dimension in which he viewed the Four-handed Divine Form of Krishna?

Application:

The unmanifest eternal principle is the one reality which has saturated this material world. It is therefore important that a yogi gets the insight into how this spiritual substance is distributed and how it reacts or is affected by the material world.

Knowledge about the format of righteous lifestyle is absolutely essential for a student yogi, since with that he or she can avoid a faulty interaction with the social world one encounters as one transmigrates. This is not simply a matter of reading books and hearing lectures by persons who know **Bhagavad Gītā**. *It is not even a matter developing set ideas about what is faultless duty. One has to be in a state of continuous submission to the Universal Form of Krishna, which is something that was elusive to Arjuna initially when he faced the confrontation at Kurukshetra.*

Information about the other dimensions is a must for those who feel that they deserve to live in a better more trouble-free place. Hearing of such places, may ignite sufficient interest that the student might develop a burning desire to go to those places. From that could come the impetus to practice yoga seriously.

Knowledge about the eternal reality and subsequent contact with it, gives the student the opportunity to remove all doubts about what is here which is not physical, which is not perceptible to our physical senses.

Verse 10

अबुद्ध्वा यन्न गृह्णीथास्तन्मे सुमहदप्रियम्

नूनमश्रद्दधानोऽसि दुर्मेधाश्चासि पाण्डव

abuddhvā yanna gṛhṇīthāstanme sumahadapriyam
nūnamaśraddadhāno'si durmedhāścāsi pāṇḍava (1.10)

abuddhvā – loss of awareness; yan = yat = that, what; na – no, not; gṛhṇīthās = gṛhṇīthāh = loss of dimensional contact; tan = tat = that; me – to me; sumahad = sumahat = very, enormous; apriyam - not dear, disagreeable; nūnam – indeed; aśraddadhāno'si = aśraddadhānah (loss of confidence) + 'si (asi) (you are); durmedhāścāsi = durmedhāh (person with a degraded mind) + ca (and) + si (asi) (you are); pāṇḍava - O son of Paṇḍu

Your loss of awareness and loss of dimensional contact with that is really disagreeable to me. Indeed, you are a person with a degraded mind. You are faithless, O son of Paṇḍu.

Analysis:

This appears to be a completely reversed assessment of the condition of Arjuna, especially since Krishna in the *Bhagavad Gītā* repeatedly praised Arjuna for friendship, saintliness and qualification for hearing the most detailed, most esoteric information, about spiritual reality and about Krishna's dominance even over the other supernatural beings.

However when we consider that Arjuna fell apart emotionally before the battle and that Krishna had to literally lift Arjuna up psychologically, it might not be such a wonder that Arjuna lost awareness of the divine plane and lost dimensional contact with the actions of the Universal Form of Krishna.

It is interesting that Krishna expressed disfavor to Arjuna, his dear friend and transmigratory buddy. Krishna went so far as to say that Arjuna was faithless and had a degraded mind (durmedhah). Such statements are the epitome of insult to anyone in a royal family.

Application:

Student yogis must take up the task of protecting themselves from losing confidence in the spiritual practice which is detailed in the **Bhagavad Gītā**, *and in the* **Uddhava Gītā**. *If one becomes exposed to sensual energies which are focused in the material world, one will lose confidence in Krishna's information.*

Authorities in disciplic succession like to say that the cause of losing confidence is association with non-devotees. By this they mean persons who disbelieve the scriptural stories about Krishna, or people who are not interested in Krishna or are instinctively offensive to Krishna or to Krishna's ideas.

However, these conclusions of the authorities do not explain this loss of faith of Arjuna. Arjuna lived with devotees. He worked under Krishna's stipulations during the battle and immediately thereafter. He worshipped and attended deities of Krishna and of Krishna's parallel divinities.

Serious students of the yoga practice which is expounded by Krishna should take into account what happened to Arjuna. They should do everything in their power to protect themselves from losing faith and from acquiring a degraded mind which reaches a plane of consciousness, where even if they were put in the presence of Krishna, they would not be in contact with the spiritual plane.

Verse 11

स हि धर्मः सुपर्याप्तो ब्रह्मणः पदवेदने

न शक्यं तन्मया भूयस्तथा वक्तुमशेषतः

sa hi dharmaḥ suparyāpto brahmaṇaḥ padavedane
na śakyaṁ tanmayā bhūyastathā vaktumaśeṣataḥ (1.11)

sa – that; hi – surely; dharmaḥ - system of righteous duty; suparyāpto = supari (very easy) + aptah (accomplished); brahmaṇaḥ - spiritual reality; padavedane – in the lecture; na – not; śakyaṁ - possible; tan = tat = that; mayā – by me; bhūyas = bhūyah – again; tathā – as; vaktum – to speak; aśeṣataḥ - recollection

Surely, the system of righteous duty expounded in my lecture is the way to easily accomplish the spiritual reality, but my recollection of that speech is an impossibility.

Analysis:

What Krishna told Arjuna on the battlefield of Kurukshetra came about spontaneously. In fact if one makes an in-depth study of the Gita and tries to convert it into an academic course, one will have some difficulty.

It was spoken on demand, on the spur of the moment, without an academic format. Even the display of the apparition of the Universal Form was done spontaneously on request. It was not planned.

Arjuna felt that Krishna could easily replay the experience but Krishna said that was an impossibility. The method was in existence before Krishna explained it to Arjuna but that did not mean that Krishna would repeat everything verbatim.

This system of righteous duty is the application of yoga proficiency to social activities. It is karma yoga or karma which is managed efficiently by yogic insight. In the *Bhagavad Gītā* Krishna identified it as his personal method of yoga. He said he would establish it in a disciplic succession beginning with Arjuna.

Application:

Some student yogis cry out for a revelation on par with or even smaller than the one Arjuna was bestowed on the battlefield of Kurukshetra. They feel that some divine visitation, some spiritual elevation, should be awarded for increasing their faith in the path and for motivating them to practice in earnest.

These students should note that even for Arjuna a request for revelation and duplicate information was not fulfilled. In fact Krishna outright refused to even make an attempt to uplift Arjuna as before.

The war was over. The opponents of Krishna's way of social governance were departed to the hereafter. Arjuna's martial skill was not needed as before. Krishna is Arjuna's close friend. That is certain. But Krishna is also the governor of the Universal Form. From that perspective, he did not require to influence Arjuna with such emphasis as before.

The worth of Arjuna as an assistant to the Universal Form was diminished considerably after the battle. Being friendly with God is one type of relationship, being useful to God in disciplinary tasks is a completely different exchange with the Supreme Being.

Arjuna must now protect himself from being degraded in the mundane evolutionary cycle. God can always find someone else to do his work, even his unpalatable requests. Or God can do all of these himself. This suggests that all limited beings are dispensable.

Verse 12

परं हि ब्रह्म कथितं योगयुक्तेन तन्मया

इतिहासं तु वक्ष्यामि तस्मिन्नर्थे पुरातनम्

paraṁ hi brahma kathitaṁ yogayuktena tanmayā
itihāsaṁ tu vakṣyāmi tasminnarthe purātanam (1.12)

paraṁ - supreme; hi – surely; brahma – spiritual reality; kathitaṁ - was described; yogayuktena – by application of yoga technique; tan = tat = that; mayā – by me; itihāsaṁ - history; tu – now; vakṣyāmi – I will speak; tasmin – that which; narthe = arthe = on the basis of; purātanam – of the ancient

Surely, that Supreme Spiritual Reality described by me previously was experienced by the application of a yoga technique. Now I will speak on the basis of ancient history.

Analysis:

The Vedic educational system was based on ancient history and established archaic information. Thus Krishna resumed that system and abandoned the independent declarations which he gave in the *Bhagavad Gītā*. He will again give information with and without respect to the ancient information but that would be to Uddhava when clarifying the idea of total renunciation of opportunities and the utilities of bhakti yoga and jnana yoga.

Many people think that since Krishna is the Supreme Personality among all deities, he should give revelations on demand, especially when requested by a dear devotee like Arjuna. However that opinion was demolished by this statement of Krishna where he admitted that what he showed Arjuna as the Universal form and as the Four-handed divinity, was done by the application of a specific yoga kriya technique. It was a deliberate action on the mystic level of existence. Krishna had no intentions of using that technique on this occasion.

Application:

Student yogis cannot expect that Krishna or any of the parallel divine beings will offer revelatory visions or apparitions, as Arjuna was bestowed on the battlefield. Such visions may or may not be awarded. Actually it is more a matter of getting to a divine plane through the student's endeavor to clean up his or her psychic energies so that automatically there is elevation to a higher plane.

The divine world exists side by side with the material world. It is intact and does not require assistants or visitors from this place. As the governor of the Universal Form, Krishna's primary interest in the material world, as He explained in **Bhagavad Gītā*****, was to induce people to follow His idea of approved lifestyle in social dealings. In that respect, on the material side of existence, one's value to Krishna is directly related to one's willing compliance with His ideas.***

Being Krishna's friend in no way increases one's value in the material world if one is not required for enforcing and complying with such rules.

In the yoga system it is reduced to having a value for oneself and to elevate oneself using the methods explained by Krishna for spiritual upliftment. The devotee should not expect that Krishna would elevate anyone who does not endeavor for self-elevation.

Verse 13

यथा तां बुद्धिमास्थाय गतिमग्र्यां गमिष्यसि

शृणु धर्मभृतां श्रेष्ठ गदतः सर्वमेव मे

yathā tāṁ buddhimāsthāya gatimagryāṁ gamiṣyasi
śṛṇu dharmabhṛtāṁ śreṣṭha gadataḥ sarvameva me (1.13)

yathā – as, definitely; tāṁ - to that; buddhim – intellect; āsthāya – by adjusting; gatim – dimension; agryāṁ - highest; gamiṣyasi – you will achieve; śṛṇu – listen; dharmabhṛtāṁ - one who supports righteous lifestyle; śreṣṭha – best; gadataḥ -what is said, speech; sarvam – all; eva – certainly; me – from me

Definitely, by adjusting your intellect to this, you will achieve the highest dimension. Listen to what is said by me, O best of those who support righteous behavior.

Analysis:

The first yoga practice which was explained to Arjuna is buddhi-yoga, which Krishna mentioned in Chapter 2 of *Bhagavad Gītā.*

This same yoga was taught under different names like kriya yoga, Patanjali yoga, dhyana yoga and samadhi yoga.

Can this be learnt from a book?

That depends on the insight of the particular yogi. If the yogi has penetrating psychic insight he can learn this method from a book without a physical teacher. He may also learn it by contacting advanced yogis in the astral world.

The control of the intellect so that it focuses on what Krishna explained, is a feat for any student yogi. This is because the intellect is hostile to such focus. It is motivated by the kundalini life-force, which is resistant to spiritual interest.

Application:

Buddhi yoga is the yoga process taught by Patanjali as samyama. However those who are not advanced in the practice should begin the fifth step of yoga which is pratyahar sensual energy withdrawal. There is no meditation if the person has not shut down the sensual pursuits. That is done effectively by the pratyahar process of pulling in the outward-going sense energy.

A certain amount of energy is dissipated by the senses in their outward habit.

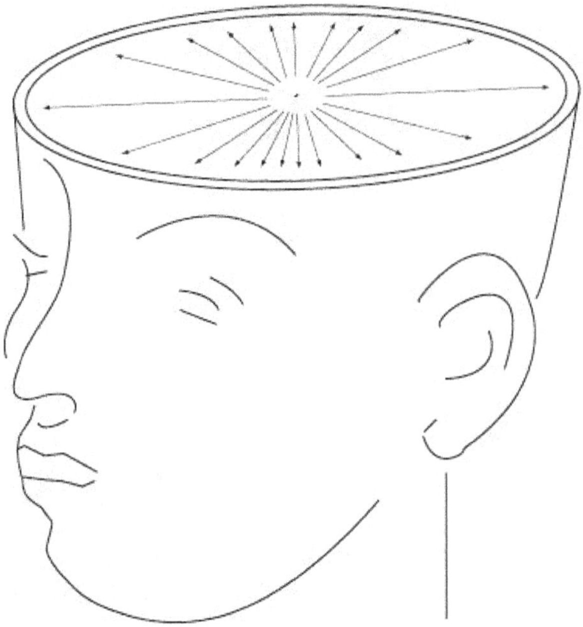

energy being drained away from core-self
by outward-bound sensual energies

This energy should be conserved if one is to progress to samyama which is the three higher stages of yoga as one sequential progression.

The situation of a yogi is nicely explained by the four Kumaras in their discussion with Priyavarta in Canto Four of the Srimad Bhagavatam. They explained that the self was like a lake. The senses were like swamp reeds. These grasses if allowed to thrive near a lake become giant plants which absorb the water.

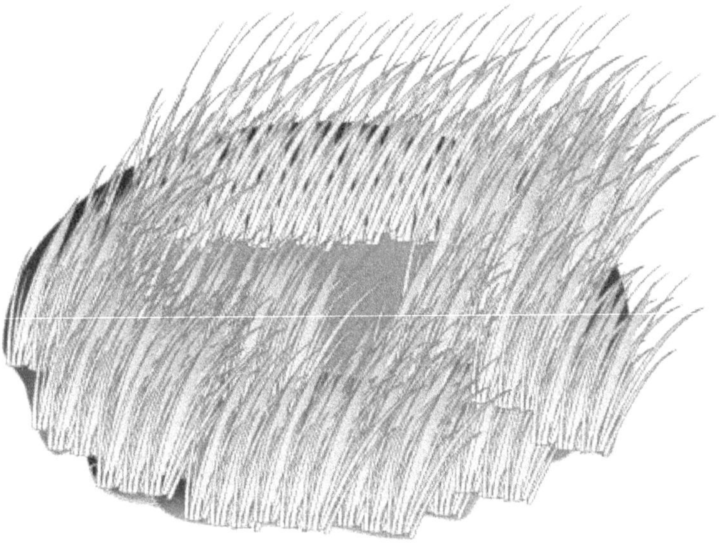

If the senses are allowed to fulfill all their desires, the self will be at risk due to loss of vital energy. The psyche will then become depressed.

The practice of pratyahar involved sitting to meditate, withdrawing the senses from the external objects, identifying the psychic energy which proceeds through the senses into the world, pulling in that energy to the core-self and totally ignoring any urge to resume the out-flow of energies.

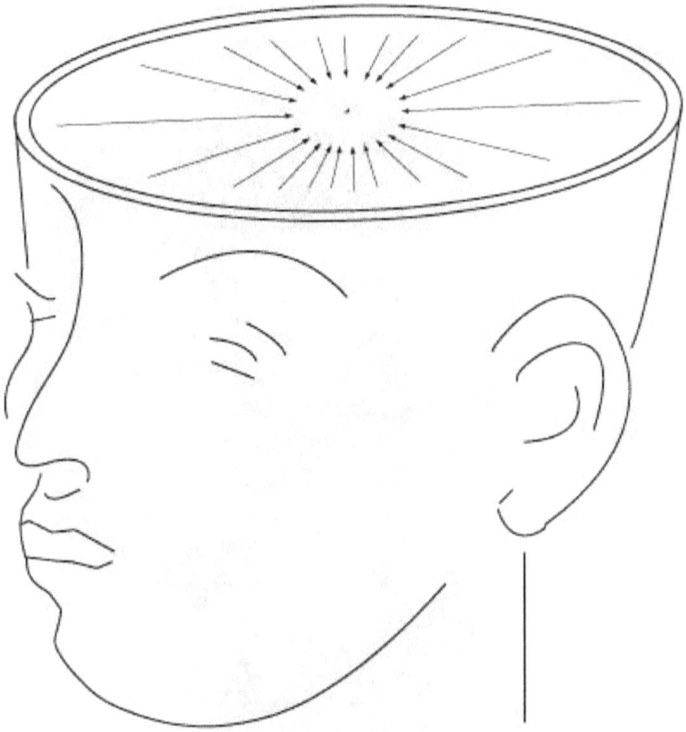

pulling in sensual energies into core-self

This is not buddhi yoga but it is preliminary to that more advanced practice.

For adjustment of the attitude and ways of operating the intellect, one should directly confront this psychic organ with intentions to shut it down.

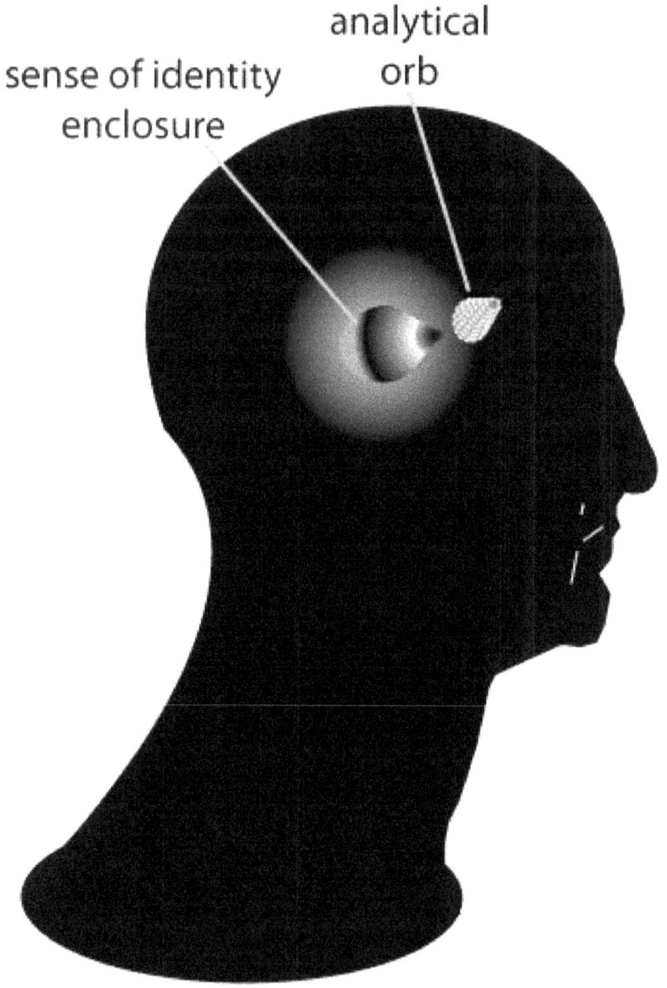

attentive I-self enclosed by sense of identity, helplessly focused on analytical orb

Patanjali in the Yoga Sutras, explained that the seer is supposed to segregate itself from the perception equipments in the psyche. These are subtle organs and the main one for visual perception is the intellect. This psychic organ is biased towards the senses. It is highly prejudiced for cooperation with the life-force. The yogi has the task of disconnecting the intellect from

the senses. The yogi must also force the intellect to abandon its visualizations for and its submissiveness to the life force.

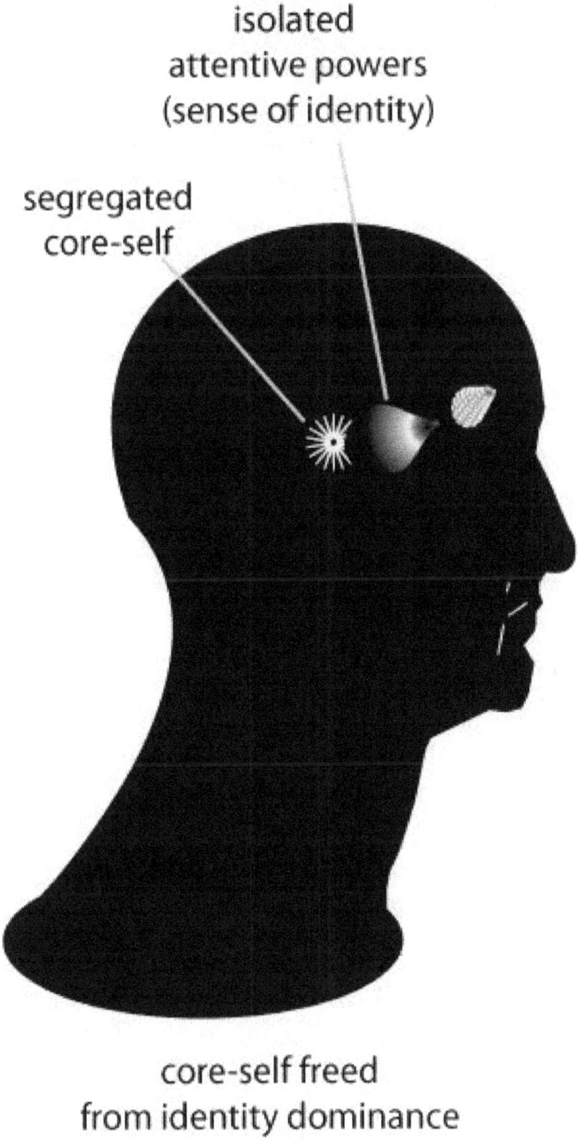

Verse 14

आगच्छद्ब्राह्मणः कश्चित्स्वर्गलोकादरिंदम

ब्रह्मलोकाच्च दुर्धर्षः सोऽस्माभिः पूजितोऽभवत्

āgacchadbrāhmaṇaḥ kaścitsvargalokādariṁdama
brahmalokācca durdharṣaḥ so'smābhiḥ pūjito'bhavat (1.14)

āgacchad - came; brāhmaṇaḥ - ritual ascetic; kaścit – once, it so happened; svargalokād = svargalokāt = from the celestial region; ariṁdama – O subduer of enemies; brahmalokāc = brahmalokāt = from the region of the local creator deity Brahma; ca – and; durdharṣaḥ - one who is difficult to locate; so'smābhiḥ = so (sah - he) + 'smābhiḥ (asmābhiḥ - by us); pūjito'bhavat = pūjito (pūjitah – duly honored) + 'bhavat (abhavat – being, existing)

O subduer of enemies, it so happened that a ritual ascetic from the celestial regions visited us. He was difficult to locate. Being from the dimension of the Creator Brahma, he was duly honored by us.

Analysis:

The dimension of Brahmā is the highest level of objective existence in this universe. To live in that place, one's subtle body has to be divested of all lower energies. Yogis who reside on that level must maintain social isolation from the lower planes. When they fail to do this, they are immediately transited to a lower plane.

A yogi who attained Brahmā's world picks and chooses which thoughts from which persons can reach him. He has the power to distance himself from anyone on the lower levels.

In comparison to human beings, every resident of Brahmā's place is like a god. That place is fabulous with opulence. No endeavor is required there for the fulfillment of desires.

Krishna and other members of the Yadu royal family adored the visitor. They even performed formal welcome-rituals to greet the celestial ascetic.

Application:

An advanced yogi is valued for his insight into the unknown dimensions. He is worth everything in exchange for his knowledge about the realms hereafter.

It is difficult for anyone to break out of this physical world to experience other environments. The impetus for moving beyond the physical world, comes from persons like this ascetic and also from the Supreme Person.

Verse 15

अस्माभिः परिपृष्टश्च यदाह भरतर्षभ

दिव्येन विधिना पार्थ तच्छृणुष्वाविचारयन्

asmābhiḥ pariprṣṭaśca yadāha bharatarṣabha
divyena vidhinā pārtha tacchṛṇuṣvāvicārayan (1.15)

asmābhiḥ - by us; pariprṣṭaś = pariprṣṭah = specifically questioned; ca – and; yad = yat = what; āha – said; bharatarṣabha – O best of the Bharatas; divyena – by the divine; vidhinā – in conformity with; pārtha – O son of FĀhẠ tac = tat = that; chṛṇu = śṛṇu = listen; ṣvāvicārayan – our deliberation

O best of the Bharatas, listen to what he said, as he was specifically questioned by us in a way that was in conformity with the divine world, and with due consideration.

Analysis:

Krishna, though being aware of himself as the Supreme Person, did not on every occasion give proof of his divinity. In the *Bhagavad Gītā* when Arjuna resisted Krishna's desire for harsh treatment of the Kauravas, Krishna gave evidence of his supremacy by transiting Arjuna into a dimension where the Universal Form was displayed.

With the siddha from Brahmā's world Krishna did not display his divinity but asked questions for the benefit of others who were present. Some of the Yadu royal family did not think that Krishna was the Supreme Personality. By asking the ascetic to explain certain things, Krishna utilized their underestimation of his divinity by directing them to someone whom they respected. This person was believed to be from the celestial world and held their confidence.

Application:

Since Arjuna did not take Krishna's **Bhagavad Gītā** *discourse seriously and since he took the revelation of the Universal Form and the Four-handed Divine Form for granted, Krishna refused to even consider the redisplay of the forms. Krishna even refused to go over details about yoga and devotion. This means that student yogis should not play games with advanced teachers. They should not believe that they can get teachers to do miracles and to lecture extensively on any subject. Rather a student should inquire with interest and be in a mood to be rejected by the teacher without taking offense.*

Arjuna wanted Krishna to explain details of spirituality and the application of spiritual insight to social life, but Krishna merely quoted what was said by a highly respected ascetic who was not the Supreme Being, but who accomplished for himself transfer to the highest dimension.

When we consider the friendship between Krishna and Arjuna at Kurukshetra, and this new attitude of Krishna, we feel a certain detachment of Krishna in relation to Arjuna. Krishna perceived that his friendliness to Arjuna did Arjuna some harm in that it undermined Arjuna's respect for Krishna, resulting in Arjuna not taking Krishna's revelations and discourses seriously.

Verse 16

ब्राह्मण उवाच

मोक्षधर्मं समाश्रित्य कृष्ण यन्मानुपृच्छसि

भूतानामनुकम्पार्थं यन्मोहच्छेदनं प्रभो

brāhmaṇa uvāca
mokṣadharmaṁ samāśritya kṛṣṇa yanmānupṛcchasi
bhūtānāmanukampārthaṁ yanmohacchedanaṁ prabho (1.16)

brāhmaṇa – the ritual ascetic; uvāca – said; mokṣadharmaṁ - lifestyle resulting in liberation; samāśritya – relating to; kṛṣṇa – Krishna; yan = yat = which; mānupṛcchasi = ānupṛcchasi = you asked in a systemic way; bhūtānām – concerning living beings; anukampārthaṁ - what shows deep interest; yan = yat = which; mohac = mohat = from delusion; chedanaṁ - that which shatters; prabho – sir, exalted person

The ritual ascetic said: O Krishna, you asked methodically of the lifestyle which results in liberation. Being merciful to all living beings, O exalted person, you inquired of that which shatters delusion.

Analysis:

The ascetic from the heavenly world knew Krishna's tactic of not directly lecturing the family members of the Yadu royal family. He agreed to the proposal, knowing that Krishna would utilize the Yadus' lack of confidence to bring to their attention, the truths about material existence from somebody whom they wanted to honor and respect.

One great teacher might avoid explaining important subjects, and yet the same teacher may arrange for some other qualified person to provide the information. The students should not object to this. The layout of the dimensions will not change by a change of instructor.

Application:

The truth is the same even if it is spoken by a toddler. The Supreme Being cannot undo the truth or upgrade it. Thus if it is spoken by an infant or by a respectable adult, it still will not be adjusted.

It is true however, that by nature a human being has more confidence in someone whom he or she respects. The way of psychology is such that one neglects a truth which comes from an untrustworthy person. All the same one puts confidence in an untruth which is disguised as truth by a notable person.

Verse 17

तत्तेऽहं संप्रवक्ष्यामि यथावन्मधुसूदन

श्रृणुष्वावहितो भूत्वा गदतो मम माधव

tatte'haṁ saṁpravakṣyāmi yathāvanmadhusūdana
śṛṇuṣvāvahito bhūtvā gadato mama mādhava (1.17)

tat – that; te – they; 'haṁ = aham = I; saṁpravakṣyāmi – I will answer; yathāvan = yathāvat = as, appropriately; madhusūdana – O killer of Madhu; śṛṇu – listen; ṣvāvahito = ṣvāvahitah = self attentive; bhūtvā – being; gadato = gadatah = spoken; mama – by me; mādhava – O Madhava

O killer of Madhu, I will answer your inquiries appropriately. Being attentive, listen to what is said by me, O Mādhava Krishna.

Analysis:

The ascetic from the heavenly worlds recognized the divinity of Krishna, but he wanted to comply with Krishna's request for an explanation. Focusing on teaching Krishna some truths about material existence and the jump into the spiritual world, he began to explain the situations. His intention was to engage the Yadus in listening attentively.

Application:

A yogi may not get the opportunity to be directly addressed on a specific topic in spiritual life. But he should be eager to hear of such a topic when it is explained to someone else. It is nice to be personally addressed by a great teacher but one cannot rely on just that.

If in one's presence vital information is given to another, one should accept it just as if one was addressed directly.

Verse 18

कश्चिद्विप्रस्तपोयुक्तः काश्यपो धर्मवित्तमः

आससाद द्विजं कंचिद्धर्माणामागतागमम्

kaścidviprastapoyuktaḥ kāśyapo dharmavittamaḥ
āsasāda dvijaṁ kaṁciddharmāṇāmāgatāgamam (1.18)

kaścid = kaścit = anyone, who; vipras = viprah = educated ascetic; tapoyuktaḥ - person who is proficient in sensual austerity; kāśyapo – Kashyapa; dharmavittamaḥ - best of those who master religious lifestyle; āsasāda – arrived, approached; dvijaṁ - initiated ritual ascetic; kaṁcid = kaṁcit = anyone, who; dharmāṇām – of the system of righteous lifestyle; āgatāgamam – concerning the coming and going, repeated transmigrations

An educated ascetic named Kashyapa, who was proficient in sensual austerity, and who was the best of those persons who mastered righteous lifestyle, approached a well-trained ritual ascetic who was conversant with righteousness and understood the repeated transmigrations.

Analysis:

The well-respected ascetic from the heavenly world, decided to cite the inquiries and related lectures from a previous time. They were in his view most appropriate to the situation.

This style of quoting previous authorities was a signature method used in ancient India among the transcendentalists. It is valid because the truths discussed concern eternal realities such as the confrontation between the spiritual entities and material nature. That is an ongoing conflict which does not change since material nature does not yield and it remains the same no matter what.

Application:

The repeated transmigrations are the assumption of bodies in sequence as permitted by nature, with the living entity being conditioned in whatever body it is fused into.

Usually the body begins in an undeveloped form and increases in size as it matures. Once it matures, the entity who is fused into it, identifies emphatically with it. This causes the entity to neglect its enduring spiritual nature.

Verse 19

गतागते सुबहुशो ज्ञानविज्ञानपारगम्

लोकतत्त्वार्थकुशलं ज्ञातारं सुखदुःखयोः

gatāgate subahuśo jñānavijñānapāragam
lokatattvārthakuśalaṁ jñātāraṁ sukhaduḥkhayoḥ (1.19)
gatāgate subahuśo jñānavijñānapāragam
lokatattvārthakuśalaṁ jñātāraṁ sukhaduḥkhayoḥ

gatāgate = gatā (acceptance of a body) + āgate (relinquishment of a body); subahuśo = subahuśah = completely knowledgable person; jñānavijñānapāragam = jñāna (knowledge) + vijñāna (experience) + pāragam – gone over, beyond; lokatattvārthakuśalaṁ = loka (world) + tattva (essential attributes) + artha (valuable aspects) + kuśalaṁ (versed, proficient); jñātāraṁ - person with deep insight; sukhaduḥkhayoḥ - of enjoyment and misery

That well-trained ritual ascetic was in full knowledge about the acceptance and relinquishment of a body. He had boundless capacity for knowledge and experience. He was versed in whatever was of value or essential in the world. He was a person with deep insight into the aspects of enjoyment and misery.

Analysis:

This person, the second reference teacher, even though archaic, had conquered the mysteries of nature's operations which cause the living entities to transmigrate haphazardly from one form to another. He was in the world long before the time of Gautama Buddha but his achievement was no less than that super-being.

The main interest of the living entities who discover themselves as consciousness in this world is procurement of enjoyment and avoidance of misery. The ancient ascetic studied this in detail.

Application:

There comes a time in the life of a living entity, when it feels that it should forego material existence and the privileges which this existence affords. Initially the living entity feels that

it should become the master of this existence in terms of acquiring maximum enjoyment and minimum inconveniences. But after many millions of births, the entity reviews the situation and comes to the conclusion that it is impossible to successfully exploit material nature.

Then there is an effort to cull out from material nature some philosophical conclusions about the ways and means of this existence. Therefore the entities decide that even doctrines and theories are non-beneficial and the only way to go, is to split off from the material nature in all its forms and dimensions.

This ancient ascetic passed through the stages and acquired deep insight into the purpose of material nature and the value of it to a spiritual entity.

Verse 20

जातीमरणतत्त्वज्ञं कोविदं पुण्यपापयोः

द्रष्टारमुच्चनीचानां कर्मभिर्देहिनां गतिम्

jātīmaraṇatattvajñaṁ kovidaṁ puṇyapāpayoḥ
draṣṭāramuccanīcānāṁ karmabhirdehināṁ gatim (16.20)

jātīmaraṇatattvajñaṁ = jātī (birth) + maraṇa (death) + tattva (truth of) + jñaṁ (knowledge); kovidaṁ - one who is expert; puṇyapāpayoḥ = puṇya (merit) + pāpayoḥ (of fault); draṣṭāramuccanīcānāṁ = draṣṭār (observer) + amuccanīcānāṁ (of the highs and lows); karmabhirdehināṁ = karma (cultural activity) + bhir (bhih – fear, anxiety) + dehināṁ (of the embodied soul); gatim - objective

He knew the truth of birth and death. He was the expert on merits and faults. He perceived the elevation and degradation of the souls. He knew the objective of the embodied souls in terms of their anxiety and cultural work.

Analysis:

Being crafty in material existence is the way to go, if one wants to beat nature at its game. The predatory animals like the lions and eagles master the technique of advantage by exploiting the eating work of the vegetarian species. These species eat and eat and eat to grow their bodies. Then they are eaten in turn by predators who simply remain poised for the advantage of tearing apart the vegetarians.

After some time however the predators get the insight that intellectual prowess is superior to physical strength. This causes them to consider the human species which they live in fear of. After transiting into a human womb, the entities get a wider view of the scope of material nature. This leads them to the conclusion that elevation to heavenly worlds is superior to hacking out an advantageous life as the top predator on the earth.

It is in the human species, that the person comes to understand that it is not the body it uses. This occurs through detailed observation of the astral projection of the subtle body. In the animal world, such projection occurs but without objectivity. The human species affords the observational detachment during dreaming. From that the entity gets a hint of itself as being different from the innumerable bodies it transmigrated as and in.

Application:

In this material world, there is no such thing as mass liberation. Each of the entities is so varied in its transmigration experiences, that individual liberation is the only way for each of them to deal with its incarceration in the process of death, hereafter existence, birth and then death again with endless repetition. As it stands the entity is mostly conscious and observational at the time of death of the body, but then in the afterlife it has no control over the variations of consciousness. It has to accept whatever alteration of consciousness nature provides, until it loses awareness of itself as a ghost and then finds itself awake as an embryo. The awakened state as an embryo has no memory apparatus with it and so the entity assumes that as its first existence. This happens in every life in whatever species nature fuses it into.

Eventually, however, after hearing from a self realized soul, the entity makes the assumption that it must be existing on and on even though it does not know every aspect of its fate. It tries

to locate the controller or controlling force which stipulated its destiny but initially this research fails.

The entity realizes that the constant pressing need for merits is fatiguing, especially since material nature has the upper hand in all circumstances. Why play a game with a competitor who always wins? That is what it thinks. Thus it becomes discouraged and tries to renounce the adventures which material nature offers to it.

Verse 21

चरन्तं मुक्तवत्सिद्धं प्रशान्तं संयतेन्द्रियम्

दीप्यमानं श्रिया ब्राह्म्या क्रममाणं च सर्वशः

carantaṁ muktavatsiddhaṁ praśāntaṁ saṁyatendriyam
dīpyamānaṁ śriyā brāhmyā kramamāṇaṁ ca sarvaśaḥ (1.21

carantaṁ - one who moves, wanders; muktavat – just like a liberated yogi; siddhaṁ - one who is a perfected yogi, siddha; praśāntaṁ - one who is tranquil; saṁyatendriyam – one whose sensual energies are effectively restrained; dīpyamānaṁ - one who is effulgent; śriyā – one who has splendor; brāhmyā – pertaining to the spiritual reality; kramamāṇaṁ - one who roams about; ca – and; sarvaśaḥ - everywhere

Being a perfected yogi, he moved around as a siddha, a liberated soul. He was tranquil. His sensual energy were effectively restrained. He was effulgent and splendrous like spiritual reality. He roamed everywhere as desired.

Analysis:

The qualifications of a spiritual teacher are not apparent by his religious affiliation. It is not his monk status. It is not his theology degree. It is not his garments and insignia. It is not his physical body's photogenic quality. A spiritual teacher is not validated by his cultural format.

Application:

Siddhas are yogis who perfected yoga practice or certain phases of it. This gives them the right to move about invisibly through several dimensions. All siddhas have acute detachment from the spell-bounding aspects of the mind. They achieve this by exercise of detachment from the thinking part of the mind, the buddhi intellect organ in the psychic body.

This practice includes control of the kundalini life-force which goads the intellect and commands the senses to procure aspects of material existence.

The effulgence and splendor of a siddha comes from the clarification of his personal energies. The magic of it is his accomplishment of flushing out lower energies from the psyche permanently, replacing those with energies which abound in the highest levels of astral existence.

For a yogi, the category of siddha is the one which is just below the attainment of full existence in a spiritual body which has nothing to do with any levels in the astral world.

Verse 22

अन्तर्धानगतिज्ञं च श्रुत्वा तत्त्वेन काश्यपः

तथैवान्तर्हितैः सिद्धैर्यान्तं चक्रधरैः सह

antardhānagatijñaṁ ca śrutvā tattvena kāśyapaḥ
tathaivāntarhitaiḥ siddhairyāntaṁ cakradharaiḥ saha (1.22)

antardhānagatijñaṁ = antardhāna (disappearance, psychic presence) + gati (passage, course) + jñaṁ (one who knows the technique); ca – and; śrutvā – having heard; tattvena – by the essential truth known by him; kāśyapaḥ - Kashyapa; tathaivāntarhitaiḥ = tatha (as) + eva (so) + antarhitaiḥ (by disappearance); siddhair = siddhaih = by the siddha perfected yogis; yāntaṁ - passage, movement; cakradharaiḥ - by those who move like a wheel; saha - with

He knew the technique of psychic passage. He moved with the siddha perfected yogis who could disappear and who roamed everywhere like a wheel. Kashyapa having heard of his knowledge of the essential truth, desired to see him.

Analysis:

Kashyapa heard of the accomplishment of this particular siddha, and subsequently he was attracted. He harbored a desire to meet the ascetic. In such situations, the disciple feels that if he could reach such an advanced soul, he would be inspired to take seriously to practice and would attain liberation shortly.

Of course this type of thinking usually ends in frustration, since merely meeting a great yogi, does not necessarily cause rapid advancement. It does occur from time to time, that a particular student benefits in that way, but in most cases, this does not occur. In most cases the student has to take up disciplines and serve the teacher's requests. Then over time, there is accelerated progression.

Application:

The technique of psychic passage, gatijñam, is the system of rapid transfer from one dimension to the next in full consciousness. This siddhi perfection skill is attained by certain yogis. It gives them ability to transit from one astral realm to another in a jiffy. They can also make contact with physical beings through the use of psychic presence either in the mind of such persons or in the atmosphere around such persons.

Getting impetus from advanced yogis is paramount in a student's progression with spiritual life but that does not mean that a student should pester an advanced soul, or make demands of a senior yogi as if the teacher must respond to all requests. A student should ask for methods of discipline which would result in elevation over the sensual energies and control of the life-force kundalini.

The bestowal of grace on a student is totally out of his or her control. In fact in this discourse, Arjuna did not get what he wanted from Krishna, the Supreme Teacher. Arjuna wanted Krishna to display the supernatural Universal Form and the Four-handed Divine Body. He wanted also that Krishna should go over the details of everything else Krishna mentioned in the **Bhagavad Gītā**. *Arjuna had a good plan which was to carefully*

listen to Krishna again and then use the information to secure his spiritual future. Still Krishna rejected the proposal and presented instead evidence about spiritual existence and liberation which was spoken by others.

If seeing the Universal Form, gaining the darshan of it, gives inspiration to complete spiritual advancement, then why did Krishna, the Supreme Person, not give Arjuna the experience one more time?

Verse 23

संभाषमाणमेकान्ते समासीनं च तैः सह

यदृच्छया च गच्छन्तमसक्तं पवनं यथा

saṁbhāṣamāṇamekānte samāsīnaṁ ca taiḥ saha
yadṛcchayā ca gacchantamasaktaṁ pavanaṁ yathā (1.23

saṁbhāṣamāṇam – of those who assembled together; ekānte - in solitary places; samāsīnaṁ - assembled together; ca – and; taiḥ - with them; saha – with; yadṛcchayā – by chance; ca – and; gacchantam – went; asaktaṁ - unattached; pavanaṁ - wind; yathā - so

That roaming ascetic moved with those siddhas who sometimes sat together or assembled in solitary places. He went as by chance, going about unattached just like the wind. (1.23)

Analysis:

Siddhas are free from energies which are on the lower astral planes. They lose the compulsion which a departed soul feels for taking another material body. This gives them the right to wander through numerous dimensions to complete their education as to the correlation between the subtle material world and the physical world.

Their detachment is a property of their subtle forms. It is not a will-power process or an austerity.

Application:

Siddhas have other siddhas, deities and the Supreme Being for their primary association. They do on occasion give advice

and blessing to human beings. The easiest way to attract a siddha is to have a consistent yoga practice.

Yoga practice when it is steady and intense, attracts the siddhas even if they are located far away from this earthly planet. They are attracted to the intense effort of human beings who strive for liberation.

Verse 24

तं समासाद्य मेधावी स तदा द्विजसत्तमः

चरणौ धर्मकामो वै तपस्वी सुसमाहितः

प्रतिपेदे यथान्यायं भक्त्या परमया युतः

taṁ samāsādya medhāvī sa tadā dvijasattamaḥ
caraṇau dharmakāmo vai tapasvī susamāhitaḥ
pratipede yathānyāyaṁ bhaktyā paramayā yutaḥ (1.24)

taṁ - him; samāsādya – approaching; medhāvī – one who is intelligent; sa – he, that; tadā – then; dvijasattamaḥ - best of the initiated ritualists; caraṇau – two feet; dharmakāmo = dharmakāmah – one who is eager for righteous lifestyle; vai – certainly; tapasvī – yogi ascetic; susamāhitaḥ - in submission; pratipede – in submission; yathāny = yathāni = full prostration; āyaṁ - this; bhaktyā – by devotion; paramayā – by the supreme; yutaḥ - affected, felt

Then that best of the well-trained ritualists, Kashyapa, being intelligent in his own right, approached the wandering yogi. Being a person who was eager for righteous lifestyle, Kashyapa, in submission, with full prostration, fell at the feet of the ascetic, who felt Kashyapa's great devotion.

Analysis:

A student who is fortunate to meet a great soul, a siddha who achieved liberation, should jump for joy. Considering the self to be fortunate to speak to such a great person about the important subject matter of liberation, that fortunate seeker should gather the wits, think seriously about what was puzzling and submissively inquire.

Application:

The student must be intelligent in his own right, otherwise he or she will be unable to formulate the proper questions. Even if a guru explains the path to perfection in the most detailed and elaborate way, an unprepared student will not grasp what is given by the spiritual master.

Students should make every effort to tone their perception and develop spiritual insight. A spiritual master can do so much for a disciple but the student will have to make up the rest of the course by rigid austerities, persistence with practice and full disgust with the way the material energy operates this world.

Verse 25

विस्मितश्चाद्भुतं दृष्ट्वा काश्यपस्तं द्विजोत्तमम्

परिचारेण महता गुरुं वैद्यमतोषयत्

vismitaścādbhutaṁ dṛṣṭvā kāśyapastaṁ dvijottamam
paricāreṇa mahatā guruṁ vaidyamatoṣayat (1.25)

vismitah = in amazement; cādbhutaṁ = ca (and) + adbhutam (wonderful); dṛṣṭvā – seeing; kāśyapas = kāśyapah = Kashyapa; taṁ - him; dvijottamam – foremost of the trained ritualists; paricāreṇa – by exemplary conduct; mahatā – great; guruṁ = gurun = spiritual master; vaidyamatoṣayat – from sacred learning

In amazement, seeing that wonderful person, Kashyapa, the foremost of the trained ritualists, submitted to that great spiritual master who exhibited exemplary conduct and sacred knowledge.

Analysis:

Kashyapa was eager for righteous lifestyle in terms of the karma yoga instructions which Krishna gave Arjuna in the *Bhagavad Gītā*. This is not, strictly speaking, a spiritual practice. Even though that lifestyle serves the interest of the Supreme Being, it is his interest in social behavior in this world.

Karma yoga does not yield spiritual advancement but its proficiency is the platform from which to launch the self into spiritual practice. At this point in his life, Kashyapa had enough of the material world, and was seeking a way out of it, even from the supposed advantages it offers.

The visitor of Kashyapa was exemplary not only in spiritual knowledge and integrated spiritual experience but also in social dealings. This was the ideal spiritual teacher.

Application:

Kashyapa was amazed that this elevated ascetic came to contact him. He knew that a great soul does not have to give audience to anyone. He regarded the visit as a blessing and good fortune.

Verse 26

प्रीतात्मा चोपपन्नश्च श्रुतचारित्रसंयुतः

भावेन तोषयच्चैनं गुरुवृत्त्या परंतपः

prītātmā copapannaśca śrutacāritrasaṁyutaḥ
bhāvena toṣayaccainaṁ guruvṛttyā paraṁtapaḥ (1.26)

prītātmā – one who is dear to the self; copapan = ca (and) +upapan (pleasing); naś = nah = us; ca = and; śruta – education (Vedas); cāritra – activities, conduct; saṁyutaḥ - joined, combined with; bhāvena – by emotion, feeling; toṣayac = toṣayat = from pleasing; cainaṁ = ca (and) +enaṁ (this); guru – spiritual master; vṛttyā – by behavior; paraṁtapaḥ - subduer of rebels

O subduer of rebels, Kashyapa was dear to the self and pleasing to the teacher. He was educated and exhibited appropriate conduct, pleasing behavior and timeful activities in reference to the teacher.

Analysis:

These qualities are ideal for a student yogi. Without this type of character, one cannot reciprocate in earnest with a spiritual master. If one does not have these qualities, one should endeavor to develop them since without these, one will be resistant to the teachings.

Application:

Education is required because unless one gets insight into the workings of the material world, one cannot be liberated. Education means having knowledge and experience of spiritual topics. A completely ignorant person and one who has no interest in spiritual self-realization, cannot take seriously to spiritual practice. In such a person the intellectual interest would not be aroused.

A student must also take note of the idiosyncrasies of the teacher; what to do in his presence and what not to act out before him. This does not mean that the teacher can be lawless and arrogant. The teacher must be qualified in both spiritual process and social responsibility.

Verse 27

तस्मै तुष्टः स शिष्याय प्रसन्नोऽथाब्रवीद्गुरुः

सिद्धिं परामभिप्रेक्ष्य शृणु तन्मे जनार्दन

tasmai tuṣṭaḥ sa śiṣyāya prasanno'thābravīdguruḥ
siddhiṁ parāmabhiprekṣya śṛṇu tanme janārdana (1.27)

tasmai – to him; tuṣṭaḥ - satisfied; sa – he, that; śiṣyāya – by the disciple; prasanno'thābravīd = prasanno'thābravīd = prasannah (being pleased) + 'thā (athā - thus) + abravīd (abravīt - said); guruḥ - spiritual master; siddhiṁ - perfection; parām – highest; abhiprekṣya – having known, experienced; śṛṇu – hear; tan = tat = that; me – me; janārdana – maintainer of living beings

Thus being satisfied and pleased by the disciple, the tranquil spiritual master who experienced the highest perfection, spoke. Hear of this from me Janārdana, maintainer of the living beings.

Analysis:

This story is being told to Arjuna. Krishna repeats what he was told by a celestial siddha, who in turned repeated what was told to Kashyapa. The information remained valid because the human psyche is constructed in the same way as it was since the beginning of time.

Application:

If the spiritual master feels relaxed in the presence of the disciple, it is likely that some spiritual information will be divulged. Actually, a spiritual master is eager to share information about his experiences and realizations as well as what he was told by superiors.

Verse 28

विविधैः कर्मभिस्तात पुण्ययोगैश्च केवलैः

गच्छन्तीह गतिं मर्त्या देवलोकेऽपि च स्थितिम्

vividhaiḥ karmabhistāta puṇyayogaiśca kevalaiḥ
gacchantīha gatiṁ martyā devaloke'pi ca sthitim (1.28)

vividhaiḥ - by various; karma – actions; bhis = bhih = aspirations; tāta - O dear one; puṇya – pious activity; yogaiś = yogaih = by yoga practice; ca – and; kevalaiḥ - by isolation; gacchanti – they go; īha – here; gatiṁ - destination; martyā – world where bodies quickly die; devaloke – in celestial places where the lower deities reside; 'pi = api = also; ca – and; sthitim - situated

O dear one, by their various aspirations and actions, or by yoga practice, pious activity and isolation, people go to the world where bodies quickly die or are situated in the celestial places where the lower deities reside.

Analysis:

The normal routine is for a deceased person to either come back to this world as a new life form or appear in the celestial world where the lower deities permanently reside. The transit to the celestial world is temporary for most human beings because the energy which sustains them in those locations is limited. As soon as it is exhausted, their subtle bodies become de-energized and they find themselves in the astral dimensions which are adjacent to this physical world. From there they fuse into the psyche of their soon-to-be parent. Then after a time, according to the gestation rate for that species, that entity appears again in this physical world as a certain material body.

One example of this was King Yayati. He was fortunate to stay for a long period in the celestial world. He was sustained there by the socially beneficial activities he did as a king on earth. Eventually when the elevating energy of that pious life was exhausted, he found himself fading from that domain. He then realized himself as an astral being in a dimension which was near to this physical existence and he went to his living descendants for aid.

Application:

A student yogi is required to research how the soul leaves a dying body, goes to the astral world in the formation of a subtle body which contains all its psychological energy and then comes back again as an infant form of some species in complete ignorance of the former birth. How is that possible?

What happens to the individual in the interim state which results in the total loss of memory of its former life?

We perform various actions and have various aspirations which motivate us to act socially. From where do these originate? Why do we fulfill certain desires even if we know that they will bring us distress? Why are we not independent of everyone and everything else?

By yoga practice, we can attain liberation, at least that is what we are told by reliable mystics and by the person Krishna who claimed to be the Supreme Being. What is the correct yoga practice? Where is the teacher of it?

Socially-beneficial acts are the most productive form of social interaction, because it brings to the actor good circumstances in the future. However, since the actor will have no memory of the former life when it performed those beneficial actions, what is the use of this information?

By isolation one person may gain insight into how the self is influenced by others, but that does not mean that one can live without others, for it seems that there are living entities everywhere in the air, in the sea, in the land and even in the mind's environment and the astral world in which we experience realistic life in dreams.

The earth is one place and the celestial world where the lower deities reside is another. Both of these places are condemned even though the celestial places have no strenuous endeavor.

Verse 29

न क्वचित्सुखमत्यन्तं न क्वचिच्छाश्वती स्थितिः

स्थानाच्च महतो भ्रंशो दुःखलब्धात्पुनः पुनः

na kvacitsukhamatyantaṁ na kvacicchāśvatī sthitiḥ
sthānācca mahato bhraṁśo duḥkhalabdhātpunaḥ punaḥ

na – no; kvacit – where, in location; sukham – happiness; atyantaṁ - endless; na – no; kvacic = kvacit = where; chāśvatī = śāśvatī = eternal; sthitiḥ - residence; sthānāc = sthānāt = from dimension; ca – and; mahato = mahatah = highest; bhraṁśo = bhraṁśah = demotion; duḥkha – difficulty; labdhāt – from obtaining; punaḥ punaḥ = again and again

In none of these locations is there endless happiness; none of those places have eternal residence. Again and again, there is demotion from the highest dimension which one attained with difficulty.

Analysis:

The flaw in the astral heavens and paradises which are easily attained by human beings, is their automatic rejection of human beings who have exhausted the effect-energies of beneficial social acts which were performed in previous physical existences.

These regions have other disadvantages but the human being does not realize them. The human being is pleasure-hungry and thus its focus is related to that only. Thus when its pleasurable life there is terminated, the human being feels resentful about being rejected by the environment of those places.

The subtle body of a human being changes its energy level according to social activities, such that criminal acts cause that subtle body to be attracted to hellish astral worlds, while socially-beneficial acts, cause it to be attracted to the astral paradises.

The human being, if it has negative effect-energies in its psyche, may go to a hellish astral location after death. And similarly if it has positive effect-energies, it may go to an astral paradise. In either case, that individual will stay in either world for only as long as the effect-energies are not exhausted.

There is no endless happiness on earth. That is certain. There is much more happiness in the paradise regions, and still in those places, happiness comes to an end abruptly for those who were elevated to those places after life on earth.

The permanent residents of the astral paradises, are the celestial beings who use astral bodies which do not have the need for acquiring physical forms. Even for those deities and their angelic hosts, there is the specter of death when the astral paradises are destroyed through astronomical destruction like when stars or galaxies collide with one another.

Application:

After trillions and trillions of births and deaths in numerous species of life, on numerous planets, a particular living entity develops an intuition which states that this existence of gross life and lower astral life is not only fatiguing but is a complete waste of valuable time.

This conclusion is reached after accessing the highest life forms in the material world, which are those in the higher astral worlds. A mosquito feels fulfillment from its life which lasts for one summer season. A human being feels fulfillment from its life which is less than one hundred years. A celestial beings feels fulfillment from its life which may be for five billion years or more. But then such a life comes to end when the subtle material on which its life depended fizzes out.

In consideration of this some yogis aim to become siddhas who transcend all phases of the astral world and enter into the spiritual energy where deterioration has no register.

The first accomplishment is to rid one's subtle body of its tendency to rely on gross forms. After this is achieved, one should get rid of the subtle body altogether, so that one can be satisfied with the bare spiritual form of the individual spirit. These are not easy achievements.

Verse 30

अशुभा गतयः प्राप्ताः कष्टा मे पापसेवनात्

काममन्युपरीतेन तृष्णया मोहितेन च

aśubhā gatayaḥ prāptāḥ kaṣṭā me pāpasevanāt
kāmamanyuparītena tṛṣṇayā mohitena ca (1.30)

aśubhā – what is awful; gatayaḥ - states of consciousness, psychological destinations; prāptāḥ - got; kaṣṭā – tortuous, troublesome; me – by me; pāpasevanāt – due to performing; kāmamany = kāmamani = cultural activities; uparītena – improper; tṛṣṇayā – by desires; mohitena – by delusion; ca - and

Due to my performance of social crimes, I got the result of awful and tortuous states of consciousness. This was due also to improper cultural activities, desires and delusion.

Analysis:

The ascetic cited his history of social crimes through which he had to endure torturous states of consciousness as reactions within material nature. Improper cultural activities which are performed in ignorance of their effects or with knowledge of their consequence, are recorded in material nature and serve as impetus for fresh reactions in the future. These inconveniences are blended into the destiny of the entity involved.

Improper cultural activities come about due to ignorance of social norms, unawareness of past life relationships with particular souls, government policies and awkwardness produced by being served uncontrollable circumstances by providence. The conclusion is that a limited entity will never have the upper hand.

Desire and delusion are created from the same type of emotional sense-energy. This energy pervades the psyche of a living entity while it has a material body and when it is disembodied. Some of it is held in dormancy. Some is activated as a lubricant for the flow of history. Most desires are fulfilled without any understanding of its forceful impact on the future circumstances which will confront the entity.

Application:

Like this ascetic, a yogi should come to his senses, breach the membrane of the subconsciousness and review the history of past lives. If one fails to do this, one is doomed to repeated birth, repeated ignorance when acting and repeated victimization by providence. No one becomes liberated from material existence by remaining in ignorance of past lives. It is nature's procedure to keep the information from past lives under lock and key, in the subconscious, in a grey area of memory of the living entity.

Remaining in ignorance of past lives is costly for any entity, because material nature does not excuse offenses which are done in ignorance. Realizing this, yogis take a course in mystic practice which gives them the ability to penetrate the causal body where they can see the unmanifest desire energies which are to come. These energies remain in the causal form like eggs in the body of a hen which if left to the course of time, will develop into chicks one by one. A yogi cannot afford to allow material nature to continue the development of desires because nature's actions occur as an expense to the yogi.

Nature rides piggy-back on the living entities, but a yogi finds a way to throw nature off his being and thus he becomes free. Others either resist nature ineffectively or happily accept her as part of self-identity.

Verse 31

पुनः पुनश्च मरणं जन्म चैव पुनः पुनः

आहारा विविधा भुक्ताः पीता नानाविधाः स्तनाः

punaḥ punaśca maraṇaṁ janma caiva punaḥ punaḥ
āhārā vividhā bhuktāḥ pītā nānāvidhāḥ stanāḥ (1.31)

punaḥ punaś = punaḥ punah = again and again; ca – and; maraṇaṁ - death of a body; janma – birth of a form; caiva – and yet; punaḥ punaḥ - again and again; āhārā – food; vividhā – various types; bhuktāḥ - enjoyed, consumed; pītā – parents; nānā – many diverse; vidhāḥ - different types; stanāḥ - breasts

Again and again I endured death of a body, and yet again and again, I endured birth of a form. I consumed various types of food. I had many parents. I sucked on different types of breasts.

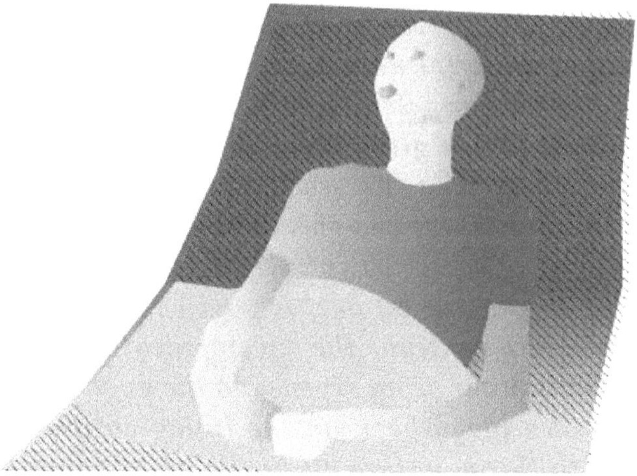

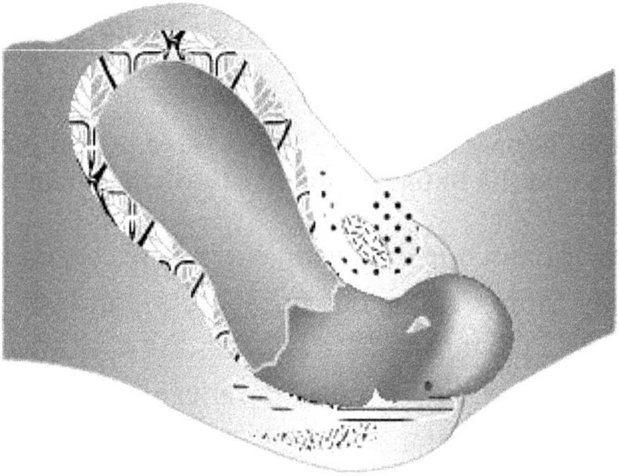

Analysis:

Even though the entities endure birth, suckling as infants, adult food consumption, death of a body, and then the repetition of this history, still there is no comprehensive recall of these actions in former bodies. Instead there is simply an instinct to go on living in whatever state of consciousness it discovers itself to be.

This instinct is stored in the kundalini life force as an evolutionary urge. It is also stored in the causal body as potent conditioned energy. This is used in the causal body to cancel out certain desire potencies. As an evolutionary urge the instinct drives the living entities to participate in the struggle for existence and so it fights its way to more efficient predatory life forms.

The suckling action is used in each species of life but it is manifested differently according to the particular life form. In all such situations, the entity who needs a body enters the psyche of the would-be parents and takes as a loan some biological material for making its new body. After getting sufficient assistance, that entity transits from infancy to adult stage and then is circumstantially and developmentally conditioned by nature to foster other disembodied entities who are in the queue for transmigrations.

Application:

It is part of the requirement that a student yogi must go back into the subconscious mind and enter into the record of past lives. This is necessary for developing the required determination to complete the austerities which would allow the entity to transit away from material existence completely. Material nature is wishing for the living entities to remain in its association forever. This desire-energy in material nature prevents the entities from sincerely striving for liberation. But if a self becomes conversant with previous lives, it can resist the encouragement provided by material nature, and attain departure to the exclusive spiritual territories.

In many lives, trillions of lives, a living entity has served as parent and has relied on others as progeny. There are obligations which it owes and benefits which it accrued in many lives. These energies are stored in material nature which will release desire-forces in its onward march through time. Even when a universe is demolished, the effect-energies from social actions, still remain intact on the causal plane. These are activated when another creation begins and suitable conditions for manifestation occurs.

In the attempt to escape from this system of manifestation in material nature, a yogi has to cross certain hurdles, the main one being the affectionate energies which were shared with other living beings in the course of the trillions of transmigrations. These energies have a magnetic charge which keeps a living entity attracted to the material cosmos. The self must make a special attempt to break the choke-hold of the affectionate energies. When that is achieved, it is freed and qualifies for entry into the spiritual universe.

Verse 32

मातरो विविधा दृष्टाः पितरश्च पृथग्विधाः

सुखानि च विचित्राणि दुःखानि च मयानघ

mātaro vividhā dṛṣṭāḥ pitaraśca pṛthagvidhāḥ
sukhāni ca vicitrāṇi duḥkhāni ca mayānagha (1.32

mātaro = mātarah = mothers; vividhā – different kinds; dṛṣṭāḥ - experienced; pitaraś = pitarah = fathers; ca – and; pṛthagvidhāḥ - various species; sukhāni – pleasures; ca – and; vicitrāṇi – variety; duḥkhāni – miseries; ca – and; mayā – by me; anagha – faultless person

I experienced different kinds of mothers and fathers in various species. O faultless person, a variety of pleasures and miseries was endured by me.

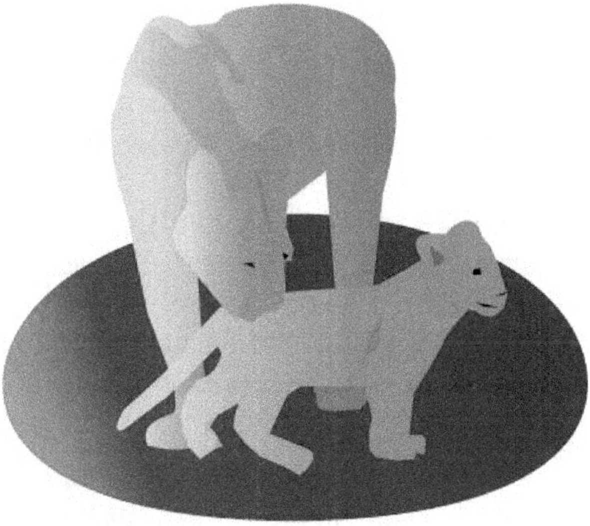

Analysis:

This yogi attained the status of siddha which meant that he could assess the value of his transmigrations. He could account his parental service-merits and know as well his obligations to others who served as parents for his numerous bodies in the various species.

In the course of material existence, pleasures and miseries must be endured regardless of whether they are desired or not. The living entity prefers pleasure but even that is awarded to it by material nature, with or without respect to its desire. Nature regulates the intensity as well as the quantity of pleasure and pain which is transmitted through the sensory energy of the self.

In the human species, the entity gets the idea that it has the upper hand over nature, but in fact, this is not true. An allowance permitted by material nature, cannot be maintained by any limited entity. Thus the siddhas have no illusions about that. They strive for full release from its dominance.

Application:

The conduit for pleasures and miseries is the kundalini life force. This psychic mechanism lays out the various nerves in the embryo. When the child is born, it is assailed with feelings and cries because of the fear of pain. Such pain is transmitted through the nerves.

Even though it does not desire miserable conditions or ill health, still it must endure whatever inconvenience it is subjected to in material nature. The self never has full autonomy over any circumstance in nature. It is not the master of nature.

Realizing this truth, a yogi decides to learn a method of freeing the self from its involvement with all aspects of material nature. Since he can never get the upper hand over it, and since it is so vast and infinite, he decides to forego his attraction to it.

The controlling location of the self's relationship with material nature is within the individual psyche. A yogi has to find the contact point between the psyche and material nature. Then he has to identify the psychic mechanism which links the core self to the sensual circuits. If the link is broken the self finds itself in exclusive spiritual existence, freed from mundane contact.

Verse 33

प्रियैर्विवासो बहुशः संवासश्चाप्रियैः सह

धननाशश्च संप्राप्तो लब्ध्वा दुःखेन तद्धनम्

priyairvivāso bahuśaḥ saṁvāsaścāpriyaiḥ saha
dhananāśaśca saṁprāpto labdhvā duḥkhena taddhanam (1.33)

priyair = priyaih = concerning those who are dear; vivāso = vivāsah = separated; bahuśaḥ - time and again; saṁvāsaś = saṁvāsah = forced into association with; cāpriyaiḥ = ca (and) + āpriyaiḥ - concerning those who are disliked); saha – with; dhanan – wealth; āśaś = āśah = loss, confiscation; ca – and; saṁprāpto = saṁprāptah = endured; labdhvā – after attaining; duḥkhena – by difficult means; tad = tat = that; dhanam - wealth

Time and again I was separated from those who were dear to me and then was forced into association with those whom I disliked. After attaining wealth by difficult means, I had to endure its loss or confiscation.

Analysis:

There comes a time in a self's existence, when it realizes what options were permitted by material nature. There is no doubt that the scope of the vast mundane cosmos is way beyond the desire hopes of any entity.

The limited entities just cannot exhaust the cosmic energy. Due to nature's vastness on the subtle and gross levels of its manifestation, a realized soul comes to the conclusion that nature will maintain its control through all eternity. The only way out is to effectively renounce the need for nature.

Application:

The dance between material nature and the limited entity is ongoing with the entity attaining high levels of culture with the associated trappings in some births and not having or losing these in other births. These dual features harass the self which in conjunction with the mind feels deprived and depressed.

Learning how to distance itself from its accessory psychic adjunctions, the self takes a vacation from being linked in with material nature. This is a type of samadhi. This is permitted for a short length of time, until the entity reforms its psyche and can remain in such states for over one hour.

Within the mind, the entity discovers that it is surrounded by material nature. Its psychic organs are prejudiced for the interest of material nature, which requires the energy of the self to animate its applications. With this realization the self becomes pleased as this insight holds the key to its freedom.

Verse 34

अवमानाः सुकष्टाश्च परतः स्वजनात्तथा

शारीरा मानसाश्चापि वेदना भृशदारुणाः

avamānāḥ sukaṣṭāśca parataḥ svajanāttathā
śārīrā mānasāścāpi vedanā bhṛśadāruṇāḥ (1.34)

avamānāḥ - insults; sukaṣṭāh – terrible; ca – and; parataḥ - persons of greater status, unrelated; svajanāt – from his relatives; tathā - as well as; śārīrā - body; mānasāś = mānasāh = mind; cāpi = ca (and) + api (also); vedanā – agonies; bhṛśadāruṇāḥ - unbearable, painful

Terrible insults in the excess were endured by me, from people of greater status and from relatives as well. Unbearable painful horrors were suffered by the mind and body.

Analysis:

Material nature is one fatiguing principle. The entities who are in the social environment are a separate hassle. Those of greater status who would be expected to be pious and compassionate, are found to be criminal and harsh. These perplexities are challenging.

There is mental and physical suffering. The avenues for avoiding this are limited. In fact in many instances there seems to be no way to escape the harassment.

Application:

In the yoga practice, one learns how not to respond to the fluctuations of the emotions. This is mastered in pratyahar sensual energy withdrawal practice. If a twig is dropped into an ocean, it will find itself going upwards and downwards frequently. This is not to victimize the twig but it is necessary as part of the state of liquid energy. Just so the rhythms of material nature cause the self to endure dual transmissions of emotional energy.

Since a self cannot under any circumstances adjust the material nature in any permanent or cosmic way, that self should see that it is at a disadvantage. It should make the decision to exclude itself from nature's territory.

Verse 35

प्राप्ता विमानननाश्चोग्रा वधबन्धाश्च दारुणाः

पतनं निरये चैव यातनाश्च यमक्षये

prāptā vimānanāścogrā vadhabandhāśca dāruṇāḥ
patanaṁ niraye caiva yātanāśca yamakṣaye (1.35)

prāptā – endured; vimānanāś = vimānanāh = indignities; cogrā = ca (and) + ugrā (horrible); vadha – death, killing; bandhāś = bandhāh = imprisonment; ca – and; dāruṇāḥ - miserable conditions; patanaṁ - sent down; niraye - in hell; caiva – and so; yātanāś = yātanāh = punishments; ca – and; yamakṣaye – in the realm of the deity who judges hereafter

I endured horrible indignities, vicious deaths, imprisonments and miserable conditions. I was sent into hellish conditions and was painfully punished in the realm of the deity who judges hereafter.

Analysis:

Some religions profess a deity who judges departed souls. Some say that the Supreme God does this. Others deny it entirely. It is reasonable to assume that if there are astral realms where departed souls exist, there must be social organization in those places. If there is social organization there will be approved behaviors and condemned acts. There will be administration of that society.

The ascetic could recall situations in which he was subjected to horrible indignities, vicious deaths, imprisonments and miserable conditions while using human bodies but there were also hellish conditions in the astral realms hereafter. There were courts and judges who enforced punishments on the subtle bodies of the deceased for some antisocial or criminal actions performed during the earthly life.

Application:

A yogi should not be reckless in social acts. Nature tracks down all offenders sooner or later, and administers compensatory energies. Knowing this a yogi should learn how to reduce social expenditures to the minimum and should eliminate the need for criminal and antisocial behavior.

Nature does not accept the practice of spiritual discipline as an excuse for not dealing with social liabilities. Therefore it is best to reduce the social interactions to a minimum so that the liabilities are within one's means. If a yogi expands social contacts, he or she must expect extended commitments within material nature. To reduce the obligations one has to reduce the social outlay.

Verse 36

जरा रोगाश्च सततं वासनानि च भूरिशः

लोकेऽस्मिन्ननुभूतानि द्वंद्वजानि भृशं मया

jarā rogāśca satataṁ vāsanāni ca bhūriśaḥ
loke'sminnanubhūtāni dvaṁdvajāni bhṛśaṁ mayā (1.36)

jarā – old age; rogāś = rogāh = disease; ca – and; satataṁ - constant; vāsanāni – disasters; ca – and; bhūriśaḥ - more than sufficient; loke'smin – in this world; nanubhūtāni = anubhūtāni – perception;

dvaṁdvajāni – dual conditions; bhṛśaṁ - psychosis which arises; mayā – by me

Old age and disease constantly assailed me. The disasters were more than sufficient. In this world, the psychosis which arises from the perception of dual conditions was felt by me.

Analysis:

The core-self is wired to the psychic equipments which detect the moods of material nature. These equipments sense various natural phenomena. The fluctuation in the sensory energy affects the core-self through signal transmission. In the psychic circuit, the core self is connected to a sense of identity which is a very sensitive transparent cloud of energy which surrounds the self. This sense of identity is in constant communication with the intellect which is the part of the mind which analyses and forms ideas.

The intellect in turn is wired to the senses, which in turn are motivated by the kundalini life force. When there are dual conditions, the intellect becomes psychotic. The sense of identity which relies on the intellect, follows that behavior. The core-self in turn takes on the attitude of the sense of identity. In this way whatever the senses detect has impact on the core-self.

Application:

It is the duty of a student yogi to study the design of the psyche. It is not the duty of God or the spiritual teacher to redesign the psyche in a simpler configuration. In fact the deity and the spiritual teacher cannot redesign a psyche which came about naturally by the conjunction of a core self and material nature. If there are flaws in the psyche these flaws exist because of the creative process of material nature. Neither God nor the spiritual teacher can dictate the formation methods of material nature. Thus the only alternative is for the disciple to review the construction of the psyche, get advice on how to reform it, apply such advice and experience the benefit of those changes. This must be done individually.

The dual conditions of material nature attack the feelings of a living entity. How can it do that? What is the connection between the dual conditions of heat and cold, happiness and distress and the core self? Is there a direct connect between cold weather for instance and the core self? If the core self is in the astral world and does not have a material body, will it be affected by cold weather which freezes material bodies?

What is the intellect? How do thoughts occur? Why is the core-self affected happily or sadly by certain thoughts?

A student yogi should research this and find out the link between what happens in the material world and its impact on the self which is a transcendental principle.

Verse 37

ततः कदाचिन्निर्वेदान्निकारान्निकृतेन च

लोकतन्त्रं परित्यक्तं दुःखार्तेन भृशं मया

ततः सिद्धिरियं प्राप्ता प्रसादादात्मनो मया

tataḥ kadācinnirvedānnikārānnikṛtena ca
lokatantraṁ parityaktaṁ duḥkhārtena bhṛśaṁ mayā
tataḥ siddhiriyaṁ prāptā prasādādātmano mayā (1.37)

tataḥ - then; kadācin = kadācit = it happened; nirvedān = nirvedāt = from disgust; nikārān = nikārāt = overwhelming; nikṛtena – by a depression; ca – and; loka – world; tantraṁ - operations; parityaktaṁ - total abandonment; duḥkhār= duḥkhān = miseries; tena – by this; bhṛśaṁ - fatiguing circumstances; mayā – by me; tataḥ - then; siddhir = siddhih = spiritual perfection; iyaṁ - this; prāptā – attained; prasādād = prasādāt = by the favor; ātmano = ātmanah = of the self; mayā – by me

Then, it so happened, that an overwhelming disgust and a depression was felt by me. Subsequently, I totally abandoned the fatiguing operations of this world with its miseries. Then being conversant with that detachment, and by the favor of the self, I attained spiritual perfection.

Analysis:

One has to gain the favor of the spiritual self, which is to say that the self must bless itself as the core-self, segregate itself from the rest of the psyche, assess its value to itself and then work to gain leverage over the psychic components which implicate the self in the operations of material nature.

Is it necessary for the self to reach a stage of disgust and abandonment in depression, before it can make the decision to review its relationship with material nature? From the evidence presented by the elevated ascetic, it appears that the self must first become disgusted and abjectly depressed before it can turn itself about and seriously consider its predicament.

Application:

A student yogi should not wait for full disgust and dejection. He or she should assess the worth of the core-self and then make a decision to upset the influence the other psychic components exert over the self. Material nature will always harass the self. That will never end. Thus it is up to the self to invoke in itself sufficient impetus for liberation. If there is another environment, another cosmos, somewhere else which is devoid of material nature, then the core-self should hustle up and migrate to that transcendental location. If there is no such place, then the self is condemned to perpetual conflict in this mundane situation.

Verse 38

नाहं पुनरिहागन्ता लोकानालोकयाम्यहम्

आ सिद्धेरा प्रजासर्गादात्मनो मे गतिः शुभा

nāhaṁ punarihāgantā lokānālokayāmyaham
ā siddherā prajāsargādātmano me gatiḥ śubhā (1.38)

nāhaṁ = na (never) + aham (I); punarihāgantā = punar (again) + iha (here) + āgantā (come, be involved); lokān – worlds; ālokayāmy = ālokayāmi = observe; aham – I; ā – until the time of; siddher = siddheḥ = of perfection; ā – until; prajā – beings; sargād = sargāt = up to end of the creation; ātmano = ātmanah = of the self; me – by me; gatiḥ = destination; śubhā - auspicious

I will never again be involved here. I observe the worlds. From the time of my perfection to the time of the end of these beings in the creation, the auspicious destinations attained by the self will be noted by me.

Analysis:

It seems that the siddha reached spiritual perfection in so far as it can be attained while remaining in the mundane universe. He admitted that he would be in this existence up to the time of the end of these beings. This pertains to the end of the subtle bodies of these beings, a time in which everything manifested as this cosmos will go into non-manifestation.

The ascetic carefully noted the auspicious or favorable destinations which could be attained in this cosmos. None of these was his ultimate objective, but they were the best this nature had to offer, and he took note it.

Application:

An inquiry regarding the liberation of this ascetic is this: Why did he have to wait for the summary conclusion of this cosmos? Why could he not exit from this system at the time of his perfection?

The answer is that even a perfected being does not have absolute freedom. Even that person must work with natural cause and effect. The ascetic was free to move in the various dimensions of this cosmos but he was not free to fully transcend the time content of this universe. Is there a deity controlling transits out of this cosmic place? Is there a supernatural corridor which cordons this place?

Verse 39

उपलब्धा द्विजश्रेष्ठ तथेयं सिद्धिरुत्तमा

इतः परं गमिष्यामि ततः परतरं पुनः

ब्रह्मणः पदमव्यग्रं मा ते भूदत्र संशयः

upalabdhā dvijaśreṣṭha tatheyaṁ siddhiruttamā
itaḥ paraṁ gamiṣyāmi tataḥ parataraṁ punaḥ
brahmaṇaḥ padamavyagraṁ mā te bhūdatra saṁśayaḥ (1.39)

upalabdhā – having obtained; dvija – well-trained ascetic; śreṣṭha – best; tatheyaṁ = tathā(as) + eyaṁ (this); siddhir = siddhih = perfection; uttamā – highest; itaḥ - thereafter; paraṁ - higher; gamiṣyāmi – I will go; tataḥ - then; parataraṁ - even higher; punaḥ - again; brahmaṇaḥ - exclusive spiritual existence; padam – level, position; avyagraṁ - definitely; mā – not; te – you; bhūd – know; atra – here; saṁśayaḥ - doubt

O best of the well-trained ascetics, having obtained the highest perfection, I will go to the highest dimension. Then again, I will go even higher. I will definitely attain the level of exclusive spiritual existence. You should harbor no doubts on this subject.

Analysis:

The perfected ascetic had not attained exclusive spiritual existence at the time of answering the worthy questions of Kashyapa. However he assured that he would reach that level sometime in the future. In the meantime, he researched and assessed the higher dimensions.

Application:

The ascetic said he would go to the highest dimension for which he was qualified. However he graciously alerted that after attaining that highest dimension he would again go even higher until he reached the level of exclusive spiritual existence, brahman.

This is instructive since some neophyte yogis feel that they should and will reach the highest level once and for all. However the staircase to spiritual perfection has many steps.

As soon as one surmounts one, one perceives another. The quest is challenging to say the least. The ascetic did not indulge Kashyapa with a promise for reaching perfection in one achievement. He was honest and laid out the course taken by a yogi.

Verse 40

नाहं पुनरिहागन्ता मर्त्यलोकं परंतप

प्रीतोऽस्मि ते महाप्राज्ञ ब्रूहि किं करवाणि ते

nāhaṁ punarihāgantā martyalokaṁ paraṁtapa
prīto'smi te mahāprājña brūhi kiṁ karavāṇi te

nāhaṁ = na (never) + ahaṁ (I); punar = punah = again; ihāgantā = iha (here) + āgantā (return); martyalokaṁ - world where bodies quickly die; paraṁtapa – scorcher of foes; prīto = prītah = pleased; 'smi = asmi = I am; te – you; mahā – great; prājña – insight; brūhi – say; kiṁ - what; karavāṇi – what to do; te - you

I will never again return here to the world where bodies quickly reach their end. I am pleased with you. O person of great insight, say what I can do for you.

Analysis:

Even though he could not get out of the cosmos, he attained a state of perfection which allowed him to never again take birth in the material world in a place where the life of the body is of very short duration.

He willingly associated with Kashyapa who was serious about attaining the same type of spiritual perfection, but he would soon close off his affiliation with physical existence.

Application:

When one perfected entity is no longer required to manifest in the physical world, other yogis who are on the verge of perfection, remain available to students. Assistance for spiritual elevation is always forthcoming.

Verse 41

यदीप्सुरुपपन्नस्त्वं तस्य कालोऽयमागतः

अभिजाने च तदहं यदर्थं मा त्वमागतः

अचिरात्तु गमिष्यामि येनाहं त्वामचूचुदम्

yadīpsurupapannastvaṁ tasya kālo'yamāgataḥ
abhijāne ca tadahaṁ yadarthaṁ mā tvamāgataḥ
acirāttu gamiṣyāmi yenāhaṁ tvāmacūcudam (1.41)

yad – what; īpsur = īpsuh = desirous, eager to know; upapannas = upapannah = overtaken by; tvaṁ - you; tasya – of this; kālo = kālah = time; 'yam = ayam = this; āgataḥ - come; abhijāne – in knowing, aware of; ca – and; tad = tat = that; ahaṁ - I; yad = yat = which; arthaṁ - value, reason; mā – not; tvam – you; āgataḥ - approached, contacted; acirāt – shortly; tu – but; gamiṣyāmi – I will go; yenāhaṁ = yena (by which) + aham (I); tvām – you; acūcudam - prompted, indicated

The time is now! Express what you are eager to know. Actually I am aware of the reason you contacted me. I will go shortly. Thus I informed you.

Analysis:

This was Kashyapa's last opportunity to question this perfected entity.

Application:

A student yogi should not take an advanced teacher for granted. One should not assume that the teacher will always be available. Association with an advanced soul is taken for granted only by those who are arrogant or foolish. One becomes arrogant when one is unable to properly assess the value of a teacher, especially when one thinks that one has the same level of spiritual insight as the teacher.

Being an expert at some cultural aspects and being proud of the self's assumption of a superior body, like that in an aristocratic culture or that in a ruling race of people, a disciple carries with him or her, a certain arrogance which serves to deprive the self of a sense of appreciation for an advanced entity. Usually such disciples find every fault of an advanced soul and use those discoveries as a reason not to take the instructions of the senior person. Of course this does nothing to aid that student in spiritual advancement.

A spiritual teacher does not have to be perfect in everything he does. What is required of him is perfection in practice, particularly he should have a persistent spiritual practice which yields for him steady advancement. His flaws in social operations and in other things which are not really related to spiritual development are irrelevant really.

The two accounts, the social one and the one of the personal psyche upliftment and control, should not be assessed as one principle. These should be sorted so that the disciple can focus on the teacher's spiritual practice and the validity of that.

Verse 42

भृशं प्रीतोऽस्मि भवतश्चारित्रेण विचक्षण

परिपृच्छ यावद्भवते भाषेयं यत्तवेप्सितम्

bhṛśaṁ prīto'smi bhavataścāritreṇa vicakṣaṇa
paripṛccha yāvadbhavate bhāṣeyaṁ yattavepsitam (1.42)

bhṛśaṁ - very; prīto = prītah = pleased; 'smi = asmi = I am; bhavataś = bhavatah = great soul; cāritreṇa – by your behavior; vicakṣaṇa – mature; paripṛccha - inquire; yāvad = yāvat = which, whatever; bhavate – you; bhāṣeyaṁ - subject of interest; yat – which; tavepsitam = tave (your) + ipsetam (as much as desired)

I am very pleased, O great soul, with your mature behavior. Inquire as much as desired about whatever subject is of interest to you.

Analysis:

Great souls are not attached to controlling others, nor to having disciples to instruct. Still, if a student approaches and has an absorbent attitude, the teacher appreciates that. In all fields of teaching, submissive students who respect a teacher, regardless of his or her faults, get the best of the teacher. These students make rapid advancement through the austerities and are inspired from within their minds with visions of higher reality. This strengthens their confidence and spurs them to practice with precision and consistency.

Application:

An advanced teacher does not need students who are submissive. Still if a student is, then the teacher's advice becomes very productive in the student. In most cases of student failure, the flaw is the student's inability to sense and absorb particular disciplines of the teacher. A student whose purpose is to find fault with the teacher will resist the teacher, even when the proper methods of austerity are described.

Some students feel that if they cannot find a qualified teacher who knows the spiritual path and who is also ideal in the social sense, then they should not accept anyone as a teacher. Their approach is that providence is supposed to supply on demand a worthy teacher. But this attitude is terribly flawed.

Kashyapa must have had other teachers who were not as self-realized as this special ascetic. Does that mean that he disrespected or ridiculed those other persons who were not siddhas?

Verse 43

बहु मन्ये च ते बुद्धिं भृशं संपूजयामि च

येनाहं भवता बुद्धो मेधावी ह्यसि काश्यप

bahu manye ca te buddhiṁ bhṛśaṁ saṁpūjayāmi ca
yenāhaṁ bhavatā buddho medhāvī hyasi kāśyapa (1.43)

bahu – very; manye – I think; ca – and; te – your; buddhiṁ - intelligence; bhṛśaṁ - very, greatly; saṁpūjayāmi – I admire; ca – and; yenāhaṁ = yena (by which) + bhavatā (by you); buddho – intellect; medhāvī – one who is insightful, brillant; hyasi = hi (indeed) + asi (you are); kāśyapa - Kashyapa

I think you are very intelligent. I greatly admire you. O brilliant Kashyapa, by your insight, you recognized me.

Analysis:

A disciple who has little understanding about the level of advancement of the spiritual teacher, usually cannot assess the worth of the teacher and cannot make the best use of the information which the teacher provides. There is something to say about students who can estimate the worth of a teacher. They ask the appropriate questions and get answers which they can put into practice through spiritual discipline. For other disciples hearing from a teacher is also beneficial even though they cannot absorb as much.

A teacher is relieved to find a student who is worthy of profound conversations, since such a student acts as a container for spiritual insight. If there is no such student, the teacher is burdened with the task of passing on advanced techniques and realization through literature. The problem with literature is that when students read it without guidance, they may derive incorrect conceptions.

Application:

Spiritual advancement comes easy for some students. It is difficult to attain for others. It depends on the evolutionary status of the person. Those who have had many transmigrations where they considered the mysteries of existence, and performed austerities in previous lives to develop detachment, are the students who can make the most of an advanced teacher.

Persons who have not given material existence a thorough estimation, who have not done sensual restraint with the objective of sorting the components of the psyche, can take very little from an advanced being because they have not developed the insight which applies to psychic and spiritual reality. Still, even these persons benefit from the association of a great soul, who would never deprive them of his or her company.

Chapter 2

World of Social Action*

tasya sthānāni dṛṣṭāni trividhānīha śāstrataḥ
karmabhūmiriyaṁ bhūmiryatra tiṣṭhanti jantavaḥ (2.32)

Concerning this, it is perceived according to the authoritative texts that there are three regions. This earth where the creatures live is the world of social action. (2.32)

**This chapter heading was introduced by the translator on the basis of the verse above. The Mahābhārata does not have a chapter heading.*

Verse 1

वासुदेव उवाच

ततस्तस्योपसंगृह्य पादौ प्रश्नान्सुदुर्वचान्

पप्रच्छ तांश्च सर्वान्स प्राह धर्मभृतां वरः

vāsudeva uvāca
tatastasyopasaṁgṛhya pādau praśnānsudurvacān
papraccha tāṁśca sarvānsa prāha dharmabhṛtāṁ varaḥ (2.1)

vāsudeva – son of Vasudeva; uvāca – said; tatas = tatah = then; tasyopasaṁgṛhya = tasya (of his) + upasaṁgṛhya (gently grasping); pādau – of two feet; praśnān – answers; sudurvacān – difficult to answer; papraccha – asked; tāṁś = tān = those; ca – and; sarvān – all; sa – he, that; prāha – spoke; dharmabhṛtāṁ - advocate of righteous lifestyle; varaḥ - best

Krishna, the son of Vasudeva, said: Then gently grasping the feet of that perfected mystic, Kashyapa asked questions which were difficult to answer. The best of the advocates of righteous lifestyle spoke of all those matters.

Analysis:

Despite his detachment and power grasp over the transmigration tendency, this teacher of Kashyapa was the best of the advocates of righteous lifestyle. A perfected yogi does not encourage anyone in malicious acts, or in criminal acts, or in pretense religion. He is aware of the value of socially-beneficial acts. He supports that.

Student yogis may not give a high estimation of social acts. They rightly conclude that overall social activity is implicating. It ties up the performer and riddles his energy with urges which force him to transmigrate helplessly. Even a righteous act is binding and sets the stage for future lives in the material world. Thus a neophyte usually petitions a teacher, stating that he or she wants to terminate all social involvement.

To be practical however one has to take the Universal Form of Krishna into account. This is the form which Krishna revealed to Arjuna on the battlefield. Beneficial social acts are recommended by that deity. If one neglects that, his life will be certain misery, both on earth and hereafter.

But in any case, any sort of social act is binding and serves as the base for future mandatory transmigrations. This is why some ascetics suspect that any social entanglement will result in undesirable consequences.

One has to come to terms with the Universal Form by complying with His instructions without wanting any positive results from the activity. Service to Him should be done without need for reward, while one focuses on the issue of becoming liberated from material existence.

Application:

There is certain information which a student must get from an advanced personality. This can be acquired by physical or psychic means. If the student is sensitive, he or she could meet great souls on the astral planes and receive the required information. Otherwise it is necessary for the student to meet a teacher physically.

Much can be acquired through discovery while practicing yoga. Some can be acquired by reading books on the topic. One may also enter a hermitage or ashram and practice spiritual discipline under that regiment.

It is good to ask questions but it is not good to demand answers. Ask questions and allow seniors to answer or to ignore the requests. Most of all a student should listen attentively for answers which a senior gives on occasion especially without request.

Verse 2

काश्यप उवाच

कथं शरीरं च्यवते कथं चैवोपपद्यते

कथं कष्टाच्च संसारात्संसरन्परिमुच्यते

kāśyapa uvāca
kathaṁ śarīraṁ cyavate kathaṁ caivopapadyate
kathaṁ kaṣṭācca saṁsārātsaṁsaranparimucyate (2.2)

kāśyapa – Kashyapa; uvāca – said; kathaṁ - how; śarīraṁ - physical body; cyavate – deteriorate; kathaṁ - how; caivopapadyate = ca (and) + eva (so) + upapadyate(acquire); kathaṁ - how; kaṣṭāc = kaṣṭāt = from trouble-prone; ca – and; saṁsārāt – from the course of haphazard transmigrations; saṁsaran – course of haphazard transmigration; parimucyate – be freed, escape

Kashyapa said: How does the physical body deteriorate? How is a new one acquired? How does one who is in the trouble-ridden course of haphazard transmigrations escape from the puzzle?

Analysis:

The mystery of how the physical body deteriorates and why death becomes mandatory for all life forms is a great puzzle in material existence. Our scientists consider the solving of this mystery to be one of top priority. Many religions have flourished on the earth, because of this mystery. Such systems of faith give the follower the promise that a god or God will eventually award an eternal material body.

How is a new body acquired? This question is perplexing especially to those entities who have not experienced themselves as an astral existence which is distinct from the physical form. Even people who had out-of-the-body experiences, are perplexed about the exact process through which a spirit acquires a new body.

The living entities are moving from body to body. How is that done? Are there rules of body migration? Can one master the system of reincarnation?

Application:

A yogi studies how the body begins to deteriorate after it reaches sexual maturity. Various organs begin to operate inefficiently. Some actually shut down. Through doing asana postures, and breath infusement, a yogi has the opportunity to

study the human form in detail. The system which maintains the body is the kundalini life force. A yogi learns how to infuse this energy, which provides him with insight into various parts of the body. As a taxi driver knows the roads in a city, so the yogi by the help of kundalini perceives the subtle and gross channels through which the life force flows.

Kashyapa as the ideal student yogi, wanted to know about transmigration through various bodies, and especially about how one is fused into the parental influence through which one realizes the self as an embryo which is later delivered as a baby.

Since the entities usually cannot carry over their memories from one life to another, the only traces which they experience from the past life is their instincts. These are subjectively operated and leave the entity at a great disadvantage.

Verse 3

आत्मानं वा कथं युक्त्वा तच्छरीरं विमुञ्चति

शरीरतश्च निर्मुक्तः कथमन्यत्प्रपद्यते

ātmānaṁ vā kathaṁ yuktvā taccharīraṁ vimuñcati
śarīrataśca nirmuktaḥ kathamanyatprapadyate (2.3)

ātmānaṁ - self; vā – or; kathaṁ - how; yuktvā - being fused; tac = tat = that; charīraṁ = śarīraṁ = body; vimuñcati – release; śarīrataś = śarīratah = from the material body; ca – and; nirmuktaḥ - released; katham – how; anyat – another; prapadyate – become, acquire

Being fused into a body, how does the self become released from it? And how after being released from one, does the self become another?

Analysis:

The human being has little or no memory of what it was before becoming an embryo. During the embryo stage, it has no objectivity. However as the body's deterioration accelerates, the entity may have objectivity and can observe the fluctuations of consciousness in the body. But how is the entity finally released from the form? What does the self become after the body perishes? Is the self decayed and then reformed again like materials which deteriorate and are used to make a new formation?

Application:

The self is released from the body fully when the life force leaves the body. So long as the life force is operative in the body, the self cannot depart from the body. When the body is in a coma, the self cannot use the body but the life force keeps the body alive regardless. When however the life force leaves the body or when it is forced out of the body, then the self must accompany the life force. To understand this, a student must practice kundalini yoga and develop psychic sensitivity by doing insight meditation.

The entity goes to the astral plane in full when the physical body dies. It may go to a lower astral world, to an adjacent one or to a higher celestial place or beyond. Usually the entity goes to an adjacent astral dimension and remains there until it fuses into the body of a new parent. Once fused, it waits in the body of that person until it gets a birth opportunity through sexual intercourse or even through seminal implantation.

Material nature does not require the assistance of the self for the creation of a body for the self. It only requires the presence of the conscious or unconscious self. With that it manufactures a new body from the reproductive fluids of parents.

Verse 4

कथं शुभाशुभे चायं कर्मणी स्वकृते नरः

उपभुङ्क्ते क्व वा कर्म विदेहस्योपतिष्ठति

kathaṁ śubhāśubhe cāyaṁ karmaṇī svakṛte naraḥ
upabhuṅkte kva vā karma videhasyopatiṣṭhati (2.4)

kathaṁ -how; śubhāśubhe - sublime and degrading; cāyaṁ = ca (and) + ayam (this); karmaṇī – acts; svakṛte – his or her actions; naraḥ - person; upabhuṅkte – experience; kva – where; vā – conversely;

karma – cultural activities; videhasyopatiṣṭhati = videhasi (person without a material body) + upatiṣṭhati (manifest)

How does a human being experience his or her sublime and degrading acts? And conversely, where do the actions manifest for one who is without a material body?

Analysis:

Most human beings act but do not perceive the mechanisms in the psyche which urge the self to participate in social actions. For the most part the self contributes only attention to the operation of the body. This attention is extracted from the self impulsively. It is drawn out of the self by the life force which makes demands for attention-energy to carry out its operations.

The self does not experience all of its acts objectively. Some of them are carried out subjectively and/or involuntarily as dictated by the life force in the body and by the life forces in other bodies of other living entities.

A person who is disembodied may perform physical acts indirectly by influencing those who have bodies. This is through psychic possession where the disembodied person's willpower takes control of the will power of an entity who has a body.

Application:

If the effect-energy of a person's acts stays in the psyche of the person, where does that energy go if the person does not take another material body? Can the acts be manifested in the subtle realms of the hereafter? If those acts cannot surface in the subtle world, what happens to that energy which remains in the psyche of the soul?

Verse 5

ब्राह्मण उवाच

एवं संचोदितः सिद्धः प्रश्नांस्तान्प्रत्यभाषत

आनुपूर्व्येण वार्ष्णेय यथा तन्मे वचः शृणु

brāhmaṇa uvāca
evaṁ saṁcoditaḥ siddhaḥ praśnāṁstānpratyabhāṣata
ānupūrvyeṇa vārṣṇeya yathā tanme vacaḥ śṛṇu (2.5)

brāhmaṇa – ritual ascetic from the celestial regions; uvāca – said; evaṁ - thus; saṁcoditaḥ - as requested; siddhaḥ - perfected yogi; praśnāṁs = praśnān = answers; tān = tat = that; pratyabhāṣata – spoke; ānupūrvyeṇa – in sequence; vārṣṇeya – descendant of Vṛṣṇi; yathā – as; tan = tat = that; me – from me; vacaḥ - what was said; śṛṇu - hear

Thus as requested, the perfected yogi answered those questions in sequence. Hear from me what was said, O Krishna, descendant of Vṛṣṇi.

Analysis:

This is a reminder that this conversation was happening originally between Vaishampaiana and King Janamejaya who was the great grandson of Arjuna, the hero who was the first to learn the *Bhagavad Gītā* and to see the Universal Form of Krishna as applied to the Kuru civil war.

Vaishampaiana was a yogi who was a student of Vyasa, the grandfather of Arjuna. Vyasa entrusted Vaishampaiana with the task of reciting the history of the war of the Bharata people. This tale became known as the *Mahābhārata*.

Vaishampaiana is the one who recited the story about what Arjuna and Krishna did immediately after the battle when Krishna stayed with the Pandavas before returning to the city of Dvaraka. Once when they were at leisure in the very opulent city of the Pandavas, Arjuna took it upon himself to ask Krishna for a repeat of what happened just before the battle which was a detailed explanation of karma yoga and a revelation of how Krishna operated as the Supreme Being.

Instead of granting Arjuna's request, Krishna cited what he was told by an ascetic who came down from the celestial world of the creator-deity, Brahmā. That ascetic in turn explained what was described by a perfected yogi to Kashyapa.

Arjuna's attempt to again exploit his friendship with Krishna failed on this occasion. Krishna treated Arjuna in a harsh way because Arjuna took Krishna for granted as a friend and cousin. To be sure that Arjuna would not repeat that behavior, Krishna cited the ascetic who came down from the celestial heavens.

Application:

Many of the leaders of the disciplic succession which stems from Krishna, claim that a relationship with Krishna as a lover, friend, parent or servant, is all that is necessary for spiritual advancement of the devotee. However in this discourse we see that Krishna did not like how Arjuna was using the friendship relationship. Arjuna unwittingly abused the relationship by not taking the **Bhagavad Gītā** *discourse and the revelation of the Universal Form seriously.*

Arjuna's use of the friendship damaged the spiritual perception and blindsided him in such a way as to rupture his spiritual link with Krishna. Arjuna, by focusing on the friendship relationship with the physical body of Krishna, lost touch with the friendship he had with the spiritual body of the Lord. To save Arjuna from this, Krishna refused to relate to Arjuna in the friendly way as before. Krishna did embrace Arjuna just before he gave this discourse but that is as far as He indulged the hero.

Verse 6

सिद्ध उवाच

आयुःकीर्तिकराणीह यानि कर्माणि सेवते

शरीरग्रहणेऽन्यस्मिंस्तेषु क्षीणेषु सर्वशः

siddha uvāca
āyuḥkīrtikarāṇīha yāni karmāṇi sevate
śarīragrahaṇe'nyasmiṁsteṣu kṣīṇeṣu sarvaśaḥ (2.6)

siddha – perfected yogi; uvāca – said; āyuḥ - longevity; kīrti – fame; karāṇi – acts; iha – here; yāni – here; karmāṇi – actions; sevate – performs; śarīra – body; grahaṇe – in acquiring; 'nyasmiṁs =

anyasmin – in another; teṣu – in those; kṣīṇeṣu – in exhaustion; sarvaśaḥ - all

The perfected yogi said: Certain actions performed here result in longevity and fame. All such effects are exhausted when the individual acquires another body.

Analysis:

The two outstanding effects of social activity are longevity and fame. Sooner or later, a living entity learns how to acquire these. Longevity is important because if one does not have a healthy body which will live long, one will not enjoy cultural fulfillments. Since a human body takes so many years to reach sexual maturity and then even more years to reach financial sufficiency, good health is important.

A living entity does not have to objectively understand how to play the evolutionary game. It can learn this instinctually and that is just as effective as if it were integrated objectively. Those who develop the instinct for acquiring longevity and fame, are the ones who rule human society.

Application:

In one life, an individual may act socially in a way which solicits nature to award fame and longevity for the next body. But as it is, the duration of the fame and the extent of the longevity is measured out by material nature for its own convenience. It is done in such a way, that it quickly dissipates and leaves the entity in a fix with no fame or with ignobility and with bad health or with a terminal disease.

This happens repeatedly until the entity understands that this is a game played by material nature on the limited beings. Once a person sees that material nature has the upper hand and that it is impossible to replace nature with the self, that individual becomes reluctant to participate in social activities. Knowing that the options favor material nature and that there is no way to change the odds, a yogi becomes reluctant to participate in history.

Anyone who knows that he or she is fighting a losing battle will become reluctant to participate. However a yogi also sees that there is no choice in the matter so long as one is in a social environment which has requirements for participation.

One may perform socially beneficial acts and other philanthropic services in one life. These will cause one to be awarded with charisma and money in a future life. However in that future time, one will consume the effects of the piety from the former life. When those effects are exhausted, one will find the self taking another body to acquire some pious effects again.

Understanding this see-saw process, a yogi analyses and comes to the conclusion that it makes no sense to continue existing in such a situation of working to accumulate pious credits, then using the credits in the next body, then working again to acquire more pious credits and again taking another body to enjoy the results of the former life. When will this end?

Verse 7

आयुःक्षयपरीतात्मा विपरीतानि सेवते

बुद्धिर्व्यावर्तते चास्य विनाशे प्रत्युपस्थिते

āyuḥkṣayaparītātmā viparītāni sevate
buddhirvyāvartate cāsya vināśe pratyupasthite (2.7)

āyuḥ - longevity; kṣaya – destructive - parītātmā – empowered self; viparītāni – contrary acts; sevate – performs; buddhir = buddhih = intelligence; vyāvartate – changes, malfunctions; cāsya = ca (and) + asya (in this); vināśe – degradation; pratyupasthite – placed in position

With the longevity, that self-destructive, empowered person performs contrary acts. Due to this, his intelligence malfunctions and he becomes positioned for degradation.

Analysis:

Even though material nature, prompts the living entities to surge forward in the mundane evolutionary cycle, it has a way about it where it induces them to commit actions which in turn degrade them. When the entity climbs up the ladder of evolution from a less-skilled role to a more skilled one in a specific species, it is given insight in how to transit to a higher species. Material nature has the upper hand, because it acts as the basis for such a rise of status of anyone.

As soon as material nature establishes an entity in a higher species or in a higher status in the same species, it invariably withdraws its support. The living entity then comes tumbling down to a lower designation.

Nature has many ways to achieve its lack of support for an individual. It can make one's intelligence malfunction while buoying up or reinforcing one's confidence. That results in arrogant conclusions which bring on rapid degradation.

Application:

This empowered self got its power from material nature. Hence the real authority is material nature. The pride of the self prevents it from this admission. After acquiring pious credits from the performance of social activities which benefit the family, the country and the world, the entity is confronted by the inevitable death of its body, which is so dear to it, and which was the means for depositing those pious activities.

At death it rehashes its life's activities and culls the effect-energies which are positive. It holds that energy in its mind as a defense against adversity. When it acquires the next body material nature maps out its destiny at nature's convenience.

In some lives it reaps the benefit of its past pious action but in others the credits freeze and cannot be utilized. This is because the yarn of material nature flows out as dictated by time. Whenever material nature does not facilitate, some individuals take to antisocial acts and exhibit criminal behavior. This is urged by the same material nature which influences the intellect in making decisions.

Verse 8

सत्त्वं बलं च कालं चाप्यविदित्वात्मनस्तथा

अतिवेलमुपाश्नाति तैर्विरुद्धान्यनात्मवान्

sattvaṁ balaṁ ca kālaṁ cāpyaviditvātmanastathā
ativelamupāśnāti tairviruddhānyanātmavān (2.8)

sattvaṁ - mental clarity; balaṁ - bodily energy; ca – and; kālaṁ - time, opportunity; cāpy = ca (and) + api (also); aviditvātmanas – person who has no insight about the spiritual self; tathā – thus; ativelam – too late; upāśnāti – he eats; tair = taih = them, their; viruddhāny = viruddhani = what runs contrary; anātmavān – like one who is against the self

Despite mental clarity, bodily energy, and opportunity, that person who has no insight about the spiritual self, eats when it is too late and thus acts in other contrary ways just as if he were someone who was against the self.

Analysis:

A simple and routine matter such as eating, should be regulated by the self in its long-ranged interest. However this may not take place. Nature established an operation of digestion which is controlled by everything except the core-self. It takes special attention and discipline to reform the dietary method.

From the onset of its manifestation in material nature, the self struggled to wrestle control of its psyche from material nature. For the most part it failed in this effort. Usually it is forced to act against its interest.

Application:

Mental clarity, bodily energy and opportunity are assets for use by the self but the self is positioned in the psyche as a helpless power supply. Until it can change that designation, it cannot control the assets.

Of the three, namely clarity, bodily energy and opportunity, bodily energy is crucial. If someone is given an opportunity but does not have the bodily energy to utilize it, no action will be taken. If there is mental clarity but the bodily energy is on the

wane, the self will perceive correctly in one instant and then perceive incorrectly in the next. Clarity hinges on an enhanced bodily energy which is sustained throughout the individual's life.

Verse 9

यदायमतिकष्टानि सर्वाण्युपनिषेवते

अत्यर्थमपि वा भुङ्क्ते न वा भुङ्क्ते कदाचन

yadāyamatikaṣṭāni sarvāṇyupaniṣevate
atyarthamapi vā bhuṅkte na vā bhuṅkte kadācana (2.9)

yadāyam = yad (when) + ayam (this); atikaṣṭāni – harmful practices; sarvāṇy = sarvāṇi = all, many; upaniṣevate – he indulges; atyartham – in excess; api – also; vā – or; bhuṅkte – consumes; na – not; vā – or; bhuṅkte – consumes; kadācana - sometime

He indulges in many harmful practices. He consumes in excess or insufficiently.

Analysis:

The living entity does not have the absolute right to rule its psyche. Some may say that it might have that in the future if it endeavors in the right way. However looking back at the history of the self, most of its situations favored material nature. The psyche has components which are prejudiced for the interest of material nature, even when that concern is detrimental to the self.

The consumption of the psyche in material nature, is not done to please the self. In truth the self has nothing to gain in material nature except to cull out conclusions about the experiences. The psyche as a whole is concerned with consumption but the core-self gains nothing from it and thus becomes bewildered.

Application:

The kundalini life force is the psychic mechanism which operates the consumption-need. Control is gained by a yogi

who greatly restricts kundalini while infusing it with a higher energy.

Verse 10

दुष्टान्नं विषमान्नं च सोऽन्योन्येन विरोधि च

गुरु वापि समं भुङ्क्ते नातिजीर्णेऽपि वा पुनः

duṣṭānnaṁ viṣamānnaṁ ca so'nyonyena virodhi ca
guru vāpi samaṁ bhuṅkte nātijīrṇe'pi vā punaḥ (2.10)

duṣṭānnaṁ - spoilt food; viṣamānnaṁ - improperly combined food; ca – and; so'nyonyena = sa (that, he) + anyonyena (with one another); virodhi – improperly combined; ca – and; guru – heavy; vāpi – and so; samaṁ - same; bhuṅkte – digested, absorbed; nātijīrṇe'pi = na (not) + atijīrṇe – old (previous) + api (also); vā – or; punaḥ - again

He takes spoilt or improperly combined foods which are incompatible to one another. Or he takes heavy foods or again takes that before the previous meal is digested.

Analysis:

Bodily consciousness is supported by food consumption. The quantity of food, the time it is eaten, how it digested and when it is excreted are factors which affect the behavior of the material body. It is the responsibility of the entity to manage the consciousness of the body. Since the self is reliant on bodily awareness for insight, it is in its interest to eat and digest in the most efficient way.

Application:

In the practice of asana yoga postures and breath infusion practice, the self develops a sensitivity as to the correct way to eat. The increased blood circulation which the postures and breath infusion causes, makes for a very efficient use of the food eaten. This reduces over-eating.

Verse 11

व्यायाममतिमात्रं वा व्यवायं चोपसेवते

सततं कर्मलोभाद्वा प्राप्तं वेगविधारणम्

vyāyāmamatimātraṁ vā vyavāyaṁ copasevate
satataṁ karmalobhādvā prāptaṁ vegavidhāraṇam (2.11)

vyāyāmam – physical exercises; atimātraṁ - in excess; vā – or; vyavāyaṁ - regular exercise; copasevate – cohabits, live together; satataṁ - always; karma – activity; lobhād – from craving; vā – or; prāptaṁ - obtain, become conscious of the need; vega – bodily urge; vidhāraṇam - suppresses

He indulges in physical exercises in excess or he cohabits sexually as a regular practice. Due to always craving actions, he suppresses bodily urges to evacuate even when he becomes conscious of the need.

Analysis:

The operation of the body is conducted mostly by the kundalini life force, but it requires assistance from the intellect and the core-self. When the self is preoccupied with the enjoyments, it becomes distracted and fails to render assistance to the life force. This results in neglect of certain functions like prompt evacuation.

Over time if this continues the body develops constipation which results in ill health but the psyche may become accustomed to that condition even.

Application:

In the practice of yoga, a person gets the opportunity to properly assist the life force and also to advise that regulator of the body in how to maintain the form.

Verse 12

रसातियुक्तमन्नं वा दिवास्वप्नं निषेवते

अपक्वानागते काले स्वयं दोषान्प्रकोपयन्

rasātiyuktamannaṁ vā divāsvapnaṁ niṣevate
apakvānāgate kāle svayaṁ doṣānprakopayan (2.12)

rasātiyuktam = rasa (juice) + atiyuktam (excessive); annaṁ - food; vā – or; divā – daytime; svapnaṁ - sleep; niṣevate – indulges; apakvān – not ripe; āgate – not digested; kāle – in time; svayaṁ - self, person; doṣān – faults; prakopayan – make angry

He eats fruits which are excessively juicy and indulges in sleep during the daytime. He eats that which is not ripe or cannot be digested in due course. That causes the person to be anxious, angry and faulty.

Analysis:

The human body is one of the mammalian forms which are designed to be awake during the day and sleep during the night. Some other mammals are designed to sleep during the day and stay awake at night. A human can however alter its circadian rhythm so that it sleeps during the day and stays awake at night. This makes the human being more of an animal and forestalls the development of higher consciousness.

Eating habits which cause the psyche to be anxious, angry and faulty should be avoided but if the self is out of touch with higher awareness, it makes decisions which are not in its interest and which take it downwards in the mundane evolutionary cycle.

Application:

Bodily consciousness is regulated by the type of food eaten, the time the food is eaten, the amount of air breathed by the body, the type of air which is absorbed and the condition of any substance which gets into the body. A yogi is duty-bound to make sure that the consciousness of the body is not compromised through a bad diet.

Verse 13

स्वदोषकोपनाद्रोगं लभते मरणान्तिकम्

अथ चोद्बन्धनादीनि परीतानि व्यवस्यति

svadoṣakopanādrogaṁ labhate maraṇāntikam
atha codbandhanādīni parītāni vyavasyati (2.13)

sva – sel; doṣa – flaw; kopanād – from aggravation; rogaṁ - disease; labhate – acquires; maraṇāntikam – ending with death; atha – thus; codbandhan = ca (and) + udbandhan – hang oneself; ādīni – and others, similar act; parītāni – cord around; vyavasyati - exert

From aggravating the flaws in the body he acquires disease which ends in death. And thus, he may try to commit suicide by hanging with a cord or some similar activity.

Analysis:

The material body is flawed as it is, being perishable and having a law of nature which is always applicable to it for its death. However a human being should not aggravate the body's perishable nature. After getting a body, the individual spirit should do the needful to use the body to develop spiritual insight.

Application:

Some yogis do commit suicide by using pranaiama techniques of breath infusion or breath deprivation. Still most yogis merely wait for death to occur in due course. In the meantime they maximize spiritual realization and do exploration about the geography of the dimensions in which a spirit may be transited at death.

A yogi should not become a whimsical operator but should instead try to align the self with the Supreme Being and with higher yogis who use physical bodies or who exist only on subtle planes. In such association, the yogi would get directions about how to live in the body and how to depart from it.

Verse 14

तस्य तैः कारणैर्जन्तोः शरीराच्च्यवते यथा

जीवितं प्रोच्यमानं तद्यथावदुपधारय

tasya taiḥ kāraṇairjantoḥ śarīrāccyavate yathā
jīvitaṁ procyamānaṁ tadyathāvadupadhāraya (2.14)

tasya – of this; taiḥ - their; kāraṇair = kāraṇaih = of the causes and efffects; jantoḥ - of the living creature; śarīrāc = śarīrāt = from the body; cyavate – deteriorates; yathā – as a result; jīvitaṁ - living being; procyamānaṁ - describe; tad = tat = that; yathāvad – just as it is; upadhāraya – understand

From these causes and effects, there is deterioration in the body of the living creature. Therefore regarding the living being, understand it as it is, as I will describe.

Analysis:

The most in-depth and serious study for any living entity is the operation and usage of the body for spiritual purposes but human society is usually distracted with other interests. When all is said and done, whatever we may create outside of the body in the material world, has little or no meaning except for its relationship to the body. Hence the conclusion is that the body is important to the spiritual self.

The self's contact with gross objects is done through the body. Without such a body no such contact can be made. Thus for spiritual advancement one should come to that conclusion and focus on understanding the conduits which carry information from the material world to the spiritual part of the psyche.

Application:

Yoga practice involves a detailed study of the physical body, the subtle body and the individual spirit which is housed in both forms simultaneously. One will not become liberated if one does not apply the self to understanding how it is connected to the subtle and gross bodies. A living entity has interest-energy but it is impulsively applied to things which do not solve the riddle of how it is fused into the subtle and gross forms. One should extract the interest from mundane commodities and place it in researching the causes of the self's victimization by the sensual energy and life force.

Verse 15

ऊष्मा प्रकुपितः काये तीव्रवायुसमीरितः

शरीरमनुपर्यैति सर्वान्प्राणान्रुणद्धि वै

ūṣmā prakupitaḥ kāye tīvravāyusamīritaḥ
śarīramanuparyeti sarvānprāṇānruṇaddhi vai (2.15)

ūṣmā – heat; prakupitaḥ - impelled; kāye – in the body; tīvra - forceful; vāyu- -air; samīritaḥ - urged; śarīram – body; anuparyeti = anupari (penetrating every part) + iti (thus); sarvān – all; prāṇān – life force; ruṇaddhi – restricted; vai - indeed

Impelled by heat in the body, urged by the force of air in it, which penetrates every part, all energies of the life force are thereby restricted.

Analysis:

Heat is an important symptom of a living physical body. The exchange of air is an important aspect for maintaining a body. If the heat and the air in the body are not properly circulated, the body develops ill health. It may even die by heat and air congestion.

Application:

The life force which was termed the kundalini in ancient India, was a major study for serious yogis. One cannot reach an advanced stage of spiritual practice without understanding its operation and reforming it from its spiritually-negating habits.

One may wonder why it is necessary to do asana postures and physical breath infusions, if the spiritual self is not the physical body. The reason is that the spiritual self is linked to the life force which creates one body after another as the self transmigrates through numerous life forms. The condition of the body affects the efficiency of the life force. A yogi must bring the body into a state of efficiency so that the life force can invest the least amount of energy in the body's maintenance.

When this is accomplished, more energy of the life force is invested in the subtle body. This increases the self's psychic

perception. From psychic perception the self gets firsthand experience of the subtle material world which is the gateway to gaining insight into the spiritual world.

Verse 16

अत्यर्थं बलवानूष्मा शरीरे परिकोपितः

भिनत्ति जीवस्थानानि तानि मर्माणि विद्धि च

atyarthaṁ balavānūṣmā śarīre parikopitaḥ
bhinatti jīvasthānāni tāni marmāṇi viddhi ca (2.16)

atyarthaṁ - very; balavān – forceful; ūṣmā – heat; śarīre – in the body; parikopitaḥ - very impulsive; bhinatti – penetrates; jīva – living being; sthānāni – parts; tāni – those; marmāṇi – vital parts; viddhi – piercing; ca - and

Being very forceful, the heat in the body becomes very impulsive. It penetrates all vital parts of the living being.

Analysis:

When the body nears its end, the heat in the body may increase as is the case with persons who develop typhoid fever and other types of terminal conditions which physicians cannot reverse. This heat may chemically and thermally burn the vital organs to such a degree that they become useless.

Heat is created in the body by chemical reactions. That heat is expelled in the out-breath and by dissipation through the skin. However when the body becomes diseased its ability to efficiently regulate chemicals diminishes. This increases the likelihood of disease or total malfunction.

Application:

The penetration of the vital parts of the body is studied in kundalini yoga when the student yogi learns how to trace out the various nadi tubes in the subtle body. The physical body is manufactured by the life force, using the subtle body as a blueprint. Hence if the student yogi realizes the nadis through kundalini yoga, breath infusion and meditation, he or she gets direct insight into how the life force distributes its energies and maintains the psyche.

To become a siddha one has to study all components of the psyche in a very detailed way. One must also perceive every part of the subtle body visually and by pranavision which is perception through energy. This is the beginning of psychic perception with clarity. It culminates in spiritual vision when the yogi gains proficiency in samadhi practice.

Verse 17

ततः सवेदनः सद्यो जीवः प्रच्यवते क्षरन्

शरीरं त्यजते जन्तुश्छिद्यमानेषु मर्मसु

वेदनाभिः परीतात्मा तद्विद्धि द्विजसत्तम

tataḥ savedanaḥ sadyo jīvaḥ pracyavate kṣaran
śarīraṁ tyajate jantuśchidyamāneṣu marmasu
vedanābhiḥ parītātmā tadviddhi dvijasattama (2.17)

tataḥ - then; savedanaḥ - with afflictions; sadyo = sadyah = full; jīvaḥ - individual spirit; pracyavate – displaced; kṣaran – perishable body; śarīraṁ - body; tyajate – relinquishes; jantuś – entity; chidyamāneṣu – in being cut apart, afflicted in every way, deteriorate; marmasu – in the vital organs; vedanābhiḥ - with afflictions; parītātmā – around the psyche; tad = tat = this; viddhi – know; dvijasattama – best of the trained ritualists

Then the individual spirit being fully afflicted, is displaced from the perishable body. When the vital organs deteriorate in every way, the entity relinquishes the body. O best of the trained ritualists, know that the psyche suffers terribly.

Analysis:

Birth of a body which means exiting from a womb involves pain both for the host body and the embryo. Rarely do we hear of a birth which is painless for the mother. No child has said, "This is all pain," when exiting the body but from the disfigurement of the skull which is squeezed out of shape as it passes through the pelvic channel, we can assume that birth involves pain for the infant.

In fact some infants go through a small death when exiting the passage. They are revived by doctors or midwives. Some die in the passage and cannot be revived. Such are the horrors of birth, without even considering what takes place from the time the sperm implants itself in the egg of the mother and then mutates for nine solar months.

Death of a body also involves pain in most cases. Rarely does a person leave a body without physical pain to the very end. Those who have no such pain because of drugs which numb the senses of the body or because of having entered into an altered state, may deal with psychological disorders like schizophrenia, manic depression, sleep paralysis, cataleptic trance and terrifying horrible encounters on lower astral levels. Some people have beatific blissful visions at the time of death. Some of these actually go to a heavenly world thereafter.

Similar experiences are repeated again and again in each species of life the soul assumes in each birth. This drama of embodiment and body displacement is the format for life in material nature.

Application:

The technique of self displacement from a physical body at death may be learned from nature. Usually the life force operates the departure from the body, with the self complying with the exit of the life force. However through advanced meditation practices, one can learn how nature operates that system of body displacement. Just as there is astral projection into realistic dream states operated by the life force with or without the knowledge of the core-self, so there is displacement at death by the life force with or without conscious observation of the process by the spirit.

And just as a spirit can learn the astral projection process by observing the psychic mechanics of the life force, a yogi can learn the process of body displacement and gain the upper hand in routing the psychic components out of the body at death.

The main aspect of controlling the exit at death is to have the kundalini life force become habituated to travelling through the head of the body. Normally it exits through the anus or through the very end of spine or through the sexual orifice or through the navel or through the mouth. However if one becomes proficient in kundalini yoga and has trained the kundalini to come up the spine into the head, one may at the time of final exit draw the kundalini through the head of the body. This is a glorious termination of a life for a yogi.

For a masterful yogi, it does not matter if the body dies in agony or goes silently through natural causes of infirmity and old age. Since that person trained the kundalini to pass through the passage in an upward direction through the body, he will reach a higher plane in the celestial or spiritual world all depending on the extent of his advanced practice.

Sometimes by a piece of bad luck, by a twist of fate, a yogi is unable to command kundalini and it exits through a lower passage. Thus he is projected to a lower astral world or even to a hellish astral place, but then because he was proficient in practice before leaving the body, he begins his practice in the subtle body in that place. By that action, he transits to a higher dimension. Some yogis who find themselves in this predicament are stalled in the lower dimensions for a time by the pleas of other souls who are confined there. But after a time, these yogis do some practice and escape from those horrible domains.

Verse 18

जातीमरणसंविग्नाः सततं सर्वजन्तवः

दृश्यन्ते संत्यजन्तश्च शरीराणि द्विजर्षभ

jātīmaraṇasaṁvignāḥ satataṁ sarvajantavaḥ
dṛśyante saṁtyajantaśca śarīrāṇi dvijarṣabha (2.18)

jātī – birth; maraṇa – death; saṁvignāḥ - disoriented; satataṁ - always, forever; sarva – all; jantavaḥ - living beings; dṛśyante saṁtyajantaś = saṁtyajantah = being displaced; ca – and; śarīrāṇi – bodies; dvijarṣabha – best of the trained ritualists

All living beings are forever disoriented by birth and death. O best of the trained ritualists, they are observed being displaced from the material bodies.

Analysis:

No matter what, no matter what our scientists invent and develop, the puzzlement of birth and death will continue without end in the material world. Never will there be a time in the material worlds where any limited beings will effectively rule out the process of birth and death.

From the subtle world, advanced yogis observe how the process takes place and even yogis who use physical bodies do likewise when they develop psychic perception.

Application:

A student yogi must admit that material nature has the self under its control. That is the first step on the path of admission. Once one understands this, one can investigate the possibility of escape. Being forever disoriented by birth and death, the spirit is more or less confused. As soon as it gets its footing in a body, and builds for itself some security, it is forced to relinquish the form and go into a subtle world which is full of uncertainty. Nature then uses it again to formulate another body but this is done for the convenience of nature, not for the purpose of informing the soul of nature's process.

Those who realize that this system of coercion is taking place, may plan an escape from it, but it is doubtful if many of these philosophers will succeed. The system is the habit of the life force, not that of the intellect, which is merely a stooge of the kundalini instincts.

Verse 19

गर्भसंक्रमणे चापि मर्मणामतिसर्पणे

तादृशीमेव लभते वेदनां मानवः पुनः

garbhasaṁkramaṇe cāpi marmaṇāmatisarpaṇe
tādṛśīmeva labhate vedanāṁ mānavaḥ punaḥ (2.19)

garbha – womb; saṁkramaṇe – enter; cāpi – and also; marmaṇām – vital organs; atisarpaṇe – suffer violent pains; tā – that, it; dṛśīm – is observed; eva – certain; labhate – gets, is subjected to; vedanāṁ - agony; mānavaḥ - human being; punaḥ - repeatedly

They enter wombs as well, and suffer violent pains in the vital organs. It is observed that the human being is repeatedly subjected to agony.

Analysis:

Even during the sojourn in the womb the living entity feels some suffering but in that position it can neither complain to anyone nor cry out about it, except that it might complain to supernatural entities whom it may see.

In the womb the entity is alone, singled out as it were, with its psyche under lock and key while its new body is being created. It cannot move while its body is growing. It cannot leave the body or kill the body because it is not in a position to commit suicide. It has to endure that confinement until the mother's life force pushes it out of womb. Upon delivery, the infant cannot compress its nostrils to stop the breathing which keeps its body alive in the new environment.

Application:

A student yogi is required to study the birthing situation, from the time of transit of the seminal particle from the father's body into the mother's passage, through its embryonic development, until the body hardens and is exited from the womb. These studies are done by the yogi when he learns how to put his mind into trance states through which it can view the life of embryos.

Some yogis wait until they leave their bodies and then from the astral existence they check on the condition of the entities who are in wombs. Other yogis stay in a position to observe how a soul leaves a body, stays in an astral domain for a time and then becomes fused into a parent for transit as an embryo. When a yogi sees this process he or she can no longer be lured

into taking material bodies. All confusion and fantasy about birth and death are removed.

Verse 20

भिन्नसंधिरथ क्लेदमद्भिः स लभते नरः

यथा पञ्चसु भूतेषु संश्रितत्वं निगच्छति

शैत्यात्प्रकुपितः काये तीव्रवायुसमीरितः

bhinnasaṁdhiratha kledamadbhiḥ sa labhate naraḥ
yathā pañcasu bhūteṣu saṁśritatvaṁ nigacchati
śaityātprakupitaḥ kāye tīvravāyusamīritaḥ (2.20)

bhinna – split up; saṁdhir – pieces; atha – then; kledamad = kledamat = from cold water; bhiḥ - distress; sa – he; labhate - gets, suffers; naraḥ - human being; yathā – as, so; pañcasu – of give; bhūteṣu – of elements; saṁśritatvaṁ - composite mixing; nigacchati – acquired, felt; śaityāt – from cold; prakupitaḥ - agitation; kāye – in the body; tīvra – forceful; vāyu – air; samīritaḥ - moves uncomfortably

A human being suffers when the limbs are broken, and again distress comes from cold water. The composite energy of the five elements is felt. From cold there is agitation in forceful air which moves distressfully in the body.

Analysis:

There are innumerable ways of suffering in the material world. In fact the number of ways of affliction are infinite. There are life forms which attack other life forms. Some of these are microscopic, not visible to the human eye. The living entities are able to continue in material existence and not desire liberation because amidst the misery there is some happiness. In the hope of achieving happiness, the spirits deny the memory of the negative experiences and focus on whatever happiness nature yields.

Application:

Even though there is happiness in the material world, it has no spiritual value. The satisfaction one feels from doing

socially-beneficial acts is not spiritual happiness. It has worth to the Supreme Person as illustrated in the life of Arjuna, in the story of the* Bhagavad Gītā *discourse. Still, it is not a spiritual asset. Without it, the human form of life would be just like that of the other mammalian species. For social reasons it has all value and should be established and supported.

While religious people regard pious social acts as divine operations, a yogi does not estimate it in that way. He knows its value but knows that it has nothing to do with direct spiritual development. All acts in the material world, regardless of whether they are pious or impious are a distraction from the issue of attaining a spiritual environment to exist in. This is a material environment and it is unsuitable to the spiritual soul. Whatever it does to inspire a living entity to escape from it, is noteworthy.

Verse 21

यः स पञ्चसु भूतेषु प्राणापाने व्यवस्थितः

स गच्छत्यूर्ध्वगो वायुः कृच्छ्रान्मुक्त्वा शरीरिणम्

yaḥ sa pañcasu bhūteṣu prāṇāpāne vyavasthitaḥ
sa gacchatyūrdhvago vāyuḥ kṛcchrānmuktvā śarīriṇam (2.21)

yaḥ - that which; sa – it; pañcasu - in five; bhūteṣu – in elements; prāṇāpāne – in the in-breath and out-breath; vyavasthitaḥ - is situated; sa – it; gacchaty = gacchati – go; ūrdhvago = ūrdhvagah = going upwards; vāyuḥ - air; kṛcchrān – causing pain; muktvā – freed; śarīriṇam – from the body

The in-breath and out-breath are situated in the five elements which compose a body. The air goes upward and downward but it is finally freed from the body while causing pain.

Analysis:

The breathing system of the body is very important. It is so essential that eating cannot compare with it. The use of breath by the life force deserves serious introspection. A student yogi must by all means learn about the life force and its operation of the lung mechanism.

Application:

The linking element between the subtle body and the gross one is breath energy. There is no way to understand how the subtle body fuses into the gross body after dream and sleep, except through the study of how the life force procures and uses breath energy.

Even the fusion of a departed soul into the body of its would-be parent is facilitated by breath energy of the parent on the physical side of existence. When the fetus develops it relies on the breath energy of the mother's body. When it exits the womb, it is switched to its own breath procurement apparatus.

Verse 22

शरीरं च जहात्येव निरुच्छ्वासश्च दृश्यते

निरूष्मा स निरुच्छ्वासो निःश्रीको गतचेतनः

śarīraṁ ca jahātyeva nirucchvāsaśca dṛśyate
nirūṣmā sa nirucchvāso niḥśrīko gatacetanaḥ (2.22)

śarīraṁ - body; ca – and; jahāty = jahāti = gives up; eva – so, even; nirucchvāsaś = nirucchvāsaśh = without breath; ca – and; dṛśyate – it is observed; nirūṣmā – without warmth; sa – it, he; nirucchvāso = nirucchvāsah = without breath; niḥśrīko = niḥśrīkah = without beauty or vitality; gata – gone, is displaced; cetanaḥ - consciousness

It is observed that without breath, one gives up the body. Being without bodily warmth, without breath, without vitality, the consciousness is displaced from the body.

Analysis:

Even though the living entity has little knowledge about how it got a body in the womb of the mother, it may have direct knowledge about what happens just before it is displaced from the body. When, in old age, the body is near its death, it experiences a gradual and then abrupt shutdown of certain vital organs in the body.

Bodily warmth is created by chemical reactions in the body. These reactions are operated by various organs which process nutrients which come into the gut of the body. Cell vitality hinges on those nutrients and on breath which enters the body through the nostrils.

If the nutrients and the breath fail to energize the cells of the body, it loses vitality. When that happens on a wholesale basis, the self is evicted from the body, displaced as it were to the astral world.

Application:

Most people do not voluntarily give up their material bodies. In fact there is a concerted effort to avoid having to deal with being permanently displaced from the body. And yet, material nature will insist on the soul being displaced from its form.

The bonding force which keeps the core-self fused with the body, loses its adhesive grip as soon as there is no vitality in the body. Then the soul must follow the life force which is displaced from the dying or dead life form.

Before the time of death student yogis should observe how the life force is attached to the vitality of a living body. Initially a disembodied spirit on the astral plane has no connection to physical vitality. It has psychic vitality which is not linked physically. However when it becomes attracted to its would-be parent, it becomes linked to that person's physio-psychic energy. When that disembodied soul gains fusion into the feelings of its soon-to-be father, its physical vitality begins as the sperm in the father's testes. This develops further in the womb of the mother. A yogi needs to meditate on these matters to gain insight into the process of acquiring a new body.

Verse 23

ब्रह्मणा संपरित्यक्तो मृत इत्युच्यते नरः
स्रोतोभिर्यैर्विजानाति इन्द्रियार्थाञ्शरीरभृत्
तैरेव न विजानाति प्राणमाहारसंभवम्

brahmaṇā saṁparityakto mṛta ityucyate naraḥ
srotobhiryairvijānāti indriyārthāñśarīrabhṛt
taireva na vijānāti prāṇamāhārasaṁbhavam (2.23)

brahmaṇā – of the spiritual level of existence; saṁparityakto = saṁparityaktah = being totally detached; mṛta – dead; ityucyate = iti (thus) + ucyate (it is said); naraḥ - the personal body; srotobhir = srotabhih = with the psychic energy; yair = yaih = by that; vijānāti – he does perceive; indriyārthāñ – sense objects; śarīra – physical body; bhṛt – procured; tair = taih = by those; eva – even so; na – not; vijānāti he perceives; prāṇam – vital energy; āhāra – food consumed; saṁbhavam - procured

Thus the personal body, being totally detached from the spiritual level of existence, is said to be dead. Even with the same psychic energy, the soul cannot perceive the sense objects which the body procured previously. That soul was itself productive of the vital energy which was produced from food consumed by the body.

Analysis:

A body remains alive so long as a spiritual entity is connected to it in a specific way. Though it changes at every moment, a material body remains as a cohesive whole provided it is continuously supplied with vitality. The aggregate physical substances which form a living body, disintegrate as soon as the vitality becomes absent from the body. At that time, people say that it is a dead body.

The spirit departs from a dead body with its psychic accessories. These are the same energies which when linked into a living body allowed sensual perception of the material world.

Without the body to subsidize its perceptive ability, that psyche is no longer able to perceive material objects.

The physical vitality in a living body is not caused by the body, but rather by the life force of the psyche. Hence when that force is displaced from the body, the system collapses and functions as inanimate matter only.

Application:

An individual limited spirit has vast potential but it also has severe limitations. When it is displaced from a dying body, it loses physical perception. Again when it acquires a new body, it regains the physical perception at the expense of losing the psychic vision. This is how the perception operates in one realm and is simultaneously inoperative in the other. When the doors of perception to the physical world are opened, those to the psychic existence are closed and vice versa.

By practicing meditation a yogi can beat the system so that the self retains the psychic perception even while having the physical sensual ability. It requires intense samadhi practice.

Verse 24

तत्रैव कुरुते काये यः स जीवः सनातनः

तेषां यद्यद्भवेद्युक्तं संनिपाते क्वचित्क्वचित्

तत्तन्मर्म विजानीहि शास्त्रदृष्टं हि तत्तथा

tatraiva kurute kāye yaḥ sa jīvaḥ sanātanaḥ
teṣāṁ yadyadbhavedyuktaṁ saṁnipāte kvacitkvacit
tattanmarma vijānīhi śāstradṛṣṭaṁ hi tattathā (2.24)

tatraiva = tatra (here) + eva (only); kurute – does, works; kāye – in the body; yaḥ - which; sa – he, that; jīvaḥ - individual spirit; sanātanaḥ - eternal; teṣāṁ - of those; yadyad = yatyat = which ever; bhaved – become; yuktaṁ - joined, emulsified; saṁnipāte – gathers; kvacitkvacit – certain; tattan = tattat = that that; marma – vital organ; vijānīhi – know; śāstra – authoritative book; dṛṣṭaṁ - explained; hi – indeed; tat – that; tathā - so

That eternal individual soul works here on earth using a material body. Know that whatever ingredients gather together become emulsified in certain organs which are the vital parts, as explained in the authoritative books.

Analysis:

The human body is an emulsification of several ingredients which are taken from material nature. The body itself is not the person but it is identified with the person-self whose psychic energy keeps the body as one aggregate form in a living state.

The core self is just one of the components in the psyche and yet, because it is linked to other components, the social person which is identified as such and such is not the core-self alone. That person is the core self plus other psychic components plus the living body.

Application:

Student yogis must by all means, figure what the core-self is, what the intellect is, what the life force is, what the psyche which is a psychic compartment is and even what desires in the causal body are. While being housed securely in a material body, a living entity should take the opportunity to figure how the body was composed and how the self remains fused to the body. When the human body is healthy, it is a secured location from which to research the secrets of nature's formation of material bodies.

Verse 25

तेषु मर्मसु भिन्नेषु ततः स समुदीरयन्

आविश्य हृदयं जन्तोः सत्त्वं चाशु रुणद्धि वै

ततः स चेतनो जन्तुर्नाभिजानाति किंचन

teṣu marmasu bhinneṣu tataḥ sa samudīrayan
āviśya hṛdayaṁ jantoḥ sattvaṁ cāśu ruṇaddhi vai
tataḥ sa cetano janturnābhijānāti kiṁcana (2.25)

teṣu – of those; marmasu – of vital organs; bhinneṣu – deterioration, damage; tataḥ - then; sa – that; samudīrayan – aroused; āviśya –

entering; hṛdayaṁ - center of consciousness; jantoḥ - the life force; sattvaṁ - bodily awareness; cāśu = ca (and) + āśu (quickly); ruṇaddhi – restrain; vai – indeed; tataḥ - then; sa – he, it; cetano = cetanah = conscious; jantur = jantuh = soul; nābhijānāti = na (not) + abhijānāti (is aware); kiṁcana - anything

Then with the deterioration or damage of those vital organs, the life force is aroused. Quickly entering the center of consciousness, it restrains the bodily awareness. Then that soul, though conscious, is without bodily awareness.

Analysis:

Once the life force migrates from the spinal column into the center of consciousness, the soul loses awareness of the body. It may also lose awareness of everything else but only temporarily. A question may be considered: What or where is the center of consciousness? In the Sanskrit the word hṛdayaṁ is used. The most frequent meaning of this word is the physical heart. However in this case the location has to be a psychic one, because with the deterioration and damage of the vital organs, the life force will seek a psychic location and not a physical one. In fact one of the damaged or deteriorated vital organs is the physical heart.

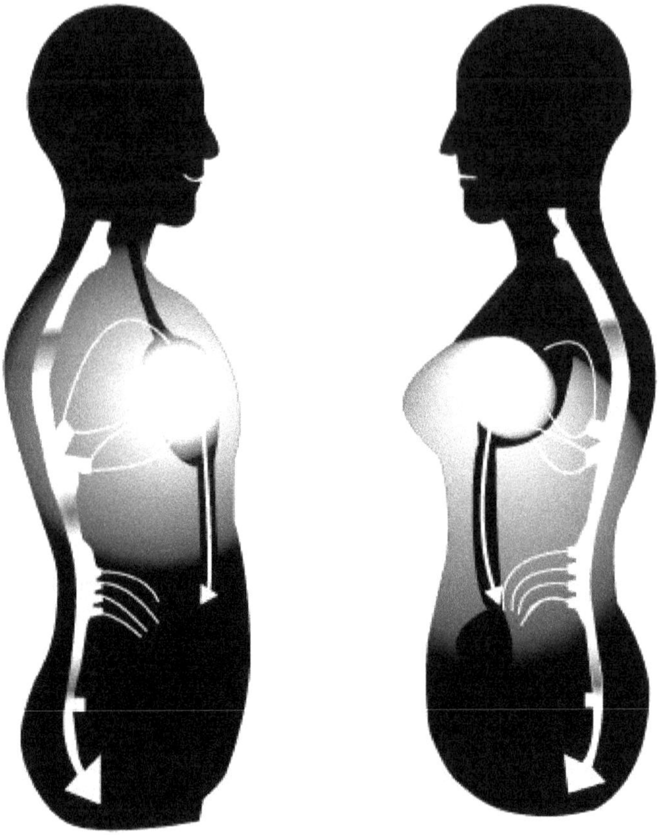

When the life force becomes aware of the total malfunction of the vital organs in the body, it panics. This is because in that situation it loses its spread of energy in the nerves and cells of the body. It becomes uprooted from the base chakra. It feels insecure. Its alliance with the intellect and the core-self loses meaning. In a panic it seeks to find the centre of consciousness. It becomes withdrawn into itself but in contact with the causal body, which is itself the real center of consciousness for the numerous movements and actions of the subtle body.

Application:

The retraction of the life force when it loses its footing in a material body is experienced once or twice in the lives of most entities. However a yogi, by practicing kundalini yoga, experiences kundalini's retraction frequently.

When the body is in great danger, like when it is in an automobile accident, or when it on the verge of drowning or when it was impacted by gunshots or assaulted by violence, the life force tries to locate the center of consciousness. What happens instead is that the life force finds itself withdrawing its electric power from the nerves and cells of the body. If it completes this action even for a moment, the core-self experiences that action as a retreat to the causal plane.

Verse 26

तमसा संवृतज्ञानः संवृतेष्वथ मर्मसु

स जीवो निरधिष्ठानश्चाव्यते मातरिश्वना

tamasā saṁvṛtajñānaḥ saṁvṛteṣvatha marmasu
sa jīvo niradhiṣṭhānaścāvyate mātariśvanā (2.26)

tamasā – dulling awareness; saṁvṛta – depressed, covered; jñānaḥ inherently conscious being; saṁvṛteṣvatha = saṁvṛteṣu (in being malfunctioned) + atha (then); marmasu – in vital organ; sa – he; jīvo = jīvah = individual soul; nira – without; dhiṣṭhānaś = dhiṣṭhānah = support; cāvyate = ca (and) + āvyate (affected); mātariśvanā - affected

The inherently conscious being is depressed by a dulling awareness, while its vital organs are still in a malfunctioned state. That individual soul being support-less is affected by the status of the airy energy in the body.

Analysis:

A fatal condition of a material body may be sudden or it may take place gradually over a period of days or years. It depends on the method used by nature to repossess the ingredients which comprise the body. As the vital organs shut down and as the cells in the body no longer respond to the electro-psychic energy of the life force, the self experiences a dulling awareness. This may be accompanied with painful feelings and with psychosis.

The individual limited spirit is reliant on several factors for its secure habitation in any dimension. When those factors are adjusted or removed, the person feels insecure. This causes shifts in its reliance and a scramble to regain its footing in the body. Of course due to the fatality, these efforts come to nil.

Application:

When the vital organs are in a terminal state and malfunction, the life force is left to itself with inefficient distribution of its psycho-physical energies. This is distressful to it and causes it to enter a state of confusion and stupor. Despite these problems and the threat of full shut down of the organs and cells, the life force clings to the body which is its only physical support. Gradually it is forced to experience itself as an inefficient energy distributor until at last it is forced to know itself as being abandoned by material nature.

A yogi should by means of deep meditation, research this, both within the self's body and within the bodies of entities who are on the verge of death. A yogi should not be ignorant of the way in which nature will evict the life force when the physical body is at its end.

Verse 27

ततः स तं महोच्छ्वासं भृशमुच्छ्वस्य दारुणम्

निष्क्रामन्कम्पयत्याशु तच्छरीरमचेतनम्

tataḥ sa taṁ mahocchvāsaṁ bhṛśamucchvasya dāruṇam
niṣkrāmankampayatyāśu taccharīramacetanam (2.27)

tataḥ - then; sa – he, it; taṁ - them; maho = maha (loud) + ucchvāsaṁ (sigh of breath); bhṛśam – harsh; ucchvasya - of breath; dāruṇam – unconscious body; niṣkrāman – outgoing, transit out; kampayaty = kampayati = quiver; āśu – quickly; tac = tat = that; charīram = śarīram - body; acetanam – without consciousness

Then it makes a loud harsh sigh of breath, which quivers the unconscious body. It quickly transits out of the unconscious body.

Analysis:

Sometimes when an old body dies or when death comes after a long illness, there is a pronounced sigh during the last in-breath and out-breath. It may also be heard only during the last out-breath. Hearing this, persons who are by the bedside of the departing soul, accept that sound as a pronouncement of death.

Sometimes the body quivers at that final moment and on the psychic side of life, the subtle body is displaced from the physical one for the final time. It then stays in the astral world. Since it is not seen by physical eyes and since its means of visibility can no longer be animated, people begin to mourn the loss of that personality who is now confined to an astral plane.

Application:

By regular meditation and by raising kundalini daily, a student yogi may learn how to shift focus from the physical to the psychic. If this is done consistently, he or she will not be focused on the life symptoms of the material body.

The yogi should keenly look for indications of cellular disintegrations, such that when the life force is on the verge of being evicted, the self can direct it upwards through the spine and into the head of the subtle body.

Sounds made by the physical body when it is near death, sounds like groaning, snoring, sighs in relation to severe pain, sighs in relation to how the air is breathing in and out, are no concern for the advanced yogi, whose mind should already be focused on the psychic and spiritual sides of life.

Verse 28

स जीवः प्रच्युतः कायात्कर्मभिः स्वैः समावृतः

अङ्कितः स्वैः शुभैः पुण्यैः पापैर्वाप्युपपद्यते

sa jīvaḥ pracyutaḥ kāyātkarmabhiḥ svaiḥ samāvṛtaḥ
aṅkitaḥ svaiḥ śubhaiḥ puṇyaiḥ pāpairvāpyupapadyate (2.28)

sa – that; jīvaḥ - individual spirit; pracyutaḥ - displaced from; kāyāt – from the body; karmabhiḥ - psychic effect-energy of action; svaiḥ - by those; samāvṛtaḥ - enveloped; aṅkitaḥ - stigmatized; svaiḥ - by his; śubhaiḥ - by spiritually uplifting; puṇyaiḥ - by socially rewarding; pāpair – by criminal effects; vāpy – and, or; upapadyate – has got

Being permanently displaced from the body, that individual spirit exists being enveloped in the psychic effect-energy of its actions. Being stigmatized by such, it has the energy of its spiritually uplifting, and socially rewarding acts as well as any criminal effects.

Analysis:

When the spirit leaves a body temporarily, people say that it is asleep. When it does so permanently, people say that it deceased. This is all well and good in so far as we are limited to physical sense perception.

Being enclosed in a subtle body, the spirit leaves the physical form at death. Within that subtle form there are other psychic components like the sense of identity, the intellect, the memory chambers, the life force energization apparatus and even the register of the causal body which transcends the subtle form. No spirit can leave a physical body unless it does so in a subtle body. This is because the spirit itself, the core-self and even its sense of identity cannot make direct contact with a physical form.

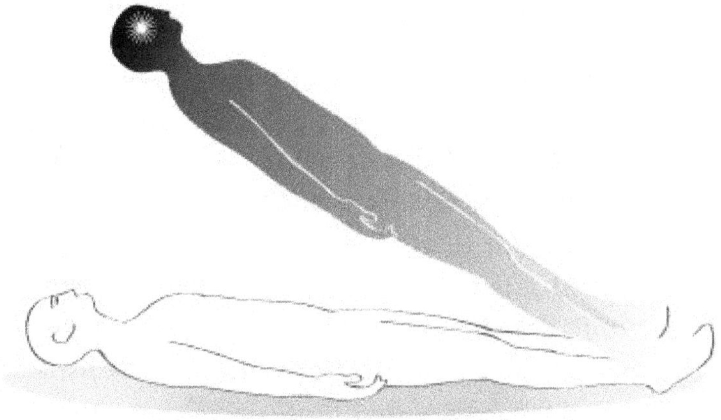

spirit fused into astral body, which is displaced permanently from the physical body at death

The psychic effect-energies of the actions committed during that lifetime, travel with the spirit in the subtle body. In fact the spirit is surrounded on all sides by that energy, which serves to keep the spirit time-bound and nature-controlled. In the *Bhagavad Gītā*, this envelope of energy which surrounds the soul is called kāmarūpa:

śrībhagavānuvāca
kāma eṣa krodha eṣa rajoguṇasamudbhavaḥ
mahāśano mahāpāpmā viddhyenamiha vairiṇam (3.37)
dhūmenāvriyate vahnir yathādarśo malena ca
yatholbenāvṛto garbhas tathā tenedamāvṛtam (3.38
āvṛtaṁ jñānametena jñānino nityavairiṇā
kāmarūpeṇa kaunteya duṣpūreṇānalena ca (3.39)
indriyāṇi mano buddhir asyādhiṣṭhānamucyate
etairvimohayatyeṣa jñānamāvṛtya dehinam (3.40)

> **The Blessed Lord said: This force is craving. This power is anger. The passionate emotion is the source. It has a great consuming power and does much damage. Recognize it as the enemy in this case.**
>
> **As the sacrificial fire is obscured by smoke, and similarly as a mirror is shrouded by dust or as an embryo is covered by skin, so a man's insight is blocked by the passionate energy.**
>
> **The discernment of educated people is adjusted by their eternal enemy which is the sense of yearning for various things. O son of Kuntī, the lusty power, is as hard to satisfy as it is to keep a fire burning.**
>
> **It is authoritatively stated that the senses, the mind and the intelligence are the combined warehouse of the passionate enemy. By these faculties, the lusty power confuses the embodied soul, shrouding his insight. (Bhagavad Gītā 3.37-40)**

Application:

The situation of the student yogi at death of the material body, should be such that there are no surprises by the destiny-enforced conditions which must be endured thereafter. The spirit is not the subtle body but that is besides the point, for until the spirit completely elevates the subtle body to the highest plane in the astral world, it will have to accept all liabilities for that form.

When a person comes to his or her senses about the misidentification of the self as the subtle body, that person still cannot banish the liabilities for that form. It may develop the ability to better regulate the subtle body's activities. Thus it may reduce those obligations.

The student yogi should be sure that during the life of the body, he or she masters astral projection. This is the minimum requirement concerning the integration of the life beyond the grave. One should understand well before the death of the body, that one will be taking the effect-energies of one's cultural involvements in the psyche at the time of death. There is a list of psychic components which are in the subtle body, just as physicians can list vital organs in the physical one. However beside that there are the highly dangerous, time-activated effect-energies which are from socially-rewarding and criminal acts. There is also the energy from any valid spiritual disciplines the person performed. Each of these energies carries particular potencies which might compel the person to reach a certain dimension in the hereafter and also to be attracted to a certain parent in the next birth.

Verse 29

ब्राह्मणा ज्ञानसंपन्ना यथावच्छ्रुतनिश्चयाः

इतरं कृतपुण्यं वा तं विजानन्ति लक्षणैः

brāhmaṇā jñānasaṁpannā yathāvacchrutaniścayāḥ
itaraṁ kṛtapuṇyaṁ vā taṁ vijānanti lakṣaṇaiḥ (2.29)

brāhmaṇā – ritually-trained ascetics; jñāna – knowledge; saṁpannā – endowed; yathā – so as; vac – speaker, speech, words; chruta = śruta = heard; niścayāḥ - fixed; itaraṁ - opposite; kṛta – act; puṇyaṁ - commendable acts; vā – or; taṁ - that; vijānanti – known by; lakṣaṇaiḥ - with characteristics

A ritually-trained ascetic who is endowed with knowledge, who heard from authoritative sources, is known by his characteristics as one with socially-commendable acts or by what is the opposite.

Analysis:

Regardless of a person's accomplishments in self realization and reality perception, the worldly persons will regard that mystic by social behavior. Thus if a realized soul commits anti-social or outright criminal acts, people will condemn him or her accordingly without giving any credit for spiritual accomplishments. The condition is that a person can be self-realized and still commit criminal acts. It happens from time to time.

It is for this reason that Lord Krishna advised all ascetics to adhere to righteous lifestyle as dictated by the Universal Form. He instructed Arjuna to do this, because that is the safest passage one may have while using a material body.

Application:

Student yogis should always try to toe the moral line. They should do nothing outlandish which will bring to them unwanted attention and condemnation. One should live peacefully in the material world side by side with those who only believe in material existence as well as those who are religious but who have no attraction to self-realization. There is no sense in stirring up the dust of public opinion. Any such involvement will consume valuable time and energy which should be used to execute psyche purification.

Krishna with his divine grace falling like the monsoon rain, left clear instructions about karma yoga in his **Bhagavad Gītā** *discourse. If one is literate and one fails to take note of that conversation then it is understood that one is preoccupied with affairs which are devoid of spiritual interest. Every yogi should learn directly from Krishna how to perform karma yoga, how to regulate the social interactions using the insight and skill attained from yoga proficiency.*

Verse 30

यथान्धकारे खद्योतं लीयमानं ततस्ततः

चक्षुष्मन्तः प्रपश्यन्ति तथा तं ज्ञानचक्षुषः

yathāndhakāre khadyotaṁ līyamānaṁ tatastataḥ
cakṣuṣmantaḥ prapaśyanti tathā taṁ jñānacakṣuṣaḥ (2.30)

yathā – as; andhakāre – moving in darkness; khadyotaṁ - firefly; līyamānaṁ - clinging, disappearing; tatastataḥ = tataḥtataḥ = now and again; cakṣuṣ - vision; mantaḥ - changing conditions; prapaśyanti – they see; tathā – as; taṁ - him; jñānacakṣuṣaḥ - insight perception

As in darkness, those with vision see the changing aspects of the firefly disappearing, now and again, so are those with insight perception (who perceive psychic reality).

Analysis:

Gross sense perception is not the full range of manifestation. One should develop subtle sense perception, which begins with psychic insight. Just as on a dark night, we surmise the continued existence of a firefly by its buzzing sound and by its repeated glowing abdomen, we can figure the individual spirit by its animated bodies and by its absence from the physical world when it loses a body. The buzzing sound of the wings of the firefly may be barely audible and yet we hear it. So one might perceive with mystic vision or bare insight the disembodied soul and its thoughts which reach us from the astral dimensions.

Application:

Student yogis should eliminate doubts about the continued existence of the spirit in the afterworld. To gain confidence in reincarnation, one should practice astral projection. One should go to the astral places, meet the astral beings, converse with them and get some idea of their situation in a place which has no physical objects.

Science is important but its denial of the astral world should be left aside by yogis. One should not get into arguments about proving the afterlife.

Verse 31

पश्यन्त्येवंविधाः सिद्धा जीवं दिव्येन चक्षुषा

च्यवन्तं जायमानं च योनिं चानुप्रवेशितम्

paśyantyevaṁvidhāḥ siddhā jīvaṁ divyena cakṣuṣā cyavantaṁ jāyamānaṁ ca yoniṁ cānupraveśitam (2.31)

paśyanty = paśyant = they see; evaṁ - thus; vidhāḥ - knowledgeable; siddhā –perfected yogi; jīvaṁ - individual soul; divyena – with divine; cakṣuṣā – with perception; cyavantaṁ - displacement from a body; jāyamānaṁ - transiting to another body from the astral world; ca – and; yoniṁ - womb; cā = ca (and) + anupraveśitam (displayed, entered, transited)

Thus with divine perception, the perfected yogis see the individual soul, as it is displaced from a body, or as it transits from the astral world to attain another form, or as it enters the womb.

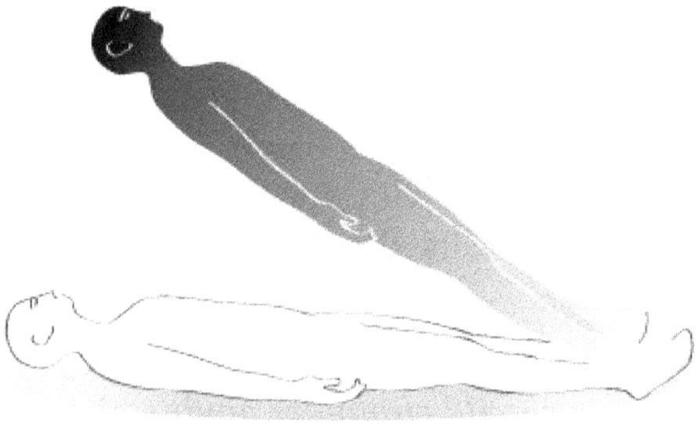

astral body leaves dead physical form

astral body is attracted to romance energy of future parents

astral body fuses into father's feelings

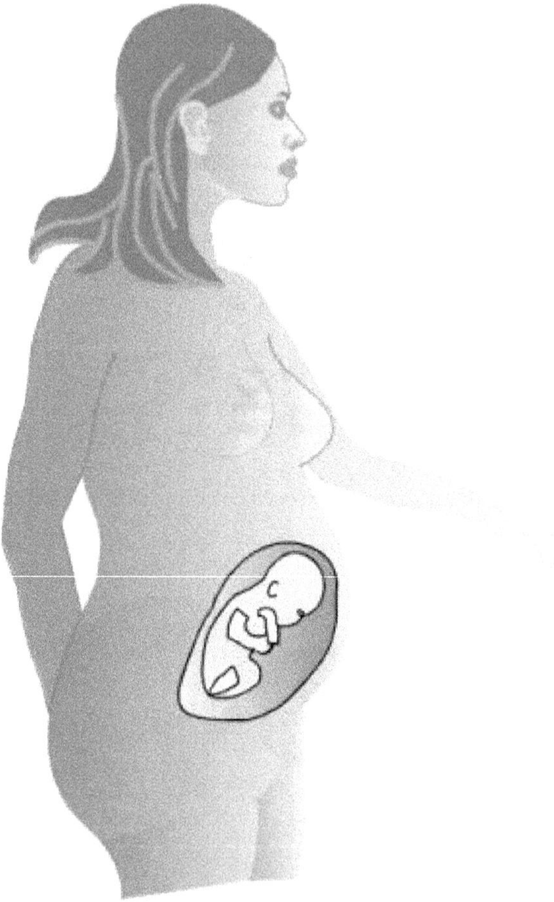

mother becomes pregnant
with compressed astral body
which was fused into father's semen

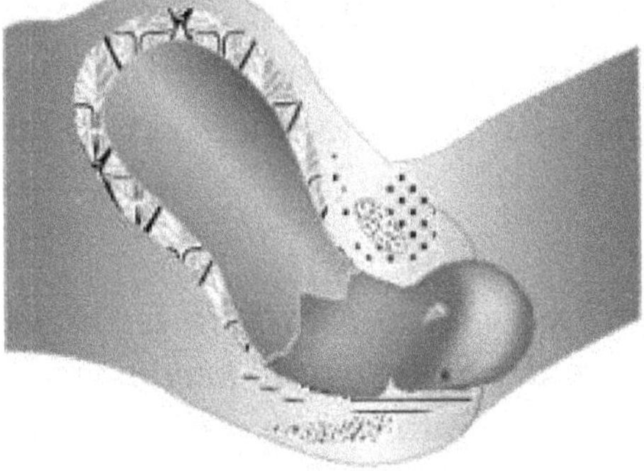

new body which is astral body
and matter which was attracted to it
is separated from mother's form

new body as toddler

Analysis:

Divine perception occurs in a variety of ways, depending on the level of the subtle body being used, or on the analytical orb in the head of the subtle body, or on the core-self itself. There is more than one means of psychic perception. An example of this variety is the vision of the Universal Form. Krishna awarded an upliftment of Arjuna's subtle body for perception of the form. But with that Arjuna could not see the Four-Handed God-Form of Krishna. Thus Arjuna made a second request for perceiving a special divine form, which even the deities from the astral world long to perceive.

It is sufficient to know that perfected beings can see the transit of a living entity from the afterlife into the womb and then back to the afterlife and then on to astral places and elsewhere.

Application:

The most difficult vision to attain is the perception of how an astral being, a departed soul, becomes a fetus. There are many theories and testimonies about how the soul gets a new body. Some say that it enters the womb at the time of conception when the father's sperm is ejected into the uterus. Others say that it enters when the sperm embeds itself in the egg of the mother. Others say that the soul enters when the body is delivered as a live baby. Regardless, the student yogi has the task to make observations, all depending on the level of developed mystic perception. Other ideas about the afterlife and about the conception of a body, do not matter. In the final consideration, it is the perception of the yogi which will count.

Verse 32

तस्य स्थानानि दृष्टानि त्रिविधानीह शास्त्रतः

कर्मभूमिरियं भूमिर्यत्र तिष्ठन्ति जन्तवः

tasya sthānāni dṛṣṭāni trividhānīha śāstrataḥ
karmabhūmiriyaṁ bhūmiryatra tiṣṭhanti jantavaḥ (2.32)

tasya – concerning this; sthānāni – regions; dṛṣṭāni – it is perceived; trividhān – three; īha – here; śāstrataḥ - according to authoritative texts; karma – social action; bhūmir = bhūmih = earth; iyaṁ - this; bhūmir= bhūmih = earth; yatra – where; tiṣṭhanti – are situated, live; jantavaḥ - creatures

Concerning this, it is perceived according to the authoritative texts that there are three regions. This earth where the creatures live is the world of social action.

Analysis:

The three regions are called bhuh, bhuva and svaha. These are not physical designations. They will not match perfectly with modern astronomical observations. Bhuh is the region of the earth. It includes some adjacent astral dimensions which though subtle, are experienced as gross.

Above that region is the bhuva region which is atmospheric and does not have any physical or near-physical lands. These places are etheric. Above these are the heavenly Svarga places where a pious human being might go after death. If one has a high register for socially-beneficial acts, it is likely that one would go to a Svarga heaven for some time after leaving the material body.

However there are regions which are higher than the Swarga heavens. These places are attained by very advanced yogis, and by great devotees of the deities who are located in such places.

Below the earth there are subterranean dimensions and hells as well.

Ultimately for a human being, it should be understood that the earth is the place for doing the work through which one would be rewarded with a transit to a Swarga heaven. While in that paradise one cannot accumulate any more piety. If one goes to the lower regions, to the hells, one will be unable to generate any piety as well. The earth is a median location in which one can either generate piety or focus on accomplishing spirituality.

Application:

Yogis will agree that this world is the place for generating good character and for executing socially-beneficial acts. However a yogi has another use of this world, which is to attain full self-realization.

A yogi leaves aside ideal cultural performance as well as criminal acts, and substitutes the lifestyle which yields spiritual elevation. In this world one can act with three objectives in mind, either benefiting others socially, exploiting others cruelly or attaining the exclusive spiritual existence.

Verse 33

ततः शुभाशुभं कृत्वा लभन्ते सर्वदेहिनः

इहैवोच्चावचान्भोगान्प्राप्नुवन्ति स्वकर्मभिः

tataḥ śubhāśubhaṁ kṛtvā labhante sarvadehinaḥ
ihaivoccāvacānbhogānprāpnuvanti svakarmabhiḥ (2.33)

tataḥ - then, in time; śubha – socially-acclaimed; āśubhaṁ - socially-condemned; kṛtvā – having done; labhante – get; sarva – all; dehinaḥ - embodied souls; ihaivoccāvacān = iha (here) + eva (so)+ ucca (elevating) + avacān (degrading); bhogān – experiences; prāpnuvanti – get; svakarmabhiḥ - their performance

In time, all embodied souls having committed socially-acclaimed or socially-condemned actions, get elevating or degrading experiences in reference to previous performance.

Analysis:

So long as a soul is within the jurisdiction of material nature, it will be confronted by the effect-reactions of its previous performance. In this respect nature has the upper hand because it lays out the various environments in which the drama of fresh actions and fly-back reactions take place.

Even though a living entity may plan the fulfillment of desires with great care, it cannot know everything about the way in which nature will hurl effect-reactions from its previous lives. Thus it may achieve some aspirations and nature will frustrate some instances as it sees fit.

Application:

The elevating and degrading experiences are a distraction from self-realization. Still, even a yogi must be attentive to some of these cultural events. It serves the yogi well, as a reminder that if he allows the self to sink into material nature again, the outcome will be favorable or unfavorable circumstances with no spiritual development. When most of the world seeks to achieve the heavens, the yogi stays secure in the aim for spiritual elevation.

Verse 34

इहैवाशुभकर्मा तु कर्मभिर्निरयं गतः

अवाक्स निरये पापो मानवः पच्यते भृशम्

तस्मात्सुदुर्लभो मोक्ष आत्मा रक्ष्यो भृशं ततः

ihaivāśubhakarmā` tu karmabhirnirayaṁ gataḥ
avāksa niraye pāpo mānavaḥ pacyate bhṛśam
tasmātsudurlabho mokṣa ātmā rakṣyo bhṛśaṁ tataḥ (2.34)

ihaivākarmā = iha (here) + eva (just so) + aśubha (socially unacceptable) + karma (act); tu – but; karmabhir - by social acts; nirayaṁ - hell hereafter; gataḥ - transit, go; avāksa – being wasted; niraye – in hell hereafter; pāpo = pāpah = faulty actors; mānavaḥ - human beings; pacyate – are tormented; bhṛśam – regularly; tasmāt – therefore, it stands to reason; sudurlabho = sudurlabhah = very difficult to achieve; mokṣa – freedom; ātmā – individual spirit; rakṣyo = rakṣyah = protected; bhṛśaṁ - especially; tataḥ - thus

Those who commit socially-unacceptable acts here on earth, transit to hell hereafter on the basis of the same acts. Being wasted, those faulty human beings are regularly tormented in hell. It stands to reason that freedom from that place is very difficult to attain. Thus the individual spirit should protect itself from that fate.

Analysis:

Given a choice between a profitable criminal act and a non-profit socially-beneficial act, the yogi should choose the socially-beneficial one. It is better to be poverty stricken without blemish, than to become wealthy through exploitive or criminal behavior. One should take care so as not to do anything which will cause the subtle body to go to a lower dimension in the afterlife.

Application:

If one develops criminal intentions and become habituated to ill-consideration, one will find it to be difficult if one decides to change. Regardless of whether it is good or bad, if one is

habituated to it, producing permanent change will take reform and discipline. A yogi should avoid bad behavior, criminal acts and occasions for expressing pride. He or she should avoid associating with those who have an insensitive conscience.

Verse 35

ऊर्ध्वं तु जन्तवो गत्वा येषु स्थानेष्ववस्थिताः

कीर्त्यमानानि तानीह तत्त्वतः संनिबोध मे

तच्छ्रुत्वा नैष्ठिकीं बुद्धिं बुध्येथाः कर्मनिश्चयात्

ūrdhvaṁ tu jantavo gatvā yeṣu sthāneṣvavasthitāḥ
kīrtyamānāni tānīha tattvataḥ saṁnibodha me
tacchrutvā naiṣṭhikīṁ buddhiṁ budhyethāḥ karmaniścayāt (2.35)

ūrdhvaṁ - ascend; tu – but; jantavo = jantavah = the entities; gatvā – being elevated; yeṣu – of their; sthāneṣv = sthāneṣu = of realms; avasthitāḥ - reside; kīrtyamānāni - describe; tānīha = tānī (they, those) + iha (here); tattvataḥ - truth; saṁnibodha – listen attentively; me – from me; tacchrutvā = tat (that) + śrutvā (having heard); naiṣṭhikīṁ - steady; buddhiṁ - intellect; budhyethāḥ - best information; karma – social action; niścayāt – be decisive

But regarding their ascent, the entities being elevated, reside in their attained realms. Listen attentively. I will describe the truth of this. Having heard this your intellect will be steady. You will have the best information and will be decisive about social actions.

Analysis:

If a soul is elevated to a celestial place in the astral realms, it will stay there for a time. Soon it will find itself back in an adjacent astral place from which deceased persons transit to take birth on the earthly planet. The duration of stay in a heavenly place, is directly related to the amount of pious activity performed in the past earthly life.

The deity of each of the heavenly places evaluates the entity's actions on earth which were in compliance with righteous lifestyle and then allows that person to stay in the heavenly world for a time.

Application:

By intuition a yogi is distrustful of the path of approved social acts. This is because his or her intuition is predisposed to attaining spiritual realization. The yogi will comply with the wishes of the Universal Form but his main interest is exemption from all sorts of social intercourses, pious types and criminal ones.

Verse 36

तारारूपाणि सर्वाणि यच्चैतच्चन्द्रमण्डलम्

यच्च विभ्राजते लोके स्वभासा सूर्यमण्डलम्

स्थानान्येतानि जानीहि नराणां पुण्यकर्मणाम्

tārārūpāṇi sarvāṇi yaccaitaccandramaṇḍalam
yacca vibhrājate loke svabhāsā sūryamaṇḍalam
sthānānyetāni jānīhi narāṇāṁ puṇyakarmaṇām (2.36)

tārā – stars; rūpāṇi – forms; sarvāṇi – all; yac = yat = which; caitac = ca (and) + etat (this); candra – moon; maṇḍalam – orbit; yac = yat = which; ca – and; vibhrājate – shining; loke – in the universe; svabhāsā – self-effulgent; sūrya – sun; maṇḍalam – orbit; sthānāny = sthānāni = locations; etāni – these; jānīhi – know; narāṇāṁ - of the people; puṇya – socially beneficial; karmaṇām - actions

Those which are the regions of all forms of the stars, the orbiting moon which shines on the earth, the self-effulgent orbiting sun, all situated in their realms; know these as the locations attained by those who perform socially-beneficial acts.

Analysis:

Persons who qualify, whose subtle bodies went through the appropriate alterations by the performance of approved selfless actions, go to a higher dimension in a subtle body which is suited to that location, either on the sun, moon or on another heavenly body.

One is promoted or demoted by the content energy of one's social actions. This happens because the subtle body is affected by association and by intention for actions. Those who do criminal action or act with the content of resentment and hate, realize themselves in the afterworld as hell-beings or horrid ghosts. This all happens because of dramatic alterations in the subtle body.

In the Bhagavad Gita, Lord Krishna gave some description of how souls move from this life to a hell in the astral world, or to a heavenly place or back into a parent body.

yard sattve pravṛddhe tu pralayaṁ yāti dehabhṛt
tadottamavidāṁ lokān amalānpratipadyate
rajasi pralayaṁ gatvā karmasaṅgiṣu jāyate
tathā pralīnastamasi mūḍhayoniṣu jāyate

When the embodied soul goes through the death experience while under the dominance of the clarifying mode, he is transferred to the pure world of those who know the Supreme.

Having gone through the death experience in the impulsive mode, the soul is born among the work-prone people; likewise when dying in the depressive mode, the soul takes birth from the wombs of the ignorant species. (14.14-15)

ūrdhvaṁ gacchanti sattvasthā madhye tiṣṭhanti rājasāḥ
jaghanyaguṇavṛttasthā adho gacchanti tāmasāḥ

Those who are anchored in clarity, go upward. Those who are impulsive are situated in the middle. Those who are habituated to the lowest influence of the material energy, the retarded people, go downward. (14.18)

Application:

Once a yogi outgrows the need for the heavenly planets, he or she is no longer attracted to the mundane heavenly world. Most religious people think that such a yogi is mistaken since he or she is reluctant to patronize a religion which promises residence in heaven after death. Some yogis shy away from

religion because their intuition tells them that it is all a farce. This means that the idea of going to a heaven for a time and then returning to this world to again generate pious acts is fatiguing and disappointing to say the least. A yogi wants to reach to an environment which is on par with the quality of the core-self. If there is a world which is subtler than the core-self, then the yogi would not be interested in it, because he will never be able to perceive a dimension which is transcendental to the spiritual self. What a yogi wants to go to a place that is 100% compatible to the self. That is realistic provided he could complete the austerities which would transit him to that place.

The performance of approved social acts cannot cause a significant enough upgrade in the status of the self. Hence some yogis reject the idea of going to heaven hereafter. They complete the austerities which result in migration to the spiritual world where the sun and moon has no presence. This place was mentioned by Krishna to Arjuna in the Bhagavad Gītā discourse:

na tadbhāsayate sūryo na śaśāṅko na pāvakaḥ
yadgatvā na nivartante taddhāma paramaṁ mama

The sun does not illuminate that place, nor the moon, nor the fire. Having gone to that location, they never return. That is My supreme residence. (15.6)

Verse 37

कर्मक्षयाच्च ते सर्वे च्यवन्ते वै पुनः पुनः

तत्रापि च विशेषोऽस्ति दिवि नीचोच्चमध्यमः

karmakṣayācca te sarve cyavante vai punaḥ punaḥ
tatrāpi ca viśeṣo'sti divi nīcoccamadhyamaḥ (2.37)

karma – energy of pious acts; kṣayāc = kṣayāt = due to consumption; ca – and; te – they; sarve – all; cyavante – demoted; vai – indeed; punaḥ punaḥ - repeatedly; tatrāpi = tatra (there) + api (also); ca – and; viśeṣo = viśeṣah = distinction; 'sti = asti = there is; divi – in the celestial regions; nīcoccamadhyamaḥ = nīca (high) + ucca (low) + madhyamaḥ (median)

After the consumption of the energy of pious acts, they are repeatedly demoted. There in the celestial regions, there is distinction as well, regarding high, low and median status.

Analysis:

A person who is a leading saint on this planet or who is a leading pious ruler might be promoted to a paradise after death. However the leading status here might not be sustained in the heavenly world. This is because it is near impossible to outshine the deities and their assistants in those heavenly places.

One who reaches heaven because of glorious political acts carries a chip on his subtle shoulder and due to that he is marked in heaven for an early dismissal because of his suppressed pride. There is a tale about a king named Yayati who made it to the heavenly world. He was demoted to the earth even before the energy-effects of his pious actions were exhausted.

To rid heaven of his obnoxious presence the Indra deity of the place merely asked Yayati if there was anyone as great or greater than him when he lived as a king on earth. Yayati without hesitation declared that of course there was no one who could compare with him. He said he never knew anyone who was as great or greater. Due to that denial his subtle body was de-energized in an instant and he found himself fading away from that place. He then realized himself in a dimension which was adjacent to this physical world.

Going to those heavenly planets and then become demoted to the earth is very frustrating and disappointing. In fact some persons after reaching this earth and finding that they are not in a comparable opulent lifestyle, subconsciously act in a suicidal manner due to manic depression.

Application:

A yogi has no use for a competitive existence. In the heavenly planets, there is competition even though it is not as

blatant or animalistic as on the earth. A yogi is simply not interested in such a place.

Instead of going to heaven after death, a mature yogi prefers to take another human body and make efforts to complete the austerities which would cause transit to the spiritual world where there is no sun or moon or electricity and where everything is blissful, self-illuminated and free from the flaws of impermanency.

Verse 38

न तत्राप्यस्ति संतोषो दृष्ट्वा दीप्ततरां श्रियम्

इत्येता गतयः सर्वाः पृथक्त्वे समुदीरिताः

na tatrāpyasti saṁtoṣo dṛṣṭvā dīptatarāṁ śriyam
ityetā gatayaḥ sarvāḥ pṛthaktve samudīritāḥ (2.38)

na – no; tatrāpy = tatra (there) + api (also); asti – there is; saṁtoṣo = saṁtoṣah = contentment; dṛṣṭvā – after seeing; dīptatarāṁ - greater effulgence; śriyam – splendour; ityetā = iti(thus) + etā (this); gatayaḥ - courses of soul transit; sarvāḥ - all; pṛthak – detailed; tve – of you; samudīritāḥ - described

Even in the celestial world, there is no contentment after one sees someone with greater effulgence and splendor. Thus details of all courses of soul transit were described by me.

Analysis:

There is no outright envy in the celestial world and there is no blatant arrogance. Still pride in the appearance of the self exists there. Through it one person compares with another person, especially those who got to the celestial places on the basis of their hard earned merits from doing socially-beneficial activities on earth.

There is also the problem of seeing others in the celestial world, whom one considers as not qualified for residence there. In the *Mahābhārata*, there is the narration of King Yudhishthira's disapproval of seeing the villain Duryodhana in the heavenly world. Since Duryodhana was a corrupt ruler, Yudhishthira condemned the means of getting to heaven when he saw the villain enjoying with others who were corrupt officials in the Kuru dynasty.

Application:

The celestial body used in the heavenly places of the higher astral world is made of light energy, like sunlight and moonlight. Still a yogi must research to know if this type of body is a spiritual body. Is that form just a souped-up version of the astral body? Or is it a spiritual body made of the core-self?

What happens to that body when the spirit leaves the heavenly world and comes down to the lower astral planes in anticipation of becoming an embryo?

Since as explained by the siddha to Kashyapa, there is modest resentment and envy in such places, it is concluded that those locales are not the ideal environment for the spiritual self.

Verse 39

उपपत्तिं तु गर्भस्य वक्ष्याम्यहमतः परम्

यथावत्तां निगदतः शृणुष्वावहितो द्विज

upapattiṁ tu garbhasya vakṣyāmyahamataḥ param
yathāvattāṁ nigadataḥ śṛṇuṣvāvahito dvija (2.39)

upapattiṁ - production; tu – but; garbhasya – of the embryo; vakṣyāmy = vakṣyāmi = I will tell; aham – I; ataḥ - then; param – after; yathāvat – regarding; tāṁ - you; nigadataḥ - explain; śṛṇu – listen; ṣvāvahito = ṣvāvahitah = rapt attention; dvija – trained ascetic

Regarding the production of the embryo, I will tell you of that after this. As I explain this to you, listen with rapt attention, O trained ascetic.

Analysis:

It is rare to get an inside view of what happens when a living entity transmigrates. Where does the person who inhabits the body go during astral projections and when the body finally dies? What does that person take to the hereafter? How can one recognize a person who is reborn in another body? Can a spirit simply refuse to take birth? Can one remain in a bodiless state forever?

Application:

The production of the embryo is a whole other study by itself. To get some insight into this process would be marvelous. Ultimately a yogi has to develop the perception to track the movements of the soul while it has a physical body and when it is permanently displaced from that form.

One person who mastered the art of viewing the movement of the spirits is Bhishma, the grandfather of the Kuru family. He tracked Princess Amba who resented him for interfering with her destiny. The Princess passed on from a female body and then took a male embryo in a dynasty which became hostile to Kurus.

Chapter 3

Similar Consciousness-Energy*

jātīmaraṇarogaiśca samāviṣṭaḥ pradhānavit
cetanāvatsu caitanyaṁ samaṁ bhūteṣu paśyati (3.31)

Though harassed by birth, death and disease, he knows the life-force energy potential. He perceives a similar consciousness-energy in all psyches which are reinforced with awareness.

**This chapter heading was introduced by the translator on the basis of the verse above. The Mahābhārata does not have a chapter heading.*

Verse 1

ब्राह्मण उवाच

शुभानामशुभानां च नेह नाशोऽस्ति कर्मणाम्

प्राप्य प्राप्य तु पच्यन्ते क्षेत्रं क्षेत्रं तथा तथा

brāhmaṇa uvāca
śubhānāmaśubhānāṁ ca neha nāśo'sti karmaṇām
prāpya prāpya tu pacyante kṣetraṁ kṣetraṁ tathā tathā (3.1)

brāhmaṇa - the elevated ascetic; uvāca – said; śubhānām – of what is asupicious; aśubhānāṁ - what is inauspicious; ca – and; neha = na (no) + iha (here); nāśo = nāśah = elimination; 'sti = asti – is; karmaṇām – of the cultural activities; prāpya prāpya = obtaining in sequence; tu – but; pacyante – express energies; kṣetraṁ kṣetraṁ - environment after environment; tathā tathā = so in order (3.1)

There is no elimination of the energy of auspicious or inauspicious social acts. Obtaining bodies in sequence, the activities express energies in various envirnoments in sequence.

Analysis:

There is no possibility of eliminating the effect-energies of auspicious and inauspicious acts. These acts will continue as after-effects of previous acts. The new acts will set into motion other effects in an endless cast of time and history.

No one, ever, will be able to put an end to the sequences of cause and effect, with an effect becoming a future cause. This will go on forever in the material world.

Application:

Even if the universe shuts down due to spend-reactive energy, the effect-potencies will go into dormancy. But they will be activated again when the universe is manifested when there is a disturbance in its equilibrium of energy. This universe was in equilibrium before and it was in disturbance prior to that. It contains the potential history even when it is not manifested. That potential emerges and acts in a sequential order when it is agitated again.

Verse 2

यथा प्रसूयमानस्तु फली दद्यात्फलं बहु

तथा स्याद्विपुलं पुण्यं शुद्धेन मनसा कृतम्

yathā prasūyamānastu phalī dadyātphalaṁ bahu
tathā syādvipulaṁ puṇyaṁ śuddhena manasā kṛtam (3.2)

yathā – as; prasūyamānas – bearing; tu – but; phalī – fruit tree; dadyāt – from yielding; phalaṁ - fruit; bahu – much; tathā – so; syād = syāt – there is; vipulaṁ - ample; puṇyaṁ - meritorious acts; śuddhena – by pure; manasā –by the mind; kṛtam - done

As during the bearing season a fruit-bearing tree yields much fruit, so meritorious acts which are done with a pure mind supply ample benefits.

Analysis:

When something is done without motive, just to get it done, with great care, without thinking that there should be a reward, the act leaves an effect-energy which will supply ample benefits sometime in the future. It may be fortune in the same life or in a future life, but it will in time reproduce a fortune return for the actor, and this is irrespective of whether the actor remembers the incidence or not.

Many people do deliberate philanthropic acts with full intent to disclaim any credit which might accrue. But material nature is not concerned with one's identity with or denial of rewards for action. It tags the actor and sees to it that the actor is rewarded sometime in the future. If the actor is resistant then material nature will find a way to disempower the actor by putting the actor in a position where he or she cannot refuse the return.

Material nature is concerned with mathematical equivalency. It does not tolerate eternal tension. Thus all initiating functions are tagged until they reach a quiescence.

Application:

Getting out of the material world with its actions and mandatory reactions, is a task in itself for a yogi. It can be done but only by exceptional individuals. This is because material nature hangs on the living entities with a very powerful adhesive. To break the bonding force requires superhuman intelligence, persistence and very good luck in the form of help from a divine being.

Material nature will hunt down the actor to deliver to him or her, whatever good or bad, favorable or unfavorable results were accrued from past actions. It distributes returns with incredible precision. It never misidentifies an actor. How then can a student yogi transcend the actions and reactions in the material world?

Verse 3

पापं चापि तथैव स्यात्पापेन मनसा कृतम्

पुरोधाय मनो हीह कर्मण्यात्मा प्रवर्तते

pāpaṁ cāpi tathaiva syātpāpena manasā kṛtam
purodhāya mano hīha karmaṇyātmā pravartate (3.3)

pāpaṁ - faulty acts; cāpi = ca (and) + api (also); tathaiva = tathā (so) + eva (even); syāt – is; pāpena – with a corrupt; manasā – with mind; kṛtam – done; purodhāya - being before; mano – mind; hīha = hi (indeed)+ iha (here); karmaṇy = karmaṇi = social activities; ātmā – self; pravartate - manifests

Faulty acts done with a corrupt mind, produce corresponding results. With the mind before it, the self manifests social activities.

Analysis:

Even though the self is tagged for actions performed by the psyche and by the physical body, the self is not the author of the actions. It is involved in permitting the acting but it is not the source of the actions. Material nature itself is the inherent root cause of the actions which are played out in the realm of nature under nature's time scale.

Operating in the mind, as subtle emotional and mental energy, material nature runs the drama of bodily acts when there is a material body for a particular spirit or psychic acts when there is just a subtle body in the astral world. In either case, the spirit only supplies a permitting energy for the acts.

This does not mean that an act will not be executed if a spirit does not permit it. In fact even if the spirit disagrees vehemently, still an act may be carried out by the psyche and by the material body. The permitting feature of the psyche is not under the full control of the objective observing aspect of the self. Failure to understand this causes the self to have an over-estimated assessment of its willpower, which is ruinous.

Application:

The default relationship between the self and the other components in the psyche is for the self to give energy to permit impulsive acts. It is the hope of God and the great souls, that the individual spirits would adjust the psyche to change the subordination of the self. There is the mind chamber. Within it there is the core-self, the sense of identity, the intellect, the memory and the sensual energies. Besides the mind chamber, there is another psychic apparatus which is called the kundalini life force. That psychic function is in the trunk of the subtle body while the mind is in the head of the subtle form. Every aspect takes energy from the core self either directly or indirectly.

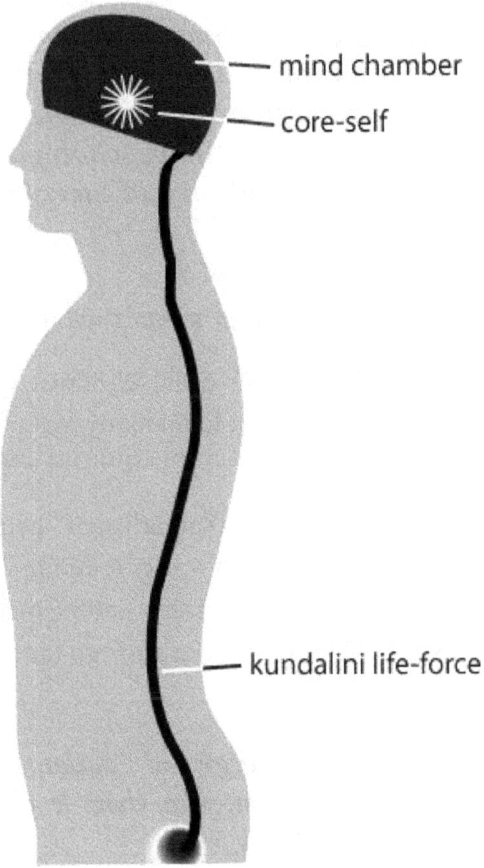

For instance the senses take energy from the life force and from the intellect. The intellect takes energy from the sense of identity and from the senses and the life force. The sense of identity takes energy from the core-self and the intellect. The kundalini life force takes energy from the sense of identity and from the intellect. In this way in various alliances, the components of the psyche interact with one another, with the core-self being the main power supply. It frequently supplies energy involuntarily because that is the system which was set up by material nature.

In kriya yoga, one is given training in how to re-order this default configuration which obviously is not in the interest of the self. So long as the mind takes the lead in making decisions about what the psyche should do, the self will be imperiled because the mind is of the same nature as material nature, and hence it has no spiritual focus. To gain a greater percentage of control the self has to institute psychological disciplines. It must cordon certain aspects of the psychological components. This requires training in meditation and energy infusion.

Verse 4

यथा कर्मसमादिष्टं काममन्युसमावृतः

नरो गर्भं प्रविशति तच्चापि शृणु चोत्तरम्

yathā karmasamādiṣṭaṁ kāmamanyusamāvṛtaḥ
naro garbhaṁ praviśati taccāpi śṛṇu cottaram (3.4)

yathā – as; karma – energy of action; samādiṣṭaṁ - being possessed; kāmamany = kāmamani = lust; usam – anger; āvṛtaḥ - overwhelmed; naro – person; garbhaṁ - womb; praviśati – enters; tac = tat = that; cāpi = ca (and) + api (also); śṛṇu – hear; cottaram = ca (and) + uttaram (explanation)

Being possessed by the energy of action, the person is overwhemled by anger and lust; like that, it enters the womb. Now hear my explanation of this.

Analysis:

The energy of desire comprises either a fulfillment-response force or a disappointment-reaction impulsion. If the desire is fulfilled by the grace of time and nature, then there is happiness and relief. If it is not, there is sadness and defiance. Usually an entity does not stop to consider the source of a desire. This is because the desire energy is usually embedded in the psyche as if it was native to the self.

Application:

Each lifetime begins with a desire energy which contains the basic drives which are to be expressed during that life. Of course the presence of such desires does not guarantee opportunities for fulfillment. In some lives those desires remain unfulfilled because material nature simply refuses to respond to them. In other lives up to ninety percent (90%) of the desires are fulfilled. In some other lives, the desires which were present just before birth and which served as the basic impetus to get the embryo, are discarded after the birth of the body, when the self finds that the circumstances are conducive to other desires which were embedded elsewhere in the psyche.

A student yogi has an ongoing task to come to terms with desire. Eventually he or she must learn how to neutralize desire energies before they burst out and greedily hunt down fulfillments.

Verse 5

शुक्रं शोणितसंसृष्टं स्त्रिया गर्भाशयं गतम्

क्षेत्रं कर्मजमाप्नोति शुभं वा यदि वाशुभम्

śukraṁ śoṇitasaṁsṛṣṭaṁ striyā garbhāśayaṁ gatam
kṣetraṁ karmajamāpnoti śubhaṁ vā yadi vāśubham (3.5)

śukraṁ - semen; śoṇita – blood; saṁsṛṣṭaṁ - fused; striyā – woman; garbhāśayaṁ - womb; gatam –entering; kṣetraṁ psyche, environment; karma – effect energy of actions; jam – produced; āpnoti – gets; śubhaṁ - pious; vā – or/and; yadi – when; vāśubham = va (or) + aśubhaṁ (despicable)

Being fused with blood and semen, entering the womb of a woman, it becomes the psyche which was produced from the effect-energy of its pious and despicable acts.

Analysis:

Material nature puts on a good show of identifying itself seamlessly with the core-self. This act of nature is so well done, that even the core-self believes it. Becoming fused into the feelings of a parent, the psyche is then fused with the biological fluids of the male parent and then with the female parent. This produces the physical result of an embryo. The core-self is so absorbed in this development that it loses its objective perception and gives itself over to the bodily awareness of the fetus.

Application:

In each life, the living entity amasses some effect-energies based on acts committed by the body. This energy goes with the spirit at the time of death. It determines what astral world the spirit will exist in during the afterlife. In the astral world, the spirit cannot generate any more effect-energy, but whatever it has in its psyche acts as an impetus to attract it to a certain type of parent.

Sometimes this attraction fails to result in the pregnancy of a specific woman. Then the self seeks out alternatives until it gets the opportunity to become a baby. Because it had certain desire-energies from the past life it comes out into the world as an infant with the impetus to achieve certain objectives. If things are not what it prefers, it feels frustrated and becomes angry.

Student yogis are trained to be tolerant and humble, so that the parents of the student's next baby form are not harassed by the infant. This gives the student yogi the opportunity to be agreeable to others who serve it in infancy.

Verse 6

सौक्ष्म्यादव्यक्तभावाच्च न स क्वचन सज्जते

संप्राप्य ब्रह्मणः कायं तस्मात्तद्ब्रह्म शाश्वतम्

तद्बीजं सर्वभूतानां तेन जीवन्ति जन्तवः

saukṣmyād avyaktabhāvācca na sa kvacana sajjate
saṁprāpya brahmaṇaḥ kāyaṁ tasmāttadbrahma śāśvatam
tadbījaṁ sarvabhūtānāṁ tena jīvanti jantavaḥ (3.6)

saukṣmyād = saukṣmyāt = due to subtlety; avyakta – unmanifest texture; bhāvāc = bhāvāt = condition of being; ca – and; na – not; sa – he, it; kvacana – somewhere; sajjate – attached, permanently fused with; saṁprāpya – obtaining; brahmaṇaḥ - spiritual energy; kāyaṁ - body; tasmāt – thus; tad – it, that; brahma – spiritual reality; śāśvatam – always; tad = tat = that, it; bījaṁ - core, reference; sarva – all; bhūtānāṁ - of the creatures; tena – by it; jīvanti – they live; jantavaḥ - living beings

Due to subtlety and the unmanifest texture of the being, it is not permanently fused with anything anywhere. It obtains a body which is based on spiritual energy. Thus it is always a spiritual reality. It is the reference of all creatures. By it, the living beings exhibit symptoms of life.

Analysis:

The fusion of the spiritual self and the other components of the psyche is apparent only because the self cannot directly be fused with physical substance or with subtle material nature. It does so indirectly through its sense of identity. The energy of the sense of identity is the highest energizing force besides the core self but it is still not on the level with the self.

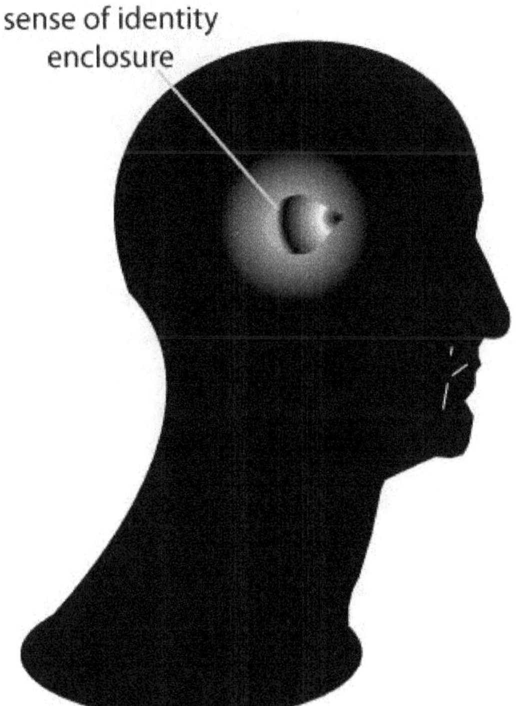

I-self enclosed by sense of identity

However unless the self masters the disciplines of yoga, it cannot realize its isolated self. When it is effectively segregated from the sense of identity it is said to be in a state of aloneness or kaivalyam. This is described nicely by Patanjali in his Yoga Sūtras:

tad abhāvāt saṁyogā abhāvaḥ
hānaṁ taddṛśeḥ kaivalyam

The elimination of the conjunction which results from the elimination of that spiritual ignorance is the withdrawal that is the total separation of the perceiver from the mundane psychology. (Yoga Sūtras 2.25)

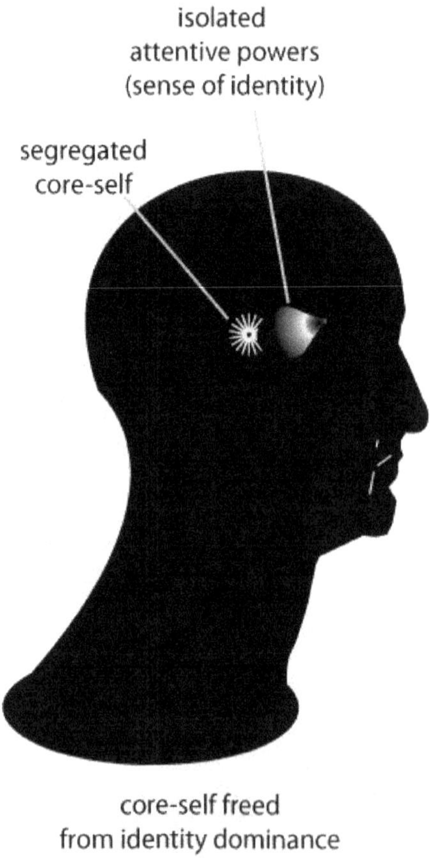

To realize the self all by itself without its adjuncts one has to practice meditation and master what Patanjali termed as samyama, which is a sequential development from deliberate linkage to the spiritual plane of consciousness to effortless linkage and then to spontaneous linkage for extended periods.

This allows the core-self to turn away from the adjuncts or accessory psychic sensors. Then the self can realize itself without a nature-derived psyche.

Application:

The linkage between the self and its sense of identity may be compared to the connection between a magnetic field and wound wires which produce electricity from movement of either the magnetism or the wires. Even though the wires are not connected physically to the magnet which produces the polarized influence, still electricity may be generated in the wires.

Even though the core-self is not directly connected to a physical body or even to a subtle body, still there is a transfer of influence from the self to the sense of identity. That sense in turn is able to attract to itself the energy of the self which it uses to gain control over the intellect and the life force. These in turn produce and control the senses and are also influenced by feedback from the sensual energies.

The most essential aspect in material existence is the core-self and yet it may struggle to free itself from the adjuncts. Yoga is the process through which it can bring to bear its separation from the other components in the psyche. The core-self must endeavor to understand how it is linked and how it can be disconnected from those components

The self did not deliberately put itself in touch with material nature, even with the subtle or psychic aspect of material nature. And yet, for it to be freed, it has to endeavor using that very same equipment.

Verse 7

स जीवः सर्वगात्राणि गर्भस्याविश्य भागशः

दधाति चेतसा सद्यः प्राणस्थानेष्ववस्थितः

ततः स्पन्दयतेऽङ्गानि स गर्भश्चेतनान्वितः

sa jīvaḥ sarvagātrāṇi garbhasyāviśya bhāgaśaḥ
dadhāti cetasā sadyaḥ prāṇasthāneṣvavasthitaḥ
tataḥ spandayate'ṅgāni sa garbhaścetanānvitaḥ (3.7)

sa – that; jīvaḥ - energy of individual spirit; sarva – all; gātrāṇi – limbs; garbhasya – of the fetus; āviśya – entering, diffused into; bhāgaśaḥ - part by part, every part; dadhāti – resides; cetasā - composite consciousness; sadyaḥ - presently; prāṇa – breath energy; sthāneṣv = sthāneṣu – of locations; avasthitaḥ - stationed, resided; - tataḥ - then; spandayate – moves; 'ṅgāni = aṅgāni = limbs; sa – it; garbhaś = garbhah = fetus; cetanā – consciousness; anvitaḥ - conditioned

The individual spirit's energy is diffused into every part of every limb of the fetus. It accepts the body's composite consciousness. It simultaneously resides in all locations where there is distribution of breath energy in the body. Then the fetus being conditioned by consciousness, moves its limbs.

Analysis:

Some people are of the opinion that the spirit takes possession of a body when that body is delivered from the womb of the mother. Others say that the spirit takes control at the time of conception when the father passes sexual fluids into the body of the mother and a portion of those fluids emulsifies in the womb and begins an embryo. And yet others feel that there is no particular moment when the soul becomes the consciousness of the fetus.

This information from a mystic ascetic explains that the spirit's energy is diffused into every part of every limb of the fetus from the very beginning of its formation in the mother's system. There was no time when the individual spirit was not present in the formation of its fetus. In fact the distribution of its consciousness throughout the body is self-evident.

Application:

The influence of the spirit occurs by its proximity to the would-be parents of its future body. This might be compared to the influence of a radio-active substance on some other material. Even though there appears to be no activity, still there will be changes in the substance if it is put within a certain distance of the radioactive isotopes.

Some persons think that since there is no physical action of a spirit fusing with the feelings and reproductive fluids of the parents, that proves that there is no spirit involved and that the fetus is merely a biological instance. This argument is further supported by modern genetic experiments where researchers are able to expand life in a test tube by providing special proteins to one or more cells which are taken from a life form.

Yogis should not contest these physical facts. But all the same, a yogi should persevere with mystic practice and develop psychic perception further, even though he or she may not be able to demonstrate to the scientific community the reality of spiritual entities.

Once its energy is used to form a fetus, the living entity is compelled to accept the composite body-awareness as itself and as its own. This might be compared to a magnet and some iron filings. If the magnet is placed within a certain distance of the filings, it will attract the filings forcibly. Then the magnet will never have the power to free itself from the filings. It will have to take possession of the filings and take them wherever it may go. The only way the magnet can release itself from the filings is to collapse its magnetic field. Of course for a magnet that is not possible. But a human being can do something to the magnet to cause it to lose its magnetic influence. Then suddenly the filings would drop from the magnet and no longer adhere to it.

The withdrawal of the self's energy from the psychic components which are the blueprint for the gross body, is executed in the pratyahar sensual energy withdrawal stage of yoga. This is the 5th of the 8 stages of yoga. In that practice, the yogi retracts his attention energy into the sense of identity. When that is done the influence of the intellect, the memories, the life force and the sensual energies collapses and no longer clings to the core-self.

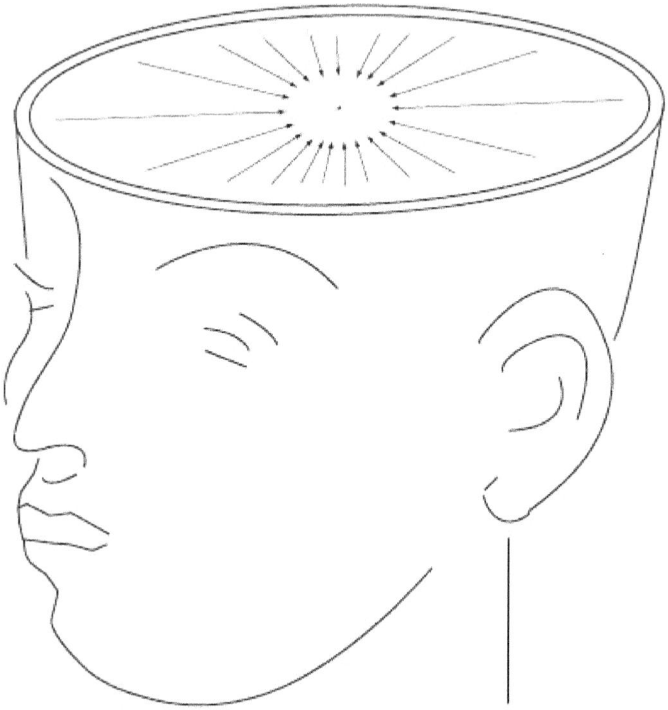

attention energy retracted into sense of identity

Verse 8

यथा हि लोहनिष्यन्दो निषिक्तो बिम्बविग्रहम्

उपैति तद्वज्जानीहि गर्भे जीवप्रवेशनम्

yathā hi lohaniṣyando niṣikto bimbavigraham
upaiti tadvajjānīhi garbhe jīvapraveśanam (3.8)

yathā – as; hi – indeed; loha – iron; niṣyando - molten; niṣikto = niṣiktah = poured; bimba – image, mold; vigraham – form; upaiti –

can, obtain; tadvaj = tatvat = for that; jānīhi – know; garbhe – in the womb; jīva – individual spirit; praveśanam - enter

As molten iron which is poured into a mould, takes the form of it, so you should know that as being similar to how the individual spirit enters the womb.

Analysis:

The psychic and physical conditions of the mother's reproductive mechanism have bearing on the conditions of the fetus which will be produced. The father's situation also has an impact. The child's effect-energies which it carried from previous lives, also figure in. The body produced is the composite effect of these forces in combination.

Application:

The body which is born for a living entity, has within it powerful forces which migrated into it as it was produced. These come from the father, the mother, the entity involved and even from the ancestors and living descendants of those ancestors. When it leaves the womb and develops into an adult body, the entity will invariably find that some traits of the body are not to its liking but it will be unable to adjust many of these unwanted features.

Verse 9

लोहपिण्डं यथा वह्निः प्रविशत्यभितापयन्

तथा त्वमपि जानीहि गर्भे जीवोपपादनम्

lohapiṇḍaṁ yathā vahniḥ praviśatyabhitāpayan
tathā tvamapi jānīhi garbhe jīvopapādanam.(3.9)

loha – iron; piṇḍaṁ - ball; yathā – as; vahniḥ - fire; praviśaty = praviśati = penetrates; abhitāpayan – heating; tathā – so; tvam – you; api – so; jānīhi – comprehend; garbhe – in the fetus; jīvopapādanam – presence of the soul

As fire penetrates a ball of iron, heating it, so you should comprehend the presence of a soul in a fetus.

Analysis:

A small quantity of heat which is in a ball of iron cannot be perceived visually by a human being, but it can be felt through the sense of touch. The spirit cannot be seen in the body by physical senses, but it can be deduced truthfully by the exhibition of consciousness and by the focalizing attitude of its awareness.

There is random awareness everywhere as is evident by the presence of static electricity in all locations. Focal awareness is an entirely different consideration just as generated electricity which surges in a power cord, has definite application.

We should assume that anytime we encounter focal awareness we are dealing with an individual spirit. It may be argued that when the fetus is in development in the womb, the evidence speaks volume about it being part of the mother's consciousness. This is true to a certain extent. As soon as the fetus' heart beat can be heard distinctly, that is evidence of it being a separate entity. But its parturition is the sure sign that it is a different personality.

Application:

A yogi should take this example seriously and by meditation begin to check the distribution of consciousness from the core-self through the sense of identity, through the intellect and kundalini, and finally through the senses out into the atmosphere. This might be similar to the filament of a light bulb, analyzing the distribution of its energy through the inside of the bulb, the glass casing, and then through the air outside the bulb. It becomes obvious that such research is subjective and intuitive.

When it researches its influence in the psyche, the self has to resort to subjective means. Even though subjective evidence is ridiculed in the scientific world, a yogi has no other recourse in this matter.

Verse 10

यथा च दीपः शरणं दीप्यमानः प्रकाशयेत्

एवमेव शरीराणि प्रकाशयति चेतना

yathā ca dīpaḥ śaraṇaṁ dīpyamānaḥ prakāśayet
evameva śarīrāṇi prakāśayati cetanā (3.10)

yathā – as; ca – and; dīpaḥ - lamp; śaraṇaṁ - house; dīpyamānaḥ - blazing; prakāśayet – illuminates; evam – thus; eva – so; śarīrāṇi - bodies; prakāśayati – gives feelings; cetanā - consciousness

As a blazing lamp illuminates a house, so consciousness gives feelings to bodies.

Analysis:

To develop confidence in this statement and to make it a statement of personal truth, one has to meditate and track the extent of bodily consciousness, expanded mental consciousness and emotional use of consciousness. Bodily consciousness is definitely a composite circumstance. This makes it difficult to analyze, partition and identify. It can be catalogued if the yogi takes the time to meditate to develop the required psychic sensitivity.

Application:

During astral projection the yogi gets definite evidence that the consciousness is composite. This is because in projection, the physical body remains alive somewhere with a minimum quantity of consciousness, while the astral body roams here and there in subtle dimensions. When the two bodies fuse together again, the physical body becomes increasingly animated by the increased influx of energy from the astral form.

In the psychology there is the spirit individual who is the source of primal energy. Thus when the astral form synchronizes back into the physical body that physique displays active personality. Each yogi must study these matters in meditation practice to come to the proper conclusion about how the spirit is related to its body.

Verse 11

यद्यच्च कुरुते कर्म शुभं वा यदि वाशुभम्

पूर्वदेहकृतं सर्वमवश्यमुपभुज्यते

yadyacca kurute karma śubhaṁ vā yadi vāśubham
pūrvadehakṛtaṁ sarvamavaśyamupabhujyate (3.11)

yadyac = yatyat = whatever; ca – and; kurute – performed; karma – activities; śubhaṁ- beneficial; vā – or; yadi – in case; vāśubham = va (or) + aśubham (degrading); pūrva – previous; deha – body; kṛtaṁ - done; sarvam – all; avaśyam – by necessity; upabhujyate – must be endured

The effects of beneficial or degrading activities which the individual soul performed in previous bodies, must be endured by necessity

Analysis:

As long as a particular spirit is in material nature, it will find that its destiny is ever related to the beneficial and degrading activities it committed in the past. Material nature keeps a tab on everything. Its log of past actions is hyper-accurate. It is concerned with returning effects to causes and with putting into balance whatever was agitated.

Application:

A living entity must endure more than just the boomerang effects of its actions. It must also deal with associative returns which involve complex conjoint energies. And there is supernatural interference which brings on other non-adjustable conditions.

Verse 12

ततस्तत्क्षीयते चैव पुनश्चान्यत्प्रचीयते

यावत्तन्मोक्षयोगस्थं धर्मं नैवावबुध्यते

tatastatkṣīyate caiva punaścānyatpracīyate
yāvattanmokṣayogasthaṁ dharmaṁ naivāvabudhyate (3.12)

tatas = tatah = then; tat – that; kṣīyate – exhausted; caiva – and also; punaś = punah = again; cānyat = ca (and) + anyat (other); pracīyate – accumulated; yāvat – until; tan = tan = that; mokṣa – liberation; yoga – yoga; sthaṁ - situated; dharmaṁ - righteous lifestyle; naivāvabudhyate = na (learn) + eva (so) + abudhyate (learnt, integrated)

Then that (effects) is exhausted and again other effects of new actions are accumulated. This continues for as long as the righteous lifestyle which situates the person in yoga and liberation is not integrated.

Analysis:

To upset the balance of power so that the individual gets some leverage and options in dealing with the reactions in material nature, one has to become proficient in advanced meditation. The reactions will keep coming regardless but an entity could make an exit from certain domains and that would put that being off limits until and unless it again it enters those territories.

It is seen that sometimes a great yogi finds peace in isolation but as soon as he is exposed to associations, his troubles begin. This is because material nature can still identify a person even if that someone attains liberation.

Application:

The righteous lifestyle which situates a person in yoga and liberation can be integrated but that practice takes many lives to complete. Due to the complications of the various phases of material nature's operations, an entity is not easily freed from this existence. Even if one masters the physical portion of nature, the subtle part which is exponentially more complicated takes time to figure and successfully transcend.

Suppose an entity attains a status that frees it from having to take material bodies. Even then it might not be free from having to live in the astral world in a subtle body which is comprising of the subtle material nature. There are trillions of angelic beings who are permanent residents of the higher astral world, and still they are not liberated from the subtle material existence. They have no idea how they could transit to pure spiritual existence. The bodies they use are celestial forms of light energy in varying colors and still those sublime forms have no facility for even considering the means of escape from those places into the exclusive spiritual world.

A human being however has an astral body which has the capability for seeking a passage to the spiritual world. However it is not an automatic feature; it is activated by a serious attempt in completing the course of higher yoga.

Verse 13

तत्र धर्मं प्रवक्ष्यामि सुखी भवति येन वै

आवर्तमानो जातीषु तथान्योन्यासु सत्तम

tatra dharmaṁ pravakṣyāmi sukhī bhavati yena vai
āvartamāno jātīṣu tathānyonyāsu sattama (3.13)

tatra – there, regarding this; dharmaṁ - righteous lifestyle; pravakṣyāmi – I will tell; sukhī – happy; bhavati – becomes; yena – by which; vai – indeed; āvartamāno = āvartamānah = revolving; jātīṣu – through births; tathānyony = tatha (as) + anyoni (another); āsu – in rapid succession; sattama – best of human beings

Regarding this, I will tell you of the righteous lifestyle, by which, the soul becomes happy, despite its revolving through births in rapid succession one after another, O best of the human beings.

Analysis:

There is no stopping the system of material nature, which churns the living entities through many births and deaths. Those who want to be liberated should plan to spend many births achieving the objective. One must carry from one life to another, the momentum influence of the desire for liberation. It should be so strong that it serves as an instinct and intuition to cause one to seek spiritual advancement anytime one becomes conscious of oneself in any place.

Application:

A student yogi should not assume an attitude of, "I will figure it out. I will liberate myself." It is not possible to become liberated without assistance from more advanced persons and especially from superior deities who maintain a presence both in the material world and in the exclusive spiritual domains.

From this end of existence, one cannot figure the required method to break out of the subtle material nature. A yogi must get assistance from more advanced souls and from divinities. The advanced mystic told Kashyapa that he would explain a process which would work to liberate a soul even as that soul is forced to transmigrate in the gripping powers of material nature.

Verse 14

दानं व्रतं ब्रह्मचर्यं यथोक्तव्रतधारणम्

दमः प्रशान्तता चैव भूतानां चानुकम्पनम्

dānaṁ vrataṁ brahmacaryaṁ yathoktavratadhāraṇam
damaḥ praśāntatā caiva bhūtānāṁ cānukampanam (3.14)

dānaṁ - contribution; vrataṁ - vow; brahmacaryaṁ - sexual isolation for attaining the spiritual plane; yathokta = yatha (according) + ukta (what was said); vrata – social rules; dhāraṇam – upholding, keeping; damaḥ - self control; praśāntatā – tranquility; caiva - and also; bhūtānāṁ - creatures; cānukampanam = ca (and) + anukampanam (social compassion)

Contributions, vows, sexual isolation for attaining the spiritual plane, keeping social rules according to traditions, sensual restraint, tranquility and social compassion to all creatures,

Analysis:

These are some aspects of the required lifestyle. It is a bit complicated but material nature has an enigmatic operation which can only be superseded by a complex mix of austerities.

Contributions

One has to be free from selfishness if one is to advance in the righteous lifestyle. One must be sensitive to take the slightest hint about giving to others, even items which one needs for oneself.

Vows

Certain vows should be taken in order to cause the self to adhere to certain restrictions and to develop resistance to habits which are detrimental to spiritual advancement. Vows may be abandoned from time to time, not whimsically but in order to adapt other vows which are more essential. Social vows which are designed to give one an elite status in a spiritual society should be avoided as these are counterproductive to psyche purification.

Sexual isolation for attaining the spiritual plane

Sexual isolation is necessary for all serious students of spiritual practice. The sexual energy is such that it acts as a counterweight to spiritual progress by keeping the affectionate energy of the self bound up either in begetting progeny or in enjoying sexual organs for pleasure sake.

As it is, the material body is designed for a downward flow of the hormonal energy to the reproductive organs. This means that nature does not sponsor the use of the hormonal energy for anything besides begetting and enjoying sexual pleasure. A special effort must be made to divert these energies up the spine into the brain in order to increase psychic perception. If the brain is starved for hormonal energy, it will be likely that a higher level of meditation will not be reached, because the subtle body will be drained by the gross form which will cause the subtle form to remain on a lower astral plane.

Overall for spiritual life, one should either be completely celibate or partially celibate with use of the hormonal energies for raising progeny. To cheat nature, one should sidestep the usage of sexual energy for pleasure purposes.

Keeping social rules according to the traditions

Traditional social rules help to lubricate the exchange between people in one category and their collective relationship with outsiders. These rules may be beneficial to one set of individuals and corrosively upset another.

In the pursuit of spiritual life one should resist traditional prejudices but one should also recognize how these customs are endorsed by material nature and are misused for gaining the upper hand.

Overall a student yogi should step aside from social discrimination when it is in one's favor and also when it deprives one of opportunities. No yogi will put an end to the disparities in material nature but all the same, a yogi should not support the biases. One should not become a crusader for social equality but in his or her own way, the yogi should not support biases either.

Sensual restraint

Sensual restraint is a must for all yogis. Without it one would be a full-time pawn of the indiscriminate but prejudiced senses which hunt for exploitative opportunities in the material world.

The senses are dedicated to the kundalini life force as its main patron while ignoring the behest of the core-self. By consistently restraining the senses, the self gains control of their pursuits and restricts their influences which implicate the psyche for irrational acts.

The sense organs such as the eyes are electrified by sensual energy which comes from both the kundalini and the analytical orb. If this energy is not curbed from most of its favorite indulgences and if its quality is not raised considerably, the self will be condemned to remain as a stooge under it.

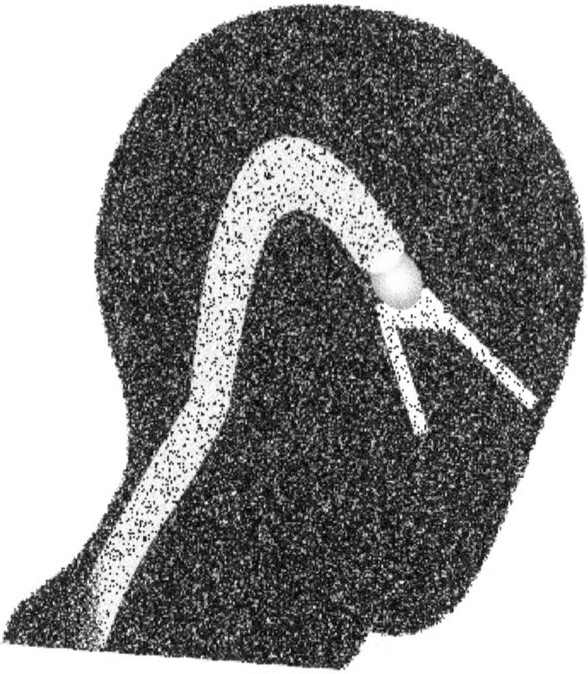

kundalini ascends through neck
and goads analytical orb (intellect),
which in turns polarises sensual energy
which electrifies the eyes

Tranquility

The quality of tranquility becomes established as soon as the senses are reigned in and the memories of previous sensual habits go into dormancy. All previous habits are still on record in material nature. Even if the individual could erase all such memories from its psyche, still material nature keeps her own log on the behaviors. One should never lose sight of the fact that material nature conducts itself irrespective of the self's participation.

At any moment if the student yogi is careless or if the self is lured, it will resume spiritually-destructive habits. Therefore one should never think that material nature is on one's side. Even when one's desires coincide with the performance of material nature, one should not lose sight of the fact that nature has its own agenda and will split off in its own direction sooner or later and leave one with the liabilities.

To remain with tranquility as a permanent feature of the psyche, a yogi should continually isolate the self from the ravaging moods which assail all selves who are involved with material nature.

Social compassion to all creatures

Social compassion to all creatures is an even attitude maintained by advanced yogis. Material nature does not always allow it, and still it is the default reactive mood of advanced souls. The strong attraction to family interest and selfish self-interest is thawed out in the nature of a yogi. That frees the self from bodily bias and opens the way for fair treatment of one and all.

When the effect-energies from the past life which caused this body are shattered, the yogi gets knowledge of past births and can divine relationships which he or she had with others in many past births. This insight is a boon for closing certain horrid chapters in the self's history.

Application:

A careless social format, plain ignorance about what to do and how to do it and outright arrogance renders no aid to a person who strives for spiritual advancement. In this world, even illusions carry a price and have value. A yogi should not abandon righteous lifestyle but all the same he or she should not become dedicated to political or religious enforcement of morality on a national or global scale.

It is sufficient for a yogi to set an example and keep the self away from those indulgences which ruin sense control and bar the way to ascension for the spirit self. There is a Supreme God. Of this there is no doubt. A yogi should do nothing to incur the disapproval of the Deity.

Verse 15

संयमश्चानृशंस्यं च परस्वादानवर्जनम्

व्यलीकानामकरणं भूतानां यत्र सा भुवि

saṁyamaścānṛśaṁsyaṁ ca parasvādānavarjanam
vyalīkānāmakaraṇaṁ bhūtānāṁ yatra sā bhuvi (3.15)

saṁyamaś = saṁyamah = proficiency in self restraint; cānṛśaṁsyaṁ ca (and) + ānṛśaṁsyaṁ (not being cruel); ca – and; paras – others; vādāna – deceptively, dishonestly; varjanam – desisting from; vyalīkā – false, deceptive; nāma – thought, name, word; karaṇaṁ - doing, causing; bhūtānāṁ - creatures; yatra – where; sā – it, that; bhuvi – on earth

...proficiency in self-restraint, not being cruel, ceasing all attempts to take the wealth of others, not acting deceptively or speaking dishonestly to any living being here in this world, not having deceptive thoughts towards any creature, here in this location,

Analysis:

Proficiency in self-restraint

Sense control is any effective means of restraining a particular sensual response. Self restraint is a wider effort to control more than one sense, or to control the entire psyche when it is forcibly pursuing things which are against the spiritual interest of the self.

When the sensual energies, the intellect, the memory and the kundalini life force gain an urge to acquire anything, these psychic pressures force the sense of identity to endorse the pursuit. Then the self feels compelled to endorse the plan. However if instead the self withholds its approval, the entire psyche freezes with the result that the self gains control over its destiny at least for the time being.

Not being cruel

There are two parts to the quality of cruelty. One is that material nature has that aspect within the archives of its being. The other is that each of the living entities acquire a cruelty streak as a tool in the arsenal needed

for participating in the struggle for existence. A yogi should research into this and distance the self from cruelty.

Weak attempts at removing the cruelty aspect of nature will do nothing substantial for any person because cruelty is permanent in material nature. One has to meditate deeply and remove oneself from the game of evolution if one intends to leave aside the cruelty trait.

The struggle for material existence will continue on and on without end. It will exist for the duration of the creation. Still a yogi should withdraw the self from participation and focus on self-realization.

Ceasing all attempts to take the wealth of others

One should desist when there is opportunity for confiscating the wealth of others. One should know when to restrain the self from easy gains. Material nature gives both socially-uplifting and socially-degrading opportunities. It is up the self to recognize when to use an advantage and when to ignore one.

Not acting deceptively or speaking dishonestly

In the struggle for survival which has to do with having a temporary body and maintaining it, one is induced repeatedly to act deceptively and give dishonest indications to others. These are natural behaviors and learned ones as well. As soon as a living entity begins to understand how material nature operates this creation, the self should make a decision to curtail all misleading acts.

Through the development of agriculture, a human beings gets the idea that for food, it might not be necessary to take advantage of other creatures. However the tendency for exploitation remains in nature. It has other usage like sports and entertainment. Later, the living being may decide that the recreational use of dishonesty should be curtailed.

When one sees that one's profile is distorted by dishonesty, one decides to abandon it. Like every other trait of material nature, deception does not leave a person merely by desire but only by inner change within the psychology. A yogi has the special task of ridding the psyche of trickery.

Not having deceptive thoughts

Thinking and scheming are the foreground of dishonest activity. If a person can control thoughts, if a person can review thoughts before they are played out, there is the likelihood that bad behavior would cease on the level of thinking and not manifest into physical or psychic acts.

As it is, the mind has this persistent tendency for deception. It gets an enjoyment from its ability to outwit others. Can the self forego or squelch this?

A yogi by intense meditations day after day, comes to observe how the mind operates. One finds a method to shift the mind away from its default methods which are supportive of the struggle for existence.

Application:

A student yogi is required to study how the self got into material existence in the first place. How did the self become fused into a psyche which has psychic organs which act in opposition to the welfare of the self? Can a yogi gain an exit from this environment? These questions may be answered by deep insight in meditation.

Verse 16

मातापित्रोश्च शुश्रूषा देवतातिथिपूजनम्

गुरुपूजा घृणा शौचं नित्यमिन्द्रियसंयमः

mātāpitrośca śuśrūṣā devatātithipūjanam
gurupūjā ghṛṇā śaucaṁ nityamindriyasaṁyamaḥ (3.16)

mātā – mother; pitroś = pitroh = father; ca – and; śuśrūṣā - serving respectfully; devatātithi = devatā (deities) + athiti (guests); pūjanam – ceremonially regarding; guru – spiritual master; pūjā – ritual honor;

ghṛṇā – empathy; śaucaṁ -being clean; nityam – always; indriya – senses; saṁyamaḥ - tightly restraining

...serving the mother and father respectfully, ceremonially regarding the deities and guests, ritually honoring the spiritual master, expressing empathy, being clean, always tightly restraining the senses,

Analysis:

Serving the mother and father respectfully

Nobody can grow from infancy to juvenile stage without kindness and selfless action by the parent or guardian. Regardless of liking or not liking that person or persons, one is still obligated for the care received. If possible one should deposit the same due care or more, to progeny. In some species the parent deposits an egg which without any more assistance, develops on its own into a functional body. In the human species, years of parental service are required to bring the infant to maturity. For this one should be grateful.

Ceremonially regarding the deities and guests

Each culture has procedures for ceremonially regarding deities and special guests. These are ancient human traditions. Deities are supernatural persons who affect the human situation without registering a physical presence. Guests require special concern because they need food and shelter.

Ritually honoring the spiritual master

It was the tradition in the time of Krishna and Arjuna, that a spiritual master should be ritually honored. Thereafter the disciple sat before the teacher for information. The teacher was regarded as an agent of the deity who could not be seen physically.

Expressing empathy

For spiritual progress a student should be in isolation. Without that one would remain in social engagement

on a full time basis, which would deprive one of the time to practice spiritual disciplines.

If a yogi meets others he should express appropriate empathy. After all, the experiences endured by others with difficulty were the same type of experiences which the yogi suffered through in the past.

On occasion a yogi should express concern for others and should share spiritual insight with those who are on the verge of understanding the losing battle they are fighting against material nature.

Being clean

A yogi should not neglect the cleaning of the body and surroundings. Being that the human body is valuable, one should not be careless with its hygiene.

Always tightly restraining the senses

Maintaining sense control on a full time basis is a strenuous endeavor. The senses are forever concerned with indulgence and addiction. A simple food like sugar can become a vice. A yogi should regard the self as being fated to always control the senses, restricting them from indulgences which cause ill-health in the body and addiction in the mind.

Application:

Selected traditional values and social procedures should be maintained. If the ascetic is out of the reach of the public, his participation in these honors is greatly reduced. This is why isolation is beneficial for yogis. So long as one is in society, among people, one is duty bound to set an example which reinforces positive traditional norms. If the ascetic feels that this consumes too much time, he or she should relocate to a place which is not frequented by people.

Verse 17

प्रवर्तनं शुभानां च तत्सतां वृत्तमुच्यते

ततो धर्मः प्रभवति यः प्रजाः पाति शाश्वतीः

pravartanaṁ śubhānāṁ ca tatsatāṁ vṛttamucyate
tato dharmaḥ prabhavati yaḥ prajāḥ pāti śāśvatīḥ (3.17)

pravartanaṁ - being a cause, stimulus; śubhānāṁ - regarding auspicious activities; ca – and; tat – that; satāṁ - those who are sincere; vṛttam - fixed; ucyate – defined; tato = tatah = then; dharmaḥ - righteous lifestyle; prabhavati – produces; yaḥ - which; prajāḥ - people; pāti – protect; śāśvatīḥ - always

...being a cause for auspicious activities; that is defined as the conduct of those who are sincere. These produce the righteous lifestyle through which the people are always protected.

Analysis:

Being a cause for auspicious activities

> *If one is in the material world, one will have to function in some role or the other. It is even more important to set an example if one is known as a saintly person, as a yogi, as a devotee, or as a religious figurehead. Those ascetics who take a back seat, who live in isolation, who are not well known, are free to live in a way which is conducive to spiritual advancement. But those who are famous must always temper their performance so as to set an example for human beings by always being engaged in auspicious activities, which benefit the public.*
>
> *Any reckless act by a well-known religious person produces a setback for the public for it brings on confusion and doubts about what is right and what is wrong. If an ascetic realizes that his exposure to society causes his spiritual progress to slow down, the way out is to move to an area where one is not well known or to go into isolation by living in the place which is frequented by wild animals.*

Application:

Common people need protection from socially–destructive activities. For them the high road of religion is to perform socially-beneficial acts. They are not attracted to full

renunciation or to full liberation. Hence if one lives among them, one is duty bound to excel in pious work, even though for liberation that has very little significance.

Verse 18

एवं सत्सु सदा पश्येत्तत्र ह्येषा ध्रुवा स्थितिः

आचारो धर्ममाचष्टे यस्मिन्सन्तो व्यवस्थिताः

evaṁ satsu sadā paśyettatra hyeṣā dhruvā sthitiḥ
ācāro dharmamācaṣṭe yasminsanto vyavasthitāḥ (3.18)

evaṁ - thus, satsu – in saintly persons; sadā – always; paśyet – see; tatra - here; hyeṣā = hi (because) + eṣā (this); dhruvā – definitely; sthitiḥ - situated; ācāro- ideal behavior; dharmam – righteous lifestyle; ācaṣṭe – inspecting; yasmin – in which; santo = santah = saintly person; vyavasthitāḥ - situated, inherent

You can see those qualities always in those who are saintly. In them it is definitely situated. On inspection the ideal behavior produces righteous lifestyle, which is inherent in those who are saintly.

Analysis:

There is an abundance of information about saintly behavior and piety in many religious books all over the world. That alone does not establish saintliness. It comes to life by a living human being who sets the example. In some this behavior is inherent. In others it is learnt. In some others it is practiced and developed over time.

Application:

A yogi should be kind to the self by seeing to it that it does not fall under subjugation of the dictatorial senses. In the world of the psyche, all psychic components like the sense of identity, the intellect, the memory, the kundalini life force and the sensual energies, should be brought to order under the jurisdiction of the core-self. Ruling benevolently, the self should not allow the various components in the psyche to deteriorate

into disorder. Each component should do its duty without infringing on the role of any other.

The sense of identity is basically a traitor but the yogi must realize that he is stuck with it for the duration of the existence of the subtle body, which is for billions of years. If you have to live with someone for many many years, it makes sense only to come to terms with that person.

The core-self should bring the sense of identity to order so that it does not destroy the self interest. Once the sense of identity is controlled, the analytical orb will do nothing which is injurious to the self. That in turn will cause the senses to respect the self. It will cause the kundalini life force to always ask permission from the self.

The memories have direct access to the analytical orb but their power can be curtailed by keeping the orb in a state of neutrality towards the sensual biases and prejudices developed in the past. Control of the personal psyche must be done by the self, not by God, not by the teacher or anyone else. The self itself must exercise this control. If it cannot do so, then it should learn how to do so from advanced teachers, even from God if the Supreme Being is available.

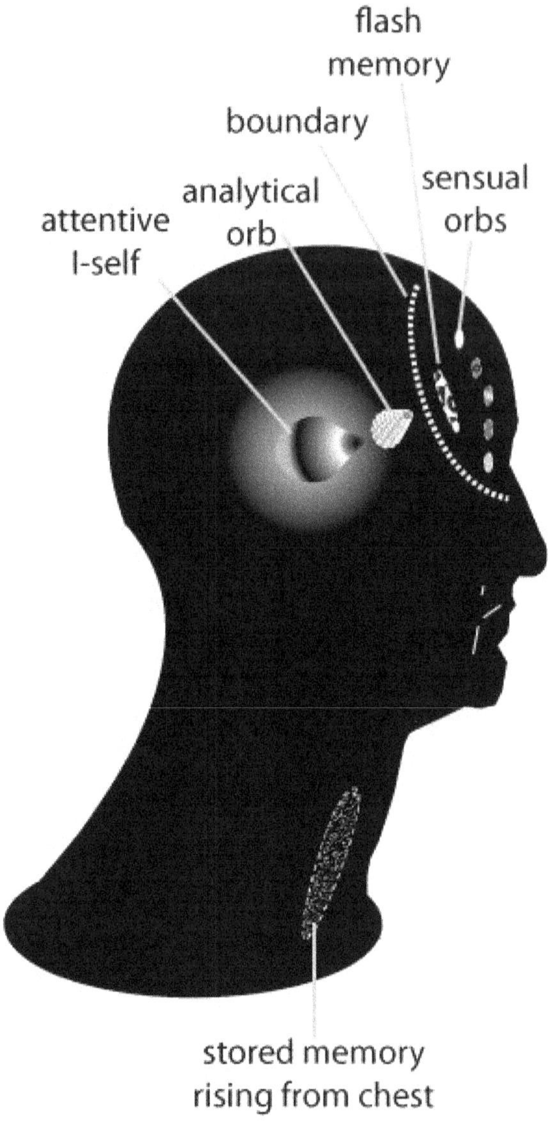
flash
memory
boundary
sensual
orbs
analytical
orb
attentive
I-self
stored memory
rising from chest

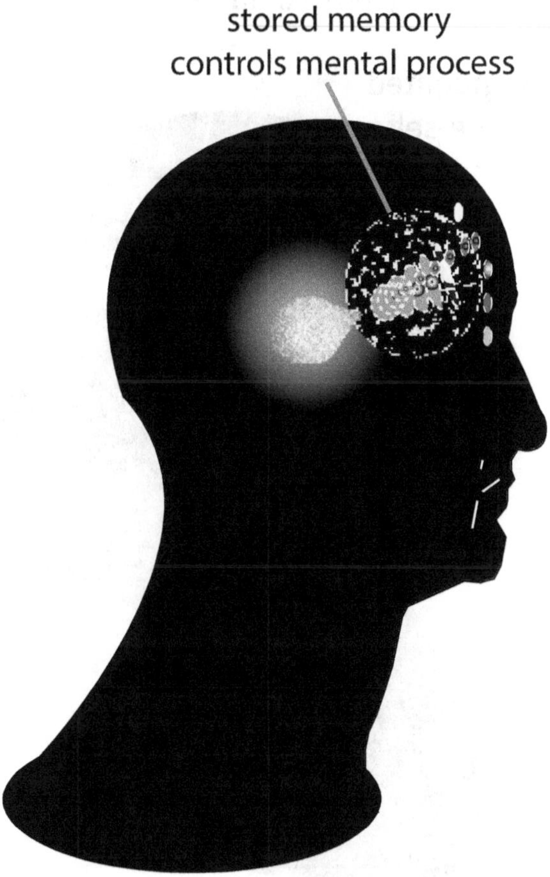
stored memory
controls mental process

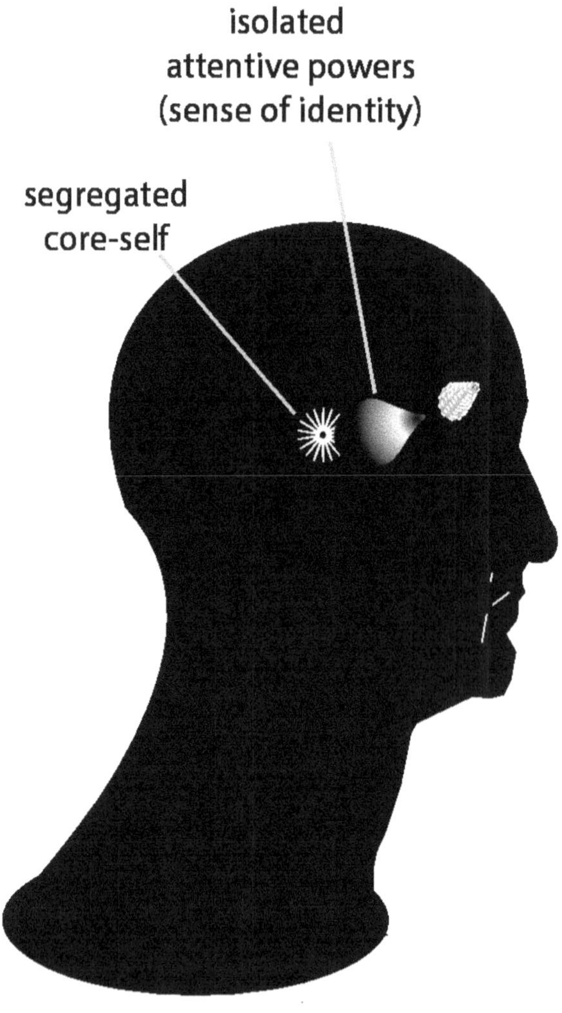

core-self freed
from identity dominance

Verse 19

तेषु तद्धर्मनिक्षिप्तं यः स धर्मः सनातनः
यस्तं समभिपद्येत न स दुर्गतिमाप्नुयात्

teṣu taddharmanikṣiptaṁ yaḥ sa dharmaḥ sanātanaḥ
yastaṁ samabhipadyeta na sa durgatimāpnuyāt (3.19)

teṣu – among them; tad = tat = that; dharman – type of lifestyle; ikṣiptaṁ - is embedded; yaḥ - which; sa – that; dharmaḥ - righteous conduct; sanātanaḥ - eternal; yas = yah = which; taṁ - it; samabhipadyeta – align itself; na – no; sa – it; durgatim – unwanted destiny; āpnuyāt - obtain

Among them is embedded the lifestyle which is the perpetual form of righteous conduct. Whosoever aligns the self to that does not obtain an unwanted destiny.

Analysis:

It is rare to stumble upon a person who exhibits and maintains always the ideal lifestyle which is supportive of keeping the self detached from material existence and also complies with the ideas of the Universal Form of the Supreme Being. Where do we find such a person who is described in this verse?

Such a person does not obtain an unwanted destiny mainly because of compliance with the equations in the mind of the Supreme Being and willingness to be neutral when entities are harshly treated by destiny. Unless one can see the past lives of a particular entity, it would be guess work to think that one knows what is right and what is wrong in regards to the effect-energies which are thrown by providence on the path of that individual.

The key word in this verse is *sanātanaḥ* which means what is perpetual, what does not change from time to time, what is applicable in every situation without exception. That is the supreme will. In the tussle between Krishna and the limited entities, between the supreme will and the limited desires, the supreme conquers all. In the long run, the supreme will proves to be the most beneficial desire there ever was.

What is that rule which applies in all times and all places, which is appropriate to every situation? It is the supreme will which comes from the mind of the Universal Form of Krishna. Arjuna requested the vision of Its apparition as revealed in the *Bhagavad Gītā* but Krishna declined to show It once again.

Application:

For a yogi, it is a calculative task to figure the ideal lifestyle which would save one from having to be reactive to the moves of material nature. The way out is to link with a super-being who transcends this nature and who can provide an escape route from this situation.

With limited insight even in the advanced stages, a yogi has no recourse but to subsidize his intelligence with assistance from the Supreme Being. One can do the very best and still one might miscalculate in some instance. The way out is to link with the Supreme Being and side with the divine views.

That will not happen if one does not purify the psyche and put it in order. Becoming a perfect being, a siddha, does not make one into the Supreme Being. Achieving the siddha stage makes an entity perceptive of the divine will, which for that person is total advantage.

Verse 20

अतो नियम्यते लोकः प्रमुह्य धर्मवर्त्मसु

यस्तु योगी च मुक्तश्च स एतेभ्यो विशिष्यते

ato niyamyate lokaḥ pramuhya dharmavartmasu
yastu yogī ca muktaśca sa etebhyo viśiṣyate (3.20)

ato = atah = thus; niyamyate – recommended behaviors; lokaḥ - world, society; pramuhya – deteriorating; dharma – righteous lifestyle; vartmasu – course; yas = yah = who; tu – but; yogī – yogi; ca – and; muktaś = muktah = one who is liberated; ca – and; sa – he; etebhyo = etebhyah = above these; viśiṣyate – defined, rated

Thus when society is deteriorating, it is the recommended behaviors which keep the situation on the course of righteous lifestyle. But the yogi, the liberated person, is rated above this.

Analysis:

Human society has a sophisticated culture which is a mystery to any other animal which observes it. The other mammals have peculiar social orders, some of which are very rigid but none except the human beings is loaded with so many complexities.

When human society deteriorates through natural disaster or man-made events, it is refashioned successfully only when certain social rules are established. The recommended behaviors which were listed in verses 14-17 of this chapter, cannot be put into practice with mere deliberation. The yogi has to change his nature so that he does these functions automatically due to his connection to a plane of existence which inspires such acts inherently. This is why the perfected yogi is rated above everyone else.

Application:

The trick of the trade of how to survive here with the least liabilities, is to line up with the divine energy from the divine world and perform with proficiency as inspired by it.

Obviously that is tricky for how can one be sure that one is in alignment with the supreme? Thus it is no joking matter. Whosoever accomplishes the connection is a blessed person indeed! During the battle of Kurukshetra, Arjuna got the fortune but later that he lost contact with the divine plane and was afraid of the consequences.

Verse 21

वर्तमानस्य धर्मेण पुरुषस्य यथा तथा

संसारतारणं ह्यस्य कालेन महता भवेत्

vartamānasya dharmeṇa puruṣasya yathā tathā
saṁsāratāraṇaṁ hyasya kālena mahatā bhavet (3.21)

vartamānasya – of the present; dharmeṇa - by righteous lifestyle; puruṣasya – of the person; yathā tathā = as so, with regularity; saṁsāratāraṇaṁ - regarding haphazard transmigrations; hy = hi = just so, because; asya – of this; kālena – by time; mahatā – great span; bhavet - occur

Regarding the person who with regularity has the righteous lifestyle, deliverance from haphazard transmigrations occurs after a great span of time.

Analysis:

This is interesting because when Krishna explained the discipline of this righteous lifestyle in the *Bhagavad Gītā,* he acclaimed the procedure as his yoga, his way of doing things. He claimed to have taught it to yogi-kings of posterity. Now he quotes an ascetic who stated that this system of righteous lifestyle (dharmena) would somehow cause the liberation of a living being but only after a great span of time.

This means that if one follows the way of karma yoga, one will become free from haphazard transmigrations after many many lives of adapting to that lifestyle.

Application:

Karma yoga is yoga expertise used to regulate one's social activities. A yogi has to understand that any course of social activities will never be a direct method for liberation from the material world. For a good situation in the future one has to perform socially-accredited acts which yield benefits for human society. But that has nothing to do with a thorough escape from the material world. If a being performs criminal acts, it is creating for itself a hellish future, either on an earthly planet or in an astral hell. Or he may become aware of the self as an animal body in a future birth.

Actions for purification of the psyche have little to do with social involvement with others. This type of action is psychological or it is physical with psychological impact. It is not an action to adjust the performance of others externally.

Verse 22

एवं पूर्वकृतं कर्म सर्वो जन्तुर्निषेवते

सर्वं तत्कारणं येन निकृतोऽयमिहागतः

evaṁ pūrvakṛtaṁ karma sarvo janturniṣevate
sarvaṁ tatkāraṇaṁ yena nikṛto'yamihāgataḥ (3.22)

evaṁ - thus; pūrva – previously; kṛtaṁ - were performed; karma – effects of action; sarvo = sarvah = all; jantur = jantuh = living being; niṣevate – endures, is destined to be; sarvaṁ - all; tat – that; kāraṇaṁ - causal basis; yena – by which; nikṛto = nikṛtah = altered; 'yamihāgataḥ = ayamihāgataḥ = ayam (this) + iha (here) + āgataḥ - arrive

Thus the living being is destined with the effects of actions which were performed previously. All such effects are the causal basis for his arrival here in an altered state.

Analysis:

The tie-down in material nature is dictated by the effect-energies of previous births. This is a handicap because the entity is prone to a lack of recall of its previous activities. Destiny, fate or providence, call it what one prefers, has the upper hand in all situations because it uses the resultant effects of past acts. It does not give the entity a winning card.

Even though in anticipation for a future life, an entity can plan and set up certain predispositions to be used in the future, nature may adjust its situation when it is unconscious in the afterlife and in the womb of the mother and so that self will become aware of itself with those alterations, temperaments which it does not have the power to abolish.

Application:

A yogi should carefully observe the operations of material nature and not be in any fantasies about what can be done to offset nature's grip over the destiny of the psyche. It is not a matter of outsmarting nature, nor of working in a way whereby one can nullify nature's control. It is rather a matter of understanding how nature operates and how its activities are either reinforced by the Supreme Being or left to nature's devices.

A puny limited self, even if it is perfected, will affect neither God nor nature. It can, however, do something about its own condition by transiting to a level of existence which is not harrying. Thus its main concern is to find a place which already exists and which is what it is desiring.

Verse 23

शरीरग्रहणं चास्य केन पूर्वं प्रकल्पितम्

इत्येवं संशयो लोके तच्च वक्ष्याम्यतः परम्

śarīra grahaṇaṁ cāsya kena pūrvaṁ prakalpitam
ityevaṁ saṁśayo loke tacca vakṣyāmyataḥ param (3.23)

śarīra – material body; grahaṇaṁ - acquiring; cāsya = ca (and) + asya (of this); kena – by which; pūrvaṁ - before; prakalpitam – transformed; ity = iti = thus; evaṁ - thus; saṁśayo = saṁśayah = doubt; loke – in human society; tac = tat = that; ca – and; vakṣyāmy = vakṣyāmi = I will mention; ataḥ - thus; param – subtle cause

By what force was it transformed to be a material body? There is doubt in human society about this. I will now mention the subtle cause.

Analysis:

When it comes to discussions about life and death, there is doubt about reincarnation, mainly because the entity does not remember its past existence. This means that if reincarnation is a fact and cannot be proven by obvious means, it has to be accepted as a belief on the basis of reliable sources like Krishna. But in any case, how should one consider that something which is not material can become a material body. The claim is that the self is not matter. Thus how can that transcendental element be transformed to the extent of identifying itself as a material body?

Application:

A yogi gets direct evidence of the spiritual identity of the core-self but that does not mean that this evidence can be shown materially to anyone else. The most basic realization about the transcendence of the spiritual self, is its discovery of itself in a subtle body in astral projections. The subtle body is not the self but it is not the physical body either. That subtle form has psychic powers which the physical body is incapable of. Experiences in it when it is displaced out of the physical form, provide the first direct evidence that the self is not the physical body and is not limited by the life duration of that form.

Verse 24

शरीरमात्मनः कृत्वा सर्वभूतपितामहः

त्रैलोक्यमसृजद्ब्रह्मा कृत्स्नं स्थावरजङ्गमम्

śarīramātmanaḥ kṛtvā sarvabhūtapitāmahaḥ
trailokyamasṛjadbrahmā kṛtsnaṁ sthāvarajaṅgamam (3.24)

śarīram – body; ātmanaḥ - himself; kṛtvā – producing; sarva – all; bhūta – creatures; pitāmahaḥ - father of fathers; trailokyam – three regions; asṛjad = asṛjat = from what is created; brahmā – Brahmā; kṛtsnaṁ - whole world, cosmos; sthāva – mobile; rajaṅgamam – of what is immobile

After producing a body for himself, Brahmā, the father of fathers of all creatures, created the cosmos, the three-partitioned world, with animate and inanimate beings.

Analysis:

Brahmā is from the Vedic pantheon of deities. He is supposed to be a supernatural being of cosmic proportions who masterminds the creation of the universe we reside in. His creative act is mental. It is not physical. From his visualizations this universe began and then evolved into its present form.

Application:

In meditation practice one encounters many beings who are worthy of honor and worship, great beings whose scope is cosmic or who are dimensional lords. Even Buddha, who was disinclined to religious practice, met deities during meditation. After enlightenment, he said that he had a discussion with this Brahmā deity.

Verse 25

ततः प्रधानमसृजच्चेतना सा शरीरिणाम्

यया सर्वमिदं व्याप्तं यां लोके परमां विदुः

tataḥ pradhānamasṛjaccetanā sā śarīriṇām
yayā sarvamidaṁ vyāptaṁ yāṁ loke paramāṁ viduḥ (3.25)

tataḥ - then; pradhānam – life force energy potential; asṛjac = asṛjat = from what was created; cetanā – consciousness; sā – that; śarīriṇām – of the embodied beings; yayā – by which; sarvam – all; idaṁ - this; vyāptaṁ - pervaded; yāṁ - this; loke – this world; paramāṁ - supreme potency; viduḥ - it is known

Then from that creation, he produced the life force energy potential of all embodied selves. By that all this is pervaded. It is known in this world as the supreme potency.

Analysis:

The life energy potential is shared by all living beings everywhere but in varying ways depending on the complexity or simplicity of the psychic and/or physical mechanisms. Some living beings only have psychic register. Those with physical register carry two charges which are physio-electric and psychic. There can be no physical reality which does not have a psychic register because the physical evolved from the psychic, just as all solid matter evolved from gaseous matter in the past.

Application:

The life force energy is for the most part randomly distributed. It can be called a chaos. However in the individual

life forms it assumes an organization and is termed as the kundalini life force in yogic conversations.

Part of the course of yoga, is the recognition and then manipulation of this life force in the interest of freeing the spirit from these life configurations which are drummed up by material nature.

Verse 26

इह तत्क्षरमित्युक्तं परं त्वमृतमक्षरम्

त्रयाणां मिथुनं सर्वमेकैकस्य पृथक्पृथक्

iha tatkṣaramityuktaṁ paraṁ tvamṛtamakṣaram
trayāṇāṁ mithunaṁ sarvamekaikasya pṛthakpṛthak (3.26)

iha – here; tat – that; kṣaram – that which is alterable; ityuktaṁ = iti (thus) + yuktaṁ - equipped; paraṁ - other; tv = tu = but; amṛtam – immortal; akṣaram – unalterable; trayāṇāṁ - of the three worlds; mithunaṁ - paired; sarvam – all; ekaikasya = eka (one) + ekasya (of one); pṛthakpṛthak – separatedly, singled out

That which is here is alterable; the other is immortal and unalterable. All species of the three worlds are paired one by one, singled, separately.

Analysis:

This means that the world we live in evolved from an immortal unalterable existence. The possibility of this however is very difficult to explain. It is a paradox since it violates logic which is that something which is immortal and unalterable should not produce something which is ever-changing and which denies immortality.

Application:

The living entity must solve the paradox of the coexistence of the spiritual and the material, of the eternal and the corruptible, for itself by referring to its core-self and the adjuncts like the material body.

Each yogi has to engage in psyche investigation on a personal level to sort the components of consciousness, to determine the feedback between the core-self and everything else. If illusion became a reality and if what is temporary has attracted what is permanent, the yogi should not rest until the self understands the dynamics of this.

Verse 27

असृजत्सर्वभूतानि पूर्वसृष्टः प्रजापतिः

स्थावराणि च भूतानि इत्येषा पौर्विकी श्रुतिः

asṛjatsarvabhūtāni pūrvasṛṣṭaḥ prajāpatiḥ
sthāvarāṇi ca bhūtāni ityeṣā paurvikī śrutiḥ (3.27)

asṛjat – he created; sarva – all; bhūtāni – living beings; pūrva – before, first; sṛṣṭaḥ - created; prajāpatiḥ - father of fathers, Brahmā; sthāvarāṇi – stationary; ca – and; bhūtāni – living beings; ityeṣā = iti (thus) + eṣā (this); paurvikī – ancient authorities; śrutiḥ - what was heard

The father of fathers, Brahmā, having first created his own body, produced all other living beings; the stationary and the mobile ones. Such is the information, which was heard from the ancient authorities.

Analysis:

If this deity created his own body, then what sort of body was that and from what form did he create the secondary body? Where did he come from? How did he get into this cosmos?

These questions would seem surprising but the same inquiry applies to humanity. Science has yet to explain where the life forms on this planet emerged from.

Application:

The yogi's task regarding the self, is to determine its origin. Is that a lost quest? Can an effect transcend its cause? Can a yogi retrogress through time and perceive how the self came to be?

Verse 28

तस्य कालपरीमाणमकरोत्स पितामहः

भूतेषु परिवृत्तिं च पुनरावृत्तिमेव च

यथात्र कश्चिन्मेधावी दृष्टात्मा पूर्वजन्मनि

tasya kālaparīmāṇamakarotsa pitāmahaḥ
bhūteṣu parivṛttiṁ ca punarāvṛttimeva ca
yathātra kaścinmedhāvī dṛṣṭātmā pūrvajanmani (3.28)

tasya – of this; kāla – time; parīmāṇam – limit, spread; akarot – designed; sa – he; pitā – father; mahaḥ - great, cosmic; bhūteṣu – of creatures; parivṛttiṁ - social activities; ca – and; punar – return; āvṛttim – return action; eva – also; ca – and; yathā – as; atra – in the physical world; kaścin = kaścit = anyone; medhāvī – wiseman; dṛṣṭa – perceived; ātmā – spiritual self; pūrva – previous; janmani - births

Regarding this, the cosmic father Brahmā designed the spread of time, the social activities of all creatures and also their return to act in the physical world after death. This information about previous births, is consistent with the experience of one who is wise and who perceives the spiritual self.

Analysis:

This means that these living beings came about from the mental action of a deity. This can neither be proven or disproven by anyone since we are not in a position to transit backwards through time and find the deity.

Let us be reasonable with ourselves and know that if anyone was to transit back in time, that person could only go back as far as the time when the self consciousness became objective to the existence around it. To pry into time before that would be impossible for the very fact, that the entity would lose objectivity at the point of origin of an observable awareness.

However a person can surmise the existence of the deity and intuit the origins by careful observation of how transcendence remains as the underlying substrata of what is manifested grossly.

Deep meditation permits an entity to transit backwards and get evidence, even though the yogi cannot bring that evidence into this time medium to share it with others.

Application:

A yogi should research both the personal and non-personal aspects of this creation. Deities should be discovered and their roles understood. The self's being should be dissected to determine the components of the psyche. Dream states should be objectified to sort imagination from subtle reality. In time a yogi might have a revelation through which the self would experience the transcendental reality. And finally, if there is a supreme deity, that person might be revealed to the yogi. If we are existing in the mind of someone, then definitely for us, that person is the Supreme Personality. The challenge is before us to locate the ultimate reality.

Verse 29

यत्प्रवक्ष्यामि तत्सर्वं यथावदुपपद्यते

सुखदुःखे सदा सम्यगनित्ये यः प्रपश्यति

कायं चामेध्यसंघातं विनाशं कर्मसंहितम्

yatpravakṣyāmi tatsarvaṁ yathāvadupapadyate
sukhaduḥkhe sadā samyaganitye yaḥ prapaśyati
kāyaṁ cāmedhyasaṁghātaṁ vināśaṁ karmasaṁhitam (3.29)

yat – what; pravakṣyāmi – I said; tat – that; sarvaṁ - all, everything; yathāvad = yathāvat = proper; upapadyate – it is fit for; sukhaduḥkhe – in pleasure and pain; sadā – always; samyaganitye – inconstancy; yaḥ - which; prapaśyati – he sees with deep insight; kāyaṁ - body; cāmedhya = ca (and, as well as) + amedhya (foul, perverse); saṁghātaṁ - aggregation; vināśaṁ - degradation; karma – social actions; saṁhitam - related

Everything I explained was proper and fit for expression. The wise one always sees with deep insight the inconstancy of pleasure and pain. That one perceives how social actions are

related to species degradation as well as to the body which is a perverse aggregation.

Analysis:

The least accomplishment of a human being, should be to research into the afterlife, to realize the segregation of a psyche which survives beyond the life of the material body.

Application:

Once a yogi experiences astral projection, and has evidence that the self will survive the death of the material body, it should consider the conditions under which it will have to take the next material form. A study of the laws of nature which relates to cause and effect is required. The entity should know what sort of action in one birth produces what sort of condition in a future appearance. Then it can adjust its activities and postures and make some input into the sculpture of fate.

Verse 30

यच्च किंचित्सुखं तच्च सर्वं दुःखमिति स्मरन्

संसारसागरं घोरं तरिष्यति सुदुस्तरम्

yacca kiṁcitsukhaṁ tacca sarvaṁ duḥkhamiti smaran
saṁsārasāgaraṁ ghoraṁ tariṣyati sudustaram (3.30)

yac = yat = which; ca – and; kiṁcit – any, every bit; sukhaṁ - happiness; tac = tat = that; ca – and; sarvaṁ - all; duḥkham – distress; iti – thus; smaran – remembers; saṁsāra – haphazard transmigration; sāgaraṁ - ocean, vast expanse; ghoraṁ - frightening; tariṣyati - he will transit beyond; sudustaram – difficult to undermine

He remembers that every bit of happiness is really a distress. He will transit beyond this frightening vast span of haphazard transmigrations which are difficult to undermine.

Analysis:

If one is certain that every bit of happiness is really a distress, one will not be able to continue in ignorance of what nature does in its alterations of bodies and forms. So long as a living entity sees a promise of happiness in these material creations, it cannot become liberated because the happiness it imagines safely offsets its insecurities and stifles interest in its origins.

Those who can perceive the vast span of haphazard transmigrations cannot continue comfortably in the transportation system of nature from life to afterlife, to life to afterlife, endlessly.

Application:

A yogi is a person who sobered-up and then saw the ghastly operations of material nature, in which the selves serve as batteries for supplying power for nature's operations. No longer wanting to be in that servile position, the yogi becomes motivated to strive for liberation.

Verse 31

जातीमरणरोगैश्च समाविष्टः प्रधानवित्

चेतनावत्सु चैतन्यं समं भूतेषु पश्यति

jātīmaraṇarogaiśca samāviṣṭaḥ pradhānavit
cetanāvatsu caitanyaṁ samaṁ bhūteṣu paśyati (3.31)

jātī – birth; maraṇa – death; rogaiś = rogaih = with disease; ca – and; samāviṣṭaḥ - harassed by; pradhānavit – he knows the life-force energy potential; cetanā – awareness; vatsu – reinforced with; caitanyaṁ - consciousness energy; samaṁ - similar; bhūteṣu - in psyches; paśyati – he perceives

Though harassed by birth, death and disease, he knows the life-force energy potential. He perceives a similar consciousness-energy in all psyches which are reinforced with awareness.

Analysis:

The life force which is the anchoring agency in material nature for the spiritual self, is the very same energy which can be used to free the self. This is because the individual life force is the counter-balance of the spiritual energy of the self.

Material nature produced the individual life force as a matching potency to a specific self. Just as by studying an image in a mirror, someone can get some objective information about the body, so by studying the features of the life force, the self can get a reflective idea of itself. That would be the beginning of the quest for liberation.

Application:

When consciousness is utilized by an individual it is termed as awareness or self-awareness. The assumption is that consciousness is everywhere and that self awareness is indicative of personality. Some say that personality is itself awareness and nothing else. The opinions vary.

The common denominator in all living bodies is self-awareness. Even if there is consciousness, if there is no self awareness in a body, people question as to whether the body is dead or alive. When the body is pronounced dead, when its life symptoms cease, people admit the absence of self awareness but no one can say that there is no consciousness, even though it might be said that there is no consciousness with self awareness. Who can prove that there is no consciousness merely because of the absence of self-awareness?

Verse 32

निर्विद्यते ततः कृत्स्नं मार्गमाणः परं पदम्

तस्योपदेशं वक्ष्यामि याथातथ्येन सत्तम

nirvidyate tataḥ kṛtsnaṁ mārgamāṇaḥ paraṁ padam
tasyopadeśaṁ vakṣyāmi yāthātathyena sattama (3.32)

nirvidyate – becoming disgusted; tataḥ - then; kṛtsnaṁ - all of this; mārgamāṇaḥ - searches for the passage; paraṁ - supreme; padam – location; tasyopadeśaṁ = tasya (of this) + upadeśaṁ (information); vakṣyāmi – I will speak; yāthātathyena – with what is factual; sattama – o best of human beings

Then, becoming disgusted with all of this, he searches for the passage to the supreme location. I will speak to you factually of this information, O best of the human beings.

Analysis:

Eventually a living entity thinks of abandoning material nature but unfortunately a decision to do this in no way causes this to cease. However persons who desire to be out of material nature, expound various philosophies.

Application:

Based on reliable information from persons like Krishna, we can assume that there is a place which is the supreme location (param padam), a place where the spiritual self will be in a compatible environment. But this information does not accomplish transit to that place for anyone. Thus what is the process for transiting? How is it done?

Verse 33

शाश्वतस्याव्ययस्याथ पदस्य ज्ञानमुत्तमम्

प्रोच्यमानं मया विप्र निबोधेदमशेषतः

śāśvatasyāvyayasyātha padasya jñānamuttamam
procyamānaṁ mayā vipra nibodhedamaśeṣataḥ (3.33)

śāśvatasyāvyayasyātha = śāśvatasya (of the eternal) + āvyayasya (of the imperishable) + atha (then); padasya – of the location; jñānam – educated person; uttamam – best; procyamānaṁ - describing; mayā – by me; vipra – educated ritualist; nibodhedam = nibodha (learn) + idam (this); aśeṣataḥ - everything

O best of the educated persons, concerning the eternal imperishable location, learn from me, O educated ritualist, as I describe everything about it.

Analysis:

At first one must hear of this from an accomplished mystic. Then one must find the ways and means of changing one's status so as to qualify for the passage.

Application:

A student yogi should acquire help from an advanced soul. Using that assistance the novice should put the advice into practice. Periodically a yoga teacher will check on the student to give more assistance and to verify the progress made.

Chapter 4

Divine Psychology*

devānāmapi devatvaṁ yuktaḥ kārayate vaśī
brahma cāvyayamāpnoti hitvā dehamaśāśvatam (4.25)

Being proficient in yoga, the person who is a master of his nature, creates for the self a divine psychology which is like that of the supernatural controllers. Having abandoned the perishable body, that person attains the imperishable spiritual world.

**This chapter heading was introduced by the translator on the basis of the verse above. The Mahābhārata does not have a chapter heading.*

Verse 1

ब्राह्मण उवाच

यः स्यादेकायने लीनस्तूष्णीं किंचिदचिन्तयन्

पूर्वं पूर्वं परित्यज्य स निरारम्भको भवेत्

brāhmaṇa uvāca
yaḥ syādekāyane līnastūṣṇīṁ kiṁcidacintayan
pūrvaṁ pūrvaṁ parityajya sa nirārambhako bhavet (4.1)

brāhmaṇa – brahmin, highly qualified ascetic; uvāca – said; yaḥ - who; syād = syāt = it may be; ekāyane - in a singular cause; līnas = līnah = absorbed in; tūṣṇīṁ = one who is calm; kiṁcid = kiṁcit = anyone; acintayan – mind without thoughts; pūrvaṁ pūrvaṁ = what came before what came before; parityajya - detaching; sa – he; nirārambhako = nirārambhakah = without endeavor, without agitation; bhavet – is, become

The highly qualified ascetic said: A person whose mind is without thoughts, who is calm, who is absorbed in one cause of an effect, which is the cause of a previous effect, he being detached, is without psychic agitation.

Analysis:

A mind without thoughts is not a common mind. To consistently achieve a mind without thoughts, yogis are advised to use the 4th stage of yoga which is pranaiama or breath infusion. This method causes the mental energy to be infused with fresh subtle air, which in turn causes the intellect to cease its thought-producing process. The conveyor belt of thought production ceases if the mind is infused with fresh energy. That is the single most important use of pranaiama breath infusion.

A thoughtless state can be attained without the use of pranaiama but again in that case, it happens because of some other method of infusion of fresh energy into the mind. This might happen accidentally or deliberately but in any case, when there are no thoughts in the mind for an extended period of time, say for instance for even five minutes, this is because there was some change in the energy content of the mind.

It is misleading to think that thought cessation is caused by a command of the will power or by a desire energy. The real cause of thought disappearance is a change of the energy in the mind.

To be absorbed in one cause of an effect, which is itself a cause of an effect, is achieved by concentration practice and also by taking help from breath infusion. There are many objectives given by various teachers. Some give a sound. Some give a location. Some give visualization. In these practices, the intent is to cause the mind to renounce everything except the desired focus.

These practices give the yogi the opportunity to develop psychic sensitivity and accurate psychic perception, something which is necessary if one is to become freed from material existence and resistant to the subtle vices which ruin self-realization.

Application:

In the yoga process, one becomes detached from the use of will power or desire force in the attainment of objectives. Will power is a major tool in the material world. Desire energy is a lubricant used by the kundalini life force to get the intellect to be fanatical about directing the body to achieve fulfillments.

A student yogi is trained to give up, to put aside, the will power and the desire force, and to focus on infusing the psyche with fresh energy. When this is done, the student notes the changes in the operation of the components of consciousness which are under the influence of the infused force.

Psychic agitation comes in many forms and shapes but all of it is based on the energy content of the mind. Hence if that energy is replaced by a higher grade of subtle force, there will be changes in the behavior of the components of the mind. The core-self in the psyche gains more control over the other components when the psyche shifts to a higher plane by breath infusion.

A student yogi observes this and then forms the conclusion that instead of struggling to control the mind when it has a low energy-content, it is easier and more effective to infuse the mind with higher energy which gives the added benefit of effortless mind control.

Verse 2

सर्वमित्रः सर्वसहः समरक्तो जितेन्द्रियः

व्यपेतभयमन्युश्च कामहा मुच्यते नरः

sarvamitraḥ sarvasahaḥ samarakto jitendriyaḥ
vyapetabhayamanyuśca kāmahā mucyate naraḥ (4.2)

sarvamitraḥ - friend of everyone; sarvasahaḥ - one who is with all; samarakto = samaraktah = one who is level-headed; jitendriyaḥ - controller of the senses; vyapeta – being devoid of; bhaya – fear; manyuś = manyuh = anger; ca – and; kāmahā – subduer of desire; mucyate – liberated; naraḥ - person

One who is the friend of everyone, who is with everyone, who is level-headed, a controller of the senses, whose nature is devoid of anger and fear, who subdues desire; that person is liberated.

Analysis:

There are many aspects to liberation. This makes it difficult to discern who is a siddha and who is not. To simplify the matter some spiritual sects issue statements which define liberation as the qualities which are demonstrated by the leaders of their particular groups. That however is not suitable for an unbiased rating.

The definition of liberation given above is not a denominational property. It is to be used individually by all student yogis, as a standard with which to gage their progress.

Becoming a friend of everyone does not mean that the student yogi runs here and there to satisfy the friendship requirements of various persons. It is an attitude of kinship and friendliness to all persons regardless of their relationship to the yogi.

A yogi is not a philanthropist nor is he or she in need of friends. The yogi realizes that everyone is a potential friend or enemy but everyone is better off in kinship rather than in animosity. The yogi is prepared to establish kinship and to decline from hostility.

Application:

At first people who try yoga practice, feel that they must apply an austerity which yields a certain quality which they desire to express. This concerns recognition by others, particularly by persons who live in the spiritual community. When one joins a spiritual group, one may be eager to get a rating as an advanced soul. This is a negative process but under pressure one may fall into the trap of wanting to express the qualities which are accredited to a liberated person.

In the advanced stage, one realizes that becoming a siddha means reaching a certain level of existence and functioning normally on that plane. It is not an effort to force saintliness into the human world. Instead of remaining on the human plane and forcing exceptional behavior, a masterful yogi shifts to a higher plane where the ideal behavior is the norm. That perfected soul is not interested to exploit devotees or student yogis. His or her interest is to associate with siddhas who live in and are focused on a higher plane. Exhibiting saintly nature and realized knowledge is not his or her intent.

Verse 3

आत्मवत्सर्वभूतेषु यश्चरेन्नियतः शुचिः

अमानी निरभीमानः सर्वतो मुक्त एव सः

ātmavatsarvabhūteṣu yaścarenniyataḥ śuciḥ
amānī nirabhīmānaḥ sarvato mukta eva saḥ (4.3)

ātmavat – like the self; sarva – all; bhūteṣu – in relation to all beings; yaś = yah = who; caren = caren = wanders, relates; niyataḥ - self-controlled; śuciḥ - pure; amānī – modest; nirabhīmānaḥ - without pride; sarvato = sarvatah = all; mukta – freed; eva – so; saḥ - he, the person

One who relates to all beings the way he regards the self, who is self-controlled, pure, who is modest, without pride, that person is free from every faults.

Analysis:

Self realization is not a business. It is not a religious foundation. It is not an exhibition. It is not a means for acquiring followers or converts. Self realization is very personal from the self to itself. It is a gift crafted and earned by the self for the self as recommended by advanced beings and by the Supreme Person.

Application:

There is a method of developing saintly qualities where a person works aggressively to restrict certain undesirable qualities and to institute the converse into one's behavior. This is the inferior method used by student yogis who just do not know any better. Their efforts are worthy of recognition but that procedure does not get the person to the higher plane in which those qualities are the normal behavior.

At some stage either by discovery or by insight given by an advanced personality, a yogi realizes that the problem is not the lower qualities but the level of existence to which the psyche is anchored. If the psyche gains access to a higher level of energy, its behavior would automatically change. This is the insight we gain when doing kriya yoga practice.

Verse 4

जीवितं मरणं चोभे सुखदुःखे तथैव च

लाभालाभे प्रियद्वेष्ये यः समः स च मुच्यते

jīvitaṁ maraṇaṁ cobhe sukhaduḥkhe tathaiva ca
lābhālābhe priyadveṣye yaḥ samaḥ sa ca mucyate (4.4)

jīvitaṁ - relating to life; maraṇaṁ - regarding what is dead; cobhe= ca (and) + ubhe (in both); sukha – enjoyment; duḥkhe – in pain; tathaiva = tathā (as) + eva (so); ca – and; lābhālābhe = lābha (acquisition) + alābhe (deprivation); priya – what is liked; dveṣye – what is disliked; yaḥ - who; samaḥ - responds the same; sa – he; ca – and; mucyate – liberated

Concerning both life and death, enjoyment and pain, acquisitions and deprivations, likes and dislikes, that person is liberated, who responds to these dualities all the same.

Analysis:

To respond to dual conditions like heat and cold, enjoyment and pain, a living body and a dead one, acquiring what is desirable and being deprived of the same, one has to be in a psychological location from which one can perceive and react to the conditions. It is not the conditions which are the problem. It is the response mechanism in the personal psyche. Thus if the response mechanism is disabled, those dual factors will no longer be an issue.

The two big problems which supersede all others in the material world are life and death. The preference is to be a healthy living body. People abhor death but if the self is securely situated in another type of life then the life of the body will not be an issue and being deprived of it would not cause distress.

Application:

The self has to get into an existential niche in which this type of behavior is the expression. The question is how to get to that psychic location. If the self could relocate there, then this behavior will be the instinct and restraint or censorship would not be required. Initially one must make attempts to adopt these behaviors by forcing the psyche to perform in a certain way and by suppressing the normal reactive attitude. However for permanent change one has to relocate the self to a place where it can absorb higher energies which make the liberated behavior the default tendency.

Verse 5

न कस्यचित्स्पृहयते नावजानाति किंचन

निर्द्वंद्वो वीतरागात्मा सर्वतो मुक्त एव सः

na kasyacitspṛhayate nāvajānāti kiṁcana
nirdvaṁdvo vītarāgātmā sarvato mukta eva saḥ (4.5)

na – no; kasyacit – anyone; spṛhayate – he neglects; nāvajānāti = na (not) + avajānāti (neglects); kiṁcana – anyone; nirdvaṁdvo = nirdvaṁdvah = neutral response to dual conditions; vīta – without; rāga – passionate emotions; ātmā – self; sarvato = sarvatah =in all respects; mukta – liberated; eva – so; saḥ - he, it

He favors no one. He neglects no one. He responds neutrally to dual conditions. His self is free of passionate emotions. He is liberated in all respects.

Analysis:

It is important to understand that regardless of what a person must do to develop these qualities and their appropriate behaviors, still the basic psychology will remain unchanged unless the psyche is relocated to a higher plane of existence. Can anyone relocate to a higher plane and still maintain a human body? That question is worthy of consideration.

Student yogis must begin on the level of the human being, with the faulty mind and mischievous life force. The student should endeavor to forcibly compel the psyche to exhibit saintly and liberated behavior. However eventually a yogi understands that this is not the permanent way to have these qualities. No matter how much one institutes these qualities, the psyche will always revert to its normal behavior which is based on the kind of energy it ingests from the environment.

The alternative is to relocate the psyche and the life force to a higher plane where the liberated behavior is the normal routine.

Application:

Each level of existence has its expressive methods of operation. If for instance one is in a tiger body, one will have the sense to kill other animals. If one uses a cow's body one will have the sense to snip grass. There are variants from psyche to psyche in each species but overall they collectively exhibit certain behaviors as a routine.

A yogi by higher meditation gets to psych out how material nature enforces certain vicious behaviors. Nature also constructs and supports certain pious acts. In all cases however good behaviors result in depriving others of their desires. If the world were ruled by a force which only permitted good acts, many beings would instantly perish.

When a yogi comes to understand that no one can adjust the overall scheme of actions on a particular plane, he or she decides to abandon this level and gain residence on a higher plane. This is of course easy to think of and difficult to achieve.

Verse 6

अनमित्रोऽथ निर्बन्धुरनपत्यश्च यः क्वचित्

त्यक्तधर्मार्थकामश्च स मुच्यते

anamitro'tha nirbandhuranapatyaśca yaḥ kvacit
tyaktadharmārthakāmaśca nirākāṅkṣī sa mucyate (4.6)

anamitro = 'anamitrah = person without enemy; 'tha = atha = then; nirbandhur = nirbandhuh = without favoring relatives; anapatyaś – anapatnah = without child; ca – and; yaḥ - who; kvacit – any time; tyakta – detached; dharmārtha = dharma (righteous lifestyle) + artha (income); kāmaś = kāmah = lusty emotion; ca – and; nirākāṅkṣī – one not stimulated by desire; sa – that person; mucyate - liberated

The person who is without enemies, who does not favor relatives, who regards no one as his child, who is detached from the benefits of righteous lifestyle, income and lusty emotion, who is not stimulated by desire; that person is factually liberated.

Analysis:

When considered, many of the prejudices and traditions favor one group of people and disenfranchise another. This is sponsored by material nature as well by those who benefit from the particular trend. A yogi must see the attitude of material nature as the underlying basis for the unfair practices in human society. Since that is the case, the living entities who express biases are superficial actors in the dramatic foldout of various species of life.

If you discover that you are not the cause of an activity and that it was endowed by material nature and enforced through life forms which were constructed by nature, you would approach the topic of liberation in a completely different way.

It is not a matter of changing the self and remaining on the same level with alterations because the underlying basis will still be there. If one stays on the same level, as soon as one relaxes, the psyche will revert to the old behaviors.

A yogi must assume the responsibility for the behavior of the psyche and also know that actually only material nature is at fault in the matter. With that one can look for a spiritual discipline through which one could eventually transit out of this environment.

Application:

When the self shifts its basis and moves away from taking so much support from material nature, it finds that its behavior becomes similar to that of a liberated soul. The key element which must be reformed is the kundalini life force mechanism, because that has the blueprint for the struggle for existence.

A student yogi should upgrade the diet of the kundalini life force by aggressive breath infusion and by repeatedly coursing the life force through the spine into the brain. As a traveler through a desert region may discard baggage which is heavy, so a yogi unlinks the self from the materialistic habits of the kundalini.

Verse 7

नैव धर्मी न चाधर्मी पूर्वोपचितहा च यः

धातुक्षयप्रशान्तात्मा निर्द्वंद्वः स विमुच्यते

naiva dharmī na cādharmī pūrvopacitahā ca yaḥ
dhātukṣayapraśāntātmā nirdvaṁdvaḥ sa vimucyate (4.7)

naiva – not even; dharmī – one who is fanatical about righteous lifestyle; na – not;cādharmī = ca (and) + adharmī (one prone to deviant social behavior); pūrvopacitahā = purva (from the previous life) + upacitahā (neutralizing the effects) ; ca – and; yaḥ - who; dhātu – evolutionary urges; kṣaya – smothering; praśāntātmā – one who is spiritually pacified; nirdvaṁdvaḥ - one who is indifferent to dual conditions; sa – that person; vimucyate – definitely liberated

The person who is not fanatical about righteous lifestyle or about deviant social behavior, who neutralizes the effects of actions performed in the previous lives, who is spiritually pacified by virtue of smothering the evolutionary urges of the present body, who is indifferent to dual conditions; that one is definitely liberated.

Analysis:

Sooner or later one should come to the conclusion that one's presence in the material world is not appreciated. Material nature does not require any specific limited entity to function, even though it must have some entities to derive power from. Being unnecessary, any self should make the effort for release. Members of the family, fellow-citizens of the community, might appreciate one's service but that is besides the point because natural nature will not allow anyone to continue in the same format for long.

The present body will be confiscated regardless of whether one desires it to be or not. Another body will be awarded in the course of history, unless one attains liberation and can relocate out of material nature's jurisdiction. It is not that the selves are running this show. Their energy is being utilized and that is all they know.

Application:

As a log is carried out to sea by currents, so the self is transmigrated from species to species, on and on endlessly until it attains liberation. The self must also accept being routed within the same species. It spends millions of years doing that, repeating the same history over and over. It can do this, because nature confiscates its log of activities after every life.

Without that memory the self assumes that its new body is its first existence. It takes up the challenge to procure food, protect the body, reproduce and locate medicines which cure disease. Eventually a self may hear about liberation from a self-realized soul. As it reflects on history, it surmises that it is being exploited by material nature. It then begins to trace the influence of nature, in regards to how nature hypnotized it and kept it confined like a horse in a paddock.

Verse 8

अकर्मा चाविकाङ्क्षश्च पश्यञ्जगदशाश्वतम्

अस्वस्थमवशं नित्यं जन्मसंसारमोहितम्

akarmā cāvikāṅkṣaśca paśyañjagadaśāśvatam
asvasthamavaśaṁ nityaṁ janmasaṁsāramohitam (4.8)

akarmā – person who is without social activities; cāvikāṅkṣaś = ca (and) + avikāṅkṣah (not expressive of desires); ca – and; paśyañ – sees, regards; jagad – world; aśāśvatam – without perpetuality; asvastham – asvatha tree; avaśaṁ - being symptomatic; nityaṁ - always; janma – birth; saṁsāra – haphazard transmigration; mohitam - delusion

A person who is without social activities, who is not expressive of desires, who regards the world as being like an Asvattha tree, without perpetuality and being always symptomatic with the delusion of birth and haphazard transmigration,

Analysis:

One who desires the world, who is lusty for physical life, cannot assess the dismal situation of the selves who transmigrate here. We can assume that outside of this solar system, there are innumerable material worlds, in which many similar circumstances occur. The expanse of the material energy is vaster than anything a limited being can imagine.

Still this does not mean that depression, disappointment or frustration can help any individual to get away from the mundane influence. One has to sober up and then research into how the core-self is fused to material nature. Is the self directly linked? Is its linkage merely a projection?

Application:

A student should associate with advanced yogis. Some siddhas use material bodies. Some are available in the astral existence. The mastership of astral projection is one of the more important accomplishments for a neophyte. That gives the opportunity to get more association from yogis who have no earthly presence. With advanced association one may learn how to perceive the opportunities nature offers as incentives for full cooperation. No limited being will ever get out of these domains without assistance. One should keep this in mind and always be on the alert for the grace of a superior soul and that of the Supreme Being.

Verse 9

वैराग्यबुद्धिः सततं तापदोषव्यपेक्षकः

आत्मबन्धविनिर्मोक्षं स करोत्यचिरादिव

vairāgyabuddhiḥ satataṁ tāpadoṣavyapekṣakaḥ
ātmabandhavinirmokṣaṁ sa karotyacirādiva (4.9)

vairāgya – detached application; buddhiḥ - intellect; satataṁ - always; tāpa – penance; doṣa – personal faults; vyapekṣakaḥ - detailed observation; ātma – self, psyche; bandha – bondage; vinirmokṣaṁ - liberation; sa – that person; karoty = karoti = does, is doing; acirād = acirāt = quickly, in a jiffy; iva – as if

...a person whose intellect is always in a detached application, one whose penance is the detailed observation of personal faults, one who is liberated from psychic bondage, that one is liberated in a jiffy.

Analysis:

To rectify the intellect, the yogi should change its energy diet. Intellectual efforts at intellect control all end in failure because the intellect's behavior is based by its energy intake. If one merely restricts it and forces it to act in a spiritually-beneficial way, it will invariably regress to its old habits. Permanent change in the conduct of this psychic organ comes about by providing a higher energy intake.

What are personal faults besides self-destructive acts which are carried out by the psyche? What is the psyche? Is it a composite of more than one psychic organ?

Application:

Many people on the spiritual quest set out to reform the self as a whole. They think that it is divisive and illusory to find partitions and components in the psyche. The fact is however that if the psyche is a composite of more than one component, each of the aspects may require a separate means of reform.

Advanced yogis have listed a core-self (atma), a sense of identity (ahamkara), an intellect (buddhi), memory (smrtih), senses (indriya) and personalized sensual energy as life force (prana or kundalini). If a student feels that it is best to treat these as one composite whole, as an undivided psyche, then this is acceptable if it brings about liberation from nature's control.

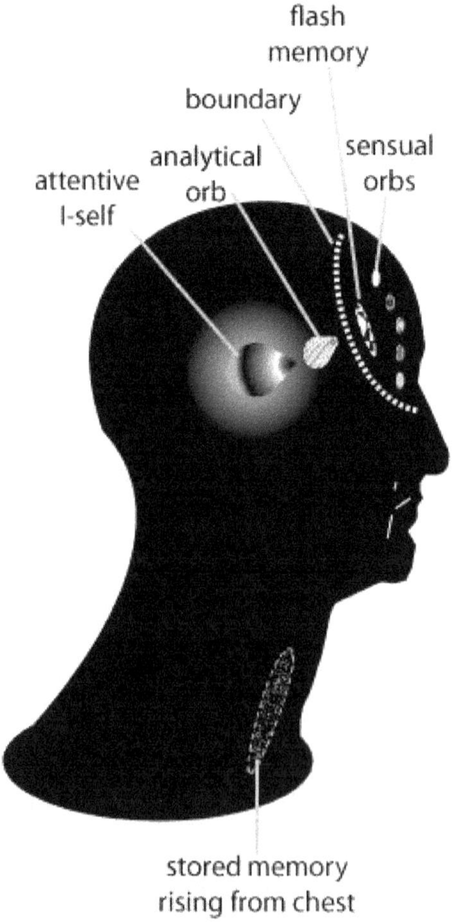

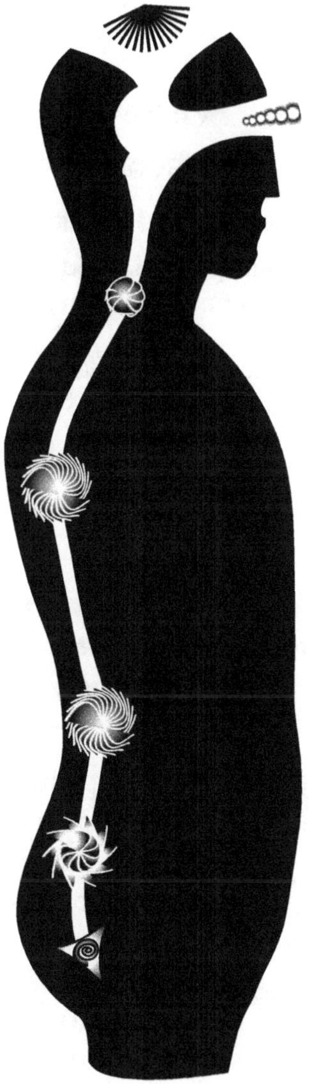

Patanjali does not endorse the idea of keeping the core-self unified with the adjuncts in the beginning stages of samyama higher meditation practice. His method is that the self should segregate itself from the means of perception and then work to purify the adjuncts. When the purification is complete and when also the self is confident of itself by itself, then Patanjali

said that one may safely unify the self with the purified means of perception.

Verse 10

अगन्धरसमस्पर्शमशब्दमपरिग्रहम्

अरूपमनभिज्ञेयं दृष्ट्वात्मानं विमुच्यते

agandharasamasparśamaśabdamaparigraham
arūpamanabhijñeyaṁ dṛṣṭvātmānaṁ vimucyate (4.10)

agandha – without fragrance; rasam – flavor; asparśam - without surface; aśabdam – without sound; aparigraham – without possessions; arūpam – without color; anabhijñeyaṁ - without education; dṛṣṭvātmānaṁ = dṛṣṭva (observing) + ātmānaṁ (of the self); vimucyate – is liberated

Without fragrance, without flavor, without a surface, without sound, without possessions, without color, without education, when the self observes itself in that way, it is liberated.

Analysis:

When all is said and done, the spiritual self will be left with nothing when it finally separates from the course of material existence. What has it gained in its transit through nature? Patanjali said that it gained experience of self-objectivity.

prakāśa kriyā sthiti śīlaṁ bhūtendriyātmakaṁ
bhogāpavargārthaṁ dṛśyam

> **What is perceived is of the nature of the mundane elements and the sense organs and is formed in clear perception, action or stability. Its purpose is to give experience or to allow liberation. (Yoga Sūtras 2.18)**

The self is conditioned with fragrance, flavor, surface, sound, possessions, color and education but it can take none of these outside the jurisdiction of material nature. Stated otherwise, the self will gain nothing from its sojourn in material nature, except perhaps the objective sense of self.

Application:

After being tossed and turned in the vast ocean of energy which is material nature, after being in trillions of lives in millions of species, the living entity may hesitate to endeavor for liberation. It invested a considerable amount of time in these travels through the life forms of matter. Should it abandon this territory and take a loss? Or should it renew its efforts to bring nature under its control?

According to the perfected yogi who instructed Kashyapa, the self will leave material nature without assets, properties, education or sensual objectives. All of that will be left behind. This is similar to the body, which comes into this world with nothing but its life. But then at death, it is deprived of everything even the life which carried it into the world.

Verse 11

पञ्चभूतगुणैर्हीनममूर्तिमदलेपकम्

अगुणं गुणभोक्तारं यः पश्यति स मुच्यते

pañcabhūtaguṇairhīnamamūrtimadalepakam
aguṇaṁ guṇabhoktāraṁ yaḥ paśyati sa mucyate (4.11)

pañca – five; bhūta – objective; guṇair – regarding the moods of nature; hīnam – without; amūrtim – without form; adalepakam – without a cause; aguṇaṁ - without perceptive moods; guṇa – mood of nature; bhoktāraṁ - experiencer; yaḥ - who; paśyati - perceives; sa – that person; mucyate – is liberated

It is not the five sense objectives, or the moods which are related. It is not a form of nature. It is without a cause. It is not a perceptive mood of nature though it experiences the attitudes. The person who perceives that is liberated.

Analysis:

When it finally leaves this scene of material nature, the unit spiritual self which is presently accommodated by material nature, will depart from this territory with nothing. In fact it can carry nothing from this zone into the exclusive spiritual domain. That other place is as subtle if not more subtle than the unit entity, and so it would not register the grossness or subtlety of material nature.

Application:

Liberation comes to one living entity after another in due course of time, according to the thrust of material nature and divine interest in the particular self. Before full liberation, an entity goes through stages of realization which take place over many lives until at last the entity loses interest in gross existence and becomes a permanent resident of the subtle material world. It is from there that the last stages of liberation are completed and the entity moves beyond this material nature.

Some yogis gain liberation directly from an earthly body but those persons are actually full time mystics even though they are in possession of a material form.

Verse 12

विहाय सर्वसंकल्पान्बुद्ध्या शारीरमानसान्

शनैर्निर्वाणमाप्नोति निरिन्धन इवानलः

vihāya sarvasaṁkalpānbuddhyā śārīramānasān
śanairnirvāṇamāpnoti nirindhana ivānalaḥ (4.12)

vihāya – disregarding; sarva – all; saṁkalpān – intentions; buddhyā – by intellect; śārīra – material body; mānasān – mind; śanair – gradually; nirvāṇam – segregation from material nature; āpnoti – obtains, accomplishes; nirindhana – fuel; ivānalaḥ = iva (like) + analaḥ (without fuel)

Disregarding through the intellect all intentions relating to the material body and the mind, he gradually becomes proficient in segregation from material nature, just as without fuel, a fire is extinguished.

Analysis:

Material nature uses the intellect as a contact agent between itself and the mind. The problem with this arrangement is that the intellect is biased towards the sensual energies and the short-termed memory. Under the circumstances it is usually unconcerned with the interest of the self.

The first accomplishment of a yogi in the process of higher meditation, is to rein in the intellect so as to force it to abandon its familiarity and submission to the sensual energy. This is achieved in the dharana deliberate linkage of the attention to a higher dimension.

The core self experiences the weakness of the intellect when that self can withdraw its interest in the activities of the intellect. These are mostly its idea and image constructions. Usually the self is entertained by the intellect in various ideas and pictures which are shown in the theatre of the intellect which is a psychic perception tool within the mind.

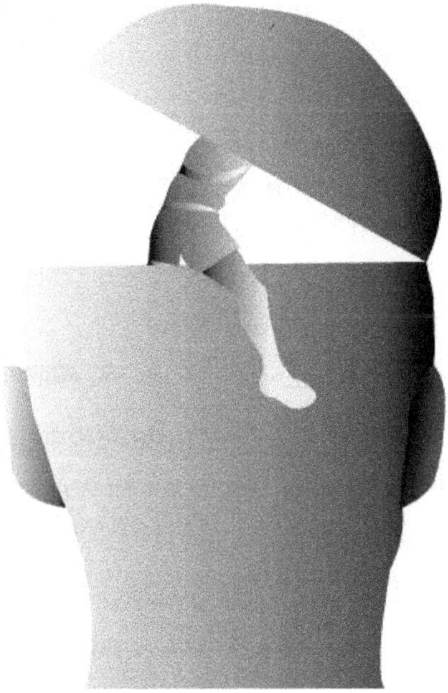

Like a foolish kid, the self positions itself to see the images and ideas which are illustrated in the intellect. Both the self and the intellect are housed in the chamber which is called the mind. Usually the sensual energies in the psyche and the sensual information from the exterior environment are filtered by the intellect. It uses the memories to evaluate its plan of action. It does this and keeps the child-like spiritual self hypnotized.

Eventually when the self wakes up to it servile position in the psyche, it decides to cut back on its viewing time within the intellect. This disempowers the intellect and the self takes note of this. After discussing this with senior yogis, the neophyte understands that the withdrawal of the self's power from the intellect would be a major victory in the quest for self control.

Application:

A neophyte finally gets it into his consciousness that if the intellect does not receive attention from the core-self, thinking and image formation ceases. The question is: Is there a definite and standard method for depriving the intellect of the attention of the core-self?

How does the core-self withdraw its interest from the intellect? Where is the core-self located? Where is the intellect positioned?

For its continued flaring, a fire requires fuel and similarly the intellect needs attention if it is to continue its theatrical performances.

Verse 13

विमुक्तः सर्वसंस्कारैस्ततो ब्रह्म सनातनम्

परमाप्नोति संशान्तमचलं दिव्यमक्षरम्

vimuktaḥ sarvasaṁskāraistato brahma sanātanam
paramāpnoti saṁśāntamacalaṁ divyamakṣaram (4.13)

vimuktaḥ - being freed; sarva – all; saṁskārais = saṁskāraih = by the subtle effects of previous actions; tato = tatah = then; brahma – spiritual reality; sanātanam – eternal; param – supreme; āpnoti – achieves; saṁśāntam – spiritual peace; acalaṁ - stable; divyam – divine; akṣaram - imperishable

Being freed from all subtle effects of previous actions, he achieves the supreme eternal spiritual reality, which is the realm

of spiritual peace and stability, and which is divine and imperishable.

Analysis:

The subtle effects of previous actions locates the original actor through his or her intellect/sense-of-identity coding. If the yogi could disconnect the sense of identity from the intellect, then he cannot be located. He cannot be made to submit to destined reactions even for the actions he committed in the most recent life.

This does not mean that a yogi wants to escape from the reactions which were due. The yogi knows that if he avoids the reactions they will occur in providence and others will be victimized by them. Therefore he voluntarily tries to clean up the effect-energies from his previous lives, especially those from his irresponsible and reckless histories.

Ultimately, a yogi leaves all such energies as they are and separates the self from any interest in the material energy. This comes about once it is understood that the self's sojourn in material nature was not its doing. It was not planned by the self. The self cannot claim responsibility for it because it was an arrangement by the inevitable combination of cosmic nature and the Supreme Being.

Application:

This freedom from having to endure a mundane providence is attained by a yogi on this side of existence before the yogi attains the exclusive spiritual world. Before one can transit to the spiritual environment, one has to be elevated to it on this side of the existential divide.

Even in the lower material world, a person who wishes to go to an astral heaven must first commit actions and develop dispositions which are compatible to such places.

Verse 14

अतः परं प्रवक्ष्यामि योगशास्त्रमनुत्तमम्

यज्ज्ञात्वा सिद्धमात्मानं लोके पश्यन्ति योगिनः

ataḥ paraṁ pravakṣyāmi yogaśāstramanuttamam
yajjñātvā siddhamātmānaṁ loke paśyanti yoginaḥ (4.14)

ataḥ - next; paraṁ - supreme; pravakṣyāmi – I will explain; yoga – yoga practice; śāstram – course; anuttamam – the best; yaj = yat = that which; jñātvā – having learnt this; siddham – perfected; ātmānaṁ - self; loke – on earth; paśyanti – see, experience; yoginaḥ - yogis

Next, I will explain the course of yoga practice, which is supreme and which is the best teaching. Having learnt this, the yogis experience the perfected self here on earth.

Analysis:

Some portions of advanced yoga can be discovered by the neophyte. The rest must be acquired from living teachers or deceased ones. No one should feel that alone, all by the self, one can discover all there is to know about spiritual perfection.

Application:

Instead of wishing to relocate to a spiritual world, one should work with an advanced yogi who can teach how to attain spirituality while one is in the material world. It is not possible to be translated to the spiritual side if one has not attained it on this side of existence.

Verse 15

तस्योपदेशं पश्यामि यथावत्तन्निबोध मे

यैर्द्वारैश्चारयन्नित्यं पश्यत्यात्मानमात्मनि

tasyopadeśaṁ paśyāmi yathāvattannibodha me
yairdvāraiścārayannityaṁ paśyatyātmānamātmani (4.15)

tasyopadeśaṁ = tasya (of this) + upadeśaṁ (instruction); paśyāmi - perceptually transmit; yathāvat – as it is; tan = tat = that; nibodha – learn; me – from me; yair = yaiḥ = by which; dvāraiś – by the dimensional opening; cārayan – transit; nityaṁ - eternal; paśyaty = paśyati = perceives; ātmānam – self; ātmani – in the psyche

I will perceptually transmit this instruction as it is. Learn from me about the dimensional opening through which one transits to the eternal and perceives the self within the psyche.

Analysis:

The journey to the spiritual side of existence uses passages from within the psyche of the individual. Some think that the passages are in the self itself. They are mistaken because the passages are in the psyche of the self. That psyche is a chamber in which the self is one of the psychic components.

Even though it is difficult to develop the required spiritual sensitivity, it can be done by a progressive and steady meditation practice in mastering the samyama advanced meditation process explained by Patanjali.

The psyche is not the self but the self is housed in the psyche. Within the psyche there are passages or gateways, dimensional openings to other worlds.

Application:

Certain techniques for self-transit to other dimensions must be learned from an advanced yogi or directly from the Supreme Being. A student should not think that teachers are unnecessary. As one progresses from the dull side of existence, one should not expect to discover every technique. Some processes must be acquired from others.

Verse 16

इन्द्रियाणि तु संहृत्य मन आत्मनि धारयेत्

तीव्रं तप्त्वा तपः पूर्वं ततो योक्तुमुपक्रमेत्

indriyāṇi tu saṁhṛtya mana ātmani dhārayet
tīvraṁ taptvā tapaḥ pūrvaṁ tato yoktumupakramet (4.16)

indriyāṇi – senses; tu – but; saṁhṛtya - withdrawing the senses; mana – mind; ātmani – core-self; dhārayet – should mentally direct; tīvraṁ extreme; taptvā – having done penance; tapaḥ - austerities; pūrvaṁ - before; tato = tatah = then; yoktum – to practice yoga; upakramet – should practice

Withdrawing the senses, one should redirect the mind to the core-self. Having done extreme austerities before, one should practice the yoga system.

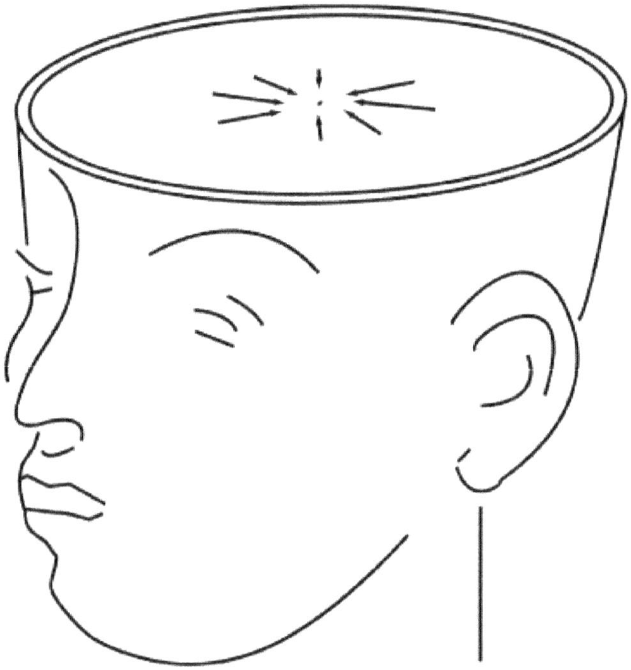

Analysis:

The 1-2-3 punch is to withdraw the senses, redirect the mind to the core-self and then practice samyama which is a sequential development in meditation. One may sit to meditate and then make mental efforts with the will power to withdraw the senses, then refocus the energy on the core-self and then internalize deeper for trance meditation. Such a procedure is not however the complete system set up as ashtanga eight-staged yoga. In classic yoga, the student should be living a righteous lifestyle which facilitates the least hassles from material nature. To do this the first two stages of yoga, namely yama restraints and niyama approved behaviors, are the practices. Before the meditation session, the yogi should practice asana postures and breath infusion techniques. The restraints and approved behavior are not practiced just before the daily meditation session. These are practiced during the day during social interaction. These are on-going whenever there is social involvement in the physical and astral worlds.

After practicing the asana postures and the pranaiama breath infusion techniques, the yogi sits to meditate. If the yogi is advanced in the 5th stage of yoga which is pratyahar sensual energy withdrawal, that practice will be completed in the first five minutes. Then the yogi will do samayama which is the last three stages of meditation practice as one sequential event.

Pratyahar is a chore which takes time, if the yogi has not practiced the postures and breath infusion practice. By these practices the pratyahar sensual energy withdrawal is accomplished in a very efficient way by the flushing out of old energy in the mind replacing it with new energy which is infused during the stretching aspects of the postures and the breathing practices.

Application:

For a yogi, the practice of yoga is easy if an expert instructor is available. Without such a person, everything relies on books and self discovery. The first two stages are ongoing practices used in daily social involvements. These first two aspects are used throughout the life of a yogi. Patanjali stated that there should be no excuse for not maintaining these commitments in regards to social behavior. If a yogi is careless in social behavior and offends morality, then he or she will experience upsets, when providence enforces penalties. To be sure not to offend the righteous lifestyle, a yogi should heed the yama restraints and niyama approved behaviors.

Here is detailed information about the eight (8) stages of yoga:

yama niyama āsana prāṇāyāma pratyāhāra
dhāraṇā dhyāna samādhayaḥ aṣṭau aṅgāni

Moral restraints, recommended behaviors, body posture, breath infusion, sensual energy withdrawal, linking of the attention to higher concentration forces or persons, effortless linkage of the attention to higher concentration forces or persons, continuous effortless linkage of the attention to higher concentration forces or persons are the eight parts of the yoga system. (Yoga Sūtras 2.29)

yama	***moral restraints***
niyama	***recommended behaviors***
āsana	***body posture***
prāṇāyāma	***breath infusion***
pratyāhāra	***sensual energy withdrawal***
dhāraṇā	***linking of the attention to higher concentration forces or persons***
dhyāna	***effortless linkage of the attention to higher concentration forces or persons***
samādhi	***continuous effortless linkage of the attention to higher concentration forces or persons***

A yogi should pay strict attention to the preliminary two stages since these are on-going in social contact with others either on the physical level or on the astral planes. There is however one special feature which is the īśvarapraṇidhānāni profound religious meditation on the Supreme Lord. Yoga is specially designed for psyche purification by segregating the core-self from its psychic adjuncts, but if there is neglect of the Supreme Being, the effort will fail. Thus Patanjali mentioned this

special feature as part of the second stage of yoga. It applies in all dealings with all reality anywhere.

Details of the First Practice:

yamāḥ moral restraints

ahiṁsā satya asteya
brahmacarya aparigrahāḥ yamāḥ

Non-violence, realism, non-stealing, sexual non-expressiveness which results in the perception of spirituality (brahman) and non-possessiveness are the moral restraints. (Yoga Sūtras 2.30)

Non-violence:

Non-violence begins with restricting the body to a vegetarian diet. Dairy products may be included but not the flesh of the cow. Meat, fish, eggs and any other type of animal or fish matter should not be used. A yogi should reform the habit of killing creatures for food. In the advanced stage of this practice, exploitation of the human species and any other species is curtailed since the yogi develops more penetrating insight which allows him to see the subtle forms of violence.

The eating of animals is a vicious activity. Once this stops the yogi develops more sensitivity towards every form of violence. However the reduction of cruelty takes place according to the facilities given to the yogi by material nature. A yogi may have lofty principles but he or she still has to accept the cues provided by destiny. The yogi should take as much facility as is possible to institute non-violence to the highest degree.

There is no flesh eating in the heavenly planets of the astral world, or on the spiritual locations in the exclusive spiritual-energy domains. Hence if a yogi desires to relocate to these places, he or she should adopt lifestyle habits which are similar to the behavior in those paradises.

Realism

Realism is developed when the yogi's psychic perception increases and when the yogi's intuition functions efficiently. When this happens the yogi is given an advantage over others because he or she can perceive situations from past life which are related to occurrences in the present. A yogi can also anticipate how material nature will lay out history in the future.

Understanding that reality is a composite of the past and present, a yogi knows that actions taken today will be figured in by providence to create the future. Thus one should do the very best to perform efficiently to curtail future inconveniences and encourage nature to give one allowances for more yoga practice. Even though material nature is not intentionally supportive of a yogi's disciplines, still if a yogi becomes less of a nuisance to nature, it will back-off and allow the practice of yoga.

Non-stealing

Stealing is an integral part of material nature. It is built into the energy of material nature. Thus its cessation is near impossible. In a world like this the complete practice of non-theft will never occur. If one is serious about ridding the self of this trait, one has to migrate into a dimension in the subtle world or in the exclusive spiritual world where there is sufficiency and free accomodations in all respect, where sublime desires can be fulfilled without endeavor and with nature being directly responsive to the individual's will.

On this planet, a yogi must first admit that complete non-stealing really means a great reduction in theft. At any moment if one loses a human body and finds the self to be the progeny of a lower species, most of the sublime actions one exhibits now will become impossible to even conceive of. This means that arrogance and pride in a pious lifestyle may cause one to become a target for demotion in the mundane evolutionary cycle.

The yogi should be humble, do the best under the circumstances and take every opportunity nature provides to practice the sublime principles but he should never forget that nature has the upper hand. She is not particularly concerned with anyone's moral stance.

Sexual non-expressiveness which results in the perception of spirituality (brahman)

Sexuality and reproduction are the two main assets used by material nature in the creation of bodies. Initially to start up the life cycle, nature only requires the proximity of the spirits. As if out of thin air, spirits are attracted to material nature and are fused into suitable material energy. This is how life begins in a material cosmos. However because of changes in the material energy, it soon becomes necessary to generate life forms through sexual access and other methods of reproduction.

Science cannot find the original conditions under which life first began, because material nature is no longer at that stage. The present phase will never return to the original conditions. In some other universe, which is still in the initial stages of formation, life will begin like a magical event, but as that place evolves it will lose those primal conditions and will branch out to the conditions which are similar to the one in our universe.

Sex was designed by nature as a conduit for responsibility, just as employment and wages are mostly used for the same objective. Since nature yields a pleasure during sexual intercourse, human beings become distracted and are blind-sided to nature's aims.

A yogi should however become detached from the need for pleasure. If this is achieved, the yogi will be able to use the hormonal energy in the body for implementing more spiritual practice. Getting a body really means achieving the adult status of that body, so as to split off from the parents and live on one's own for the fulfillment of individual desires. But if one becomes attached to sexual pleasure one's interest energy will be focused into the material body and one will forget all about spirituality.

Non-possessiveness

Originally possessions concerned tools, food and clothing. As civilization became more and more modernized other types of possession were accumulated. A yogi should master the art of having the least physical possessions. On the mental level, he or she should have a detached mood in relation to all things mundane. One should never forget that one came into the world with just a body. In the womb, one did not have even the breath. When one is displaced from the body at death one cannot directly control any physical property. And that disempowered status will remain in force until one procures another body.

Attachment of any kind takes investment of energy. Such investment robs the self of psychic focus which results in less psychic perception and more focus into the physical world. This diminishes the interest in spiritual practice. Possessions therefore should be kept to an absolute minimum.

Details of the Second Practice:

niyamāḥ approved behaviors

śauca saṅtoṣa tapaḥ svādhyāya
īśvarapraṇidhānāni niyamāḥ

Purification, contentment, austerity and profound religious meditation on the Supreme Lord are the recommended behaviors. (Yoga Sūtras 2.32)

Purification

This purification is psyche redesign. It is for the most part psychic actions, but physical hygiene is included with it in so far as the physical impacts the subtle. The energy which needs to be purified is the subtle force which is used by the psychic components, particularly those energies used by the kundalini life force.

Ancient yogis discovered and recommended pranaiama breath infusion methods which enliven the sluggish kundalini energy, causing it to become energized so that it moves up the spine into the brain. This kundalini shakti has the instinct for creature body procurement and survival of any form which it acquires. Its energy intake if not changed will cause the self to transmigrate merely on the basis of getting a gross body without respect to the inconveniences that new form would have to accept.

To purify the kundalini by deliberate methods, the ancient yogis used pranaiama breath infusion techniques to push out the old energy in the life force and to infuse it with fresh energy. This practice is continued in each session until the kundalini is so enlivened that it moves from the base chakra up the spine into the brain and into other hard to reach places like the extremities of the fingers and toes.

This one practice, kundalini yoga, causes massive energy displacement even in other components of the psyche. Through it, there is improvement in psychic perception and vision-insight.

Purification which means taking bath and such actions for improving the external condition of the material body, serve the purpose in ordinary religion and in social exchanges but it does nothing for purification of the components of the psyche. Hence it is not stressed in kriya yoga where it is considered to be a necessary but superficial chore.

Contentment

Contentment becomes a state of mind when a yogi learns how to keep desires from pressuring the psyche for fulfillments. The desire energies are in the causal body but there are some which are being incubated in the subtle form. These energies are troublesome to one and all. As for the causal form, the desires in it do not require fulfillment until those energies burst out in the subtle body. After achieving higher yoga, a yogi can keep causal energies from reaching the subtle form. This allows that ascetic to have peace of mind when meditating.

There are however desires which have already manifested or which remain dormant in the subtle form. These must be dealt with because they cannot be pushed back into the causal body. They must be neutralized by keeping them in dormancy or by fulfilling them in the most efficient way. When a yogi develops psychic perception, he or she manages these desire energies more efficiently. Some can be manifest on the astral planes without having to register on the physical level. Desires with physical requirements are humbug ideas which a yogi may fulfill if providence gives the opportunity.

A neophyte should take help from an advanced person in the art of managing these energies. If one fails to regulate these, the yoga practice will be haphazard and success will not be achieved.

In the advanced stage, a yogi remains situated with contentment of mind because of neutralizing the desires in the subtle body and because of restricting the flow of energy from the causal one into the subtle one. There is nothing to achieve in the material world, except an understanding of the nature of the individual self. There is nothing to be gained in these existences. Hence contentment is the final attitude of a living being.

Austerity

To curtail one's pleasure needs, numerous austerities need be practiced. The living being is mostly a pleasure seeker but when it understands that pleasure has a corrosive side effect, it seeks to abandon many vices.

For success in curtailing sensual needs, the living entity has to adopt austerities. The senses are involved in researching the material body and the world which is outside the body, for enjoyment. The self can effectively censor this by practicing austerities.

Profound religious meditation on the Supreme Lord

Patanjali, the author of the Yoga Sūtras, listed profound religious meditation on the Supreme Lord as one of the approved behaviors. Why did he do this since meditation is listed as a three-phased process which is the three highest stages of yoga sequentially performed.

In the stages of yoga, after this second stage of niyama approved behaviors, one should practice and perfect this meditation on the Supreme Lord. By using the Sanskrit term, īśvara, Patanjali left no room for doubt regarding whether he meant a non-personal supreme form or a Primal Personality. A yogi should assume that there is a Supreme Person. Each day should go by with the yogi thinking, "Today I will experience that Supreme Person. It will be today for sure."

<u>Details of the Third Practice:</u>

āsana postures

sthira sukham āsanam

The posture should be steady and comfortable. (Yoga Sūtras 2.46)

Postures aid the kundalini life force in its task of having to distribute nutrients and subtle energy throughout the body. The living physical body is actually two bodies in one. It is the subtle form and the physical one in fusion. Thus if postures are assumed in the physical form, they are simultaneously being done in the subtle one.

There is polluted energy in many hard to reach places in these bodies. Postures make it easy for the life force to send fresh energy to these places. This results in increased awareness in the bodies.

Details of the Fourth Practice:

prāṇāyāma breath infusion

tasmin satiśvāsa praśvāsayoḥ
gativicchedaḥ prāṇāyāmaḥ
bāhya ābhyantara stambha vṛttiḥ deśa kāla
saṁkhyābhiḥ paridṛṣṭah dărgha sūkṣmaḥ
bāhya ābhyantara viṣaya ākṣepă caturthaḥ

Once this is accomplished, breath regulation, which is the separation of the flow of inhalation and exhalation, is attained.

It has internal, external and restrictive operations, which are regulated according to the place, time and accounting, being prolonged or hardly noticed.

That which transcends the objective, external and internal breath regulation is the fourth type of breath infusement techniques. (Yoga Sūtras 2.49-52)

Pranaiama is the most important discipline for purifying the psyche. Even though water is important in purifying the physical body and the physical environment, it has no use on the inside of the psyche.

Breath infusion is the single most important method for purifying the psyche by displacing polluted used energy with fresh energy . This is done through various means of breath infusion.

Details of the Fifth Practice:

pratyāhāraḥ sensual energy withdrawal

svaviṣaya asaṁprayoge cittasya svarūpāanukāraḥ
iva indriyāṇāṁ pratyāhāraḥ

The withdrawal of the senses, is as it was, their assumption of the form of mento-emotional energy when not contacting their own objects of perception. (Yoga Sūtras 2.54)

The withdrawal of the senses takes place when the yogi can pull in his attention-energy which usually moves with rapid speed away from the core-self through the senses into the material world. This is not physical energy. This is psychic force. After repeatedly exerting mental muscles to withdraw this power from the senses, a yogi gains success at causing a reversal of the flow of energy. Then the energy comes back into the core-self rather than depart from it on a continuous basis.

This conservation of mental and emotional energy enriches meditation. It facilitates the next stage of yoga which is the effort to link to higher levels of consciousness and higher personalities who exist on those planes. A yogi experiences the practical results of sensual energy withdrawal, when the self is no longer attracted to vices, when even in the presence of opportunities for enjoyment, the self feels no compulsion to participate and turns away without regret.

Details of the Sixth Practice:

dhāraṇā linkage of attention

deśa bandhaḥ cittasya dhāraṇā

Linking of the attention to a concentration force or person, involves a restricted location in the mento-emotional energy. (Yoga Sūtras 3.1)

Even when there is mental confusion and emotional disfigurement, there is order in the psyche of the self. Mental confusion occurs in particular places in the mind. The first lesson for a student yogi when doing higher yoga is to identify the components of the mind and map their default locations.

It is very clear from the instructions of Patanjali, that in the practice of dhāraṇā linkage of the mind to higher concentration forces or persons, a restricted location is involved. The Sanskrit words are unambiguous, deśa bandhah.

When in meditation, the yogi takes the time and uses the sensitivity to identify the components of the mind, he discovers that they have default locations. The self is positioned in a specific place. The sense of identity in another. The intellect in yet another. The memories are somewhere specific. The sensual energies flow in a certain direction to a certain location. And the kundalini life force operates from a certain base.

Before one can link the attention to a higher concentration force, that other dimension must be located. The practice is not one of imagining a higher dimension. It is not a visualization exercise. During meditation when the yogi is transited to other dimensions, he or she gets factual information about the location of such places. Then an effort is made to reach those domains.

Details of the Seventh Practice:

dhyānam effortless linkage of attention

tatra pratyayaḥ ekatānatā dhyānam

When in that location, there is one continuous threadlike flow of one's instinctive interest, that is the effortless linking of the attention to a higher concentration force or person. (Yoga Sūtras 3.2)

To reach the stage of effortless linkage of the attention to higher realities, a yogi must be consistent in the practice of making the effort to link. Repeated practice results in effortless connection after some time.

Details of the Eight Practice:

samādhiḥ continuous effortless linkage of attention

tadeva arthamātranirbhāsaṁ
svarūpaśūnyam iva samādhiḥ

That same effortless linkage of the attention when experienced as illumination of the higher concentration force or person, while the yogi feels as if devoid of himself, is samādhi or continuous effortless linkage of his attention to the special person, object, or force. (Yoga Sūtras 3.3)

Samadhi happens under certain existential conditions. A yogi can put the self in a position to experience the continuous effortless linkage to higher realities by knowing how to infuse the subtle body and how to locate the core-self so as to discourage the intellect from its fantasy configurations.

Verse 17

तपस्वी त्यक्तसंकल्पो दम्भाहंकारवर्जितः

मनीषी मनसा विप्रः पश्यत्यात्मानमात्मनि

tapasvī tyaktasaṁkalpo dambhāhaṁkāravarjitaḥ
manīṣī manasā vipraḥ paśyatyātmānamātmani (4.17)

tapasvī – proficient ascetic; tyakta – detached, effectively neutralized; saṁkalpo = saṁkalpah = effect-energy from past lives; dambhāhaṁkāra = dambha (deceit, fraud) + ahaṁkāra (misplaced identity, conceit); varjitaḥ - exclude, devoid of; manīṣī – philosopher; manasā – by the mind; vipraḥ - educated yogi; paśyaty = paśyati = perceives; ātmānam – self; ātmani – in the psyche

That proficient ascetic, who effectively neutralized the effect-energy from past lives, who was devoid of conceit and deceit, that philosopher, the educated yogi, perceives the self in the psyche through clarity of mind.

Analysis:

Self-realization is the first accomplishment on the spiritual path. Without psychological clarity, the self will remain in confusion mistaking itself for this and that, and committing actions for which it will be sorry.

A self is just responsible to realize itself. When this is achieved, all other objectives come easy. There is an individual spiritual self even though some enlightened beings like Gautama Buddha denied or did not discuss the topic. There can be clarity. The self can distinguish itself without conflict and polarization.

Application:

The effect-energies from past lives are used by providence to keep all the transmigrating entities penned in. This is the way destiny handles this situation and enforces reactions for actions committed previously.

A yogi learns how to neutralize the effect-energies from his or her history. However an attitude of willingness to accept inconvenient circumstances must be the mood of the yogi, since he or she cannot nullify all historic backlashes.

Self conceit and deceit to others must be removed completely from the psyche of the yogi. This is done by infusing new energy into the kundalini life force which is the psychic apparatus which produces dishonesty and intrigue.

Verse 18

स चेच्छक्नोत्ययं साधुर्योक्तुमात्मानमात्मनि

तत एकान्तशीलः स पश्यत्यात्मानमात्मनि

sa cecchaknotyayaṁ sādhuryoktumātmānamātmani
tata ekāntaśīlaḥ sa paśyatyātmānamātmani (4.18)

sa – that person; cecchaknoty = cet (if) + śaknoti (able, could) + ayaṁ - this; sādhur = sādhuh = saintly person; yoktum – to yogically focus; ātmānam – self; ātmani – in the psyche; tata – expanded, obsessed; ekānta = eka (one) + anta (end, objective); śīlaḥ - profile, character; sa – he; paśyaty = paśyati = perceives; ātmānam – self; ātmani - in the psyche

If that saintly person could yogically focus on the self in the psyche, then being a person who is obsessed and profiled with that singular objective, he would perceive the self in the psyche.

Analysis:

There is outside on the inside, just as in a house a person may be outside a closet or an appliance may be outside the body of a person.

Clarification really means to understand that inside the psyche there are components and the core-self is not the psyche even though it is a resident of the mind chamber.

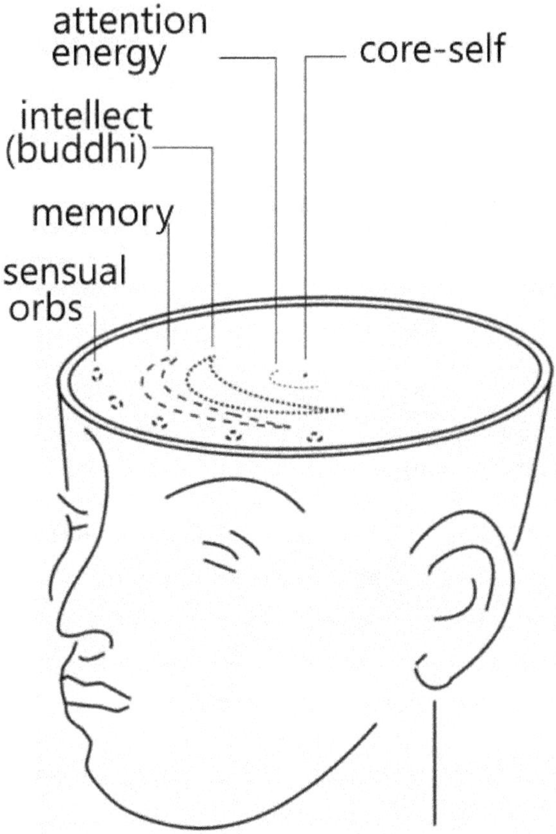

Application:

The desire to make the psyche one cohesive whole is based on the fear of facing the truth which is that the core-self is only one component in the psyche, and it does not usually control what the psyche is subjected to. However such a fear is really unwanted because perfected beings like the person who explained this *Anu Gītā* to Kashyapa, successfully faced the truth, dealt with it and attained spiritual perfection.

In the conditioned state in massive ignorance of what it is and how it is situated, the core-self seems to be doomed to remaining as a power supply for the other components in the psyche. This may cause someone to desire non-existence or to desire the conclusion of I-consciousness.

However Krishna, the Supreme Being, declared that once a spirit existed objectively in this creation as an individual entity, it cannot get rid of self-identity. If we accept this, then the only way out is to clarify what the self is and work for its autonomy and freedom from being a victim in the mind.

Verse 19

संयतः सततं युक्त आत्मवान्विजितेन्द्रियः

तथायमात्मनात्मानं साधु युक्तः प्रपश्यति

saṁyataḥ satataṁ yukta ātmavānvijitendriyaḥ
tathāyamātmanātmānaṁ sādhu yuktaḥ prapaśyati (4.19)

saṁyataḥ - total sense control; satataṁ - always; yukta – proficient in yoga practice; ātmavān – self-composed; vijitendriyaḥ - conqueror of sensual energies; tathāyam = tathā (as) + ayam (this); ātmanātmānaṁ = ātmana (by the self) + ātmānaṁ (self); sādhu – good, exceptional; yuktaḥ - being versed; prapaśyati - perceives

Having total control over the senses, being always proficient in yoga practice, being self-composed, a conqueror of the sensual energies, being like this, that one, being exceptional, being versed in yoga, perceives the self by the self.

Analysis:

Self-realization comes about only on an individual basis through individual spiritual practice and assistance from advanced entities. The advanced souls can help as much as they desire, and the student will gain no success if a certain amount of self-effort is lacking. But all the same no matter how aggressively the student practices, he or she cannot get full success without divine grace. Both factors are required.

A yogi should exert the self as much as possible and also be open to reception of grace energies and teachings from the advanced entities and from the Supreme Being.

Application:

In material existence the routine of nature is that the self only perceives physical reality and dream occurences. Most of everything else is off-limits to direct perception of a human being. However this limitation can be broken by a focus of the self on other realities. To see physically, material nature harnessed the vision energy of the self and converted that into physical sight. It is a wonder how nature achieved that. Still physical vision has given every unit psyche the idea of diversity. This has challenged the selves to identify objects and find beneficial uses for commodities.

When all is said and done however, the core-self realizes that the whole world of items has little meaning to the spiritual self. In fact the self is incompatible with the shifty presentations of material nature. When a self no longer wants to be entertained, it seeks a way out. It tries to find another world in which degeneration is not inherent.

Verse 20

यथा हि पुरुषः स्वप्ने दृष्ट्वा पश्यत्यसाविति

तथारूपमिवात्मानं साधु युक्तः प्रपश्यति

yathā hi puruṣaḥ svapne dṛṣṭvā paśyatyasāviti
tathārūpamivātmānaṁ sādhu yuktaḥ prapaśyati (4.20)

yathā – as; hi – because; puruṣaḥ - person; svapne – in a dream; dṛṣṭvā – after seeing; paśyaty = paśyati = recognises; asāviti = asau (that) + iti (it is said, thus); tathā – so; rūpam – form; ivātmānaṁ = iva (as if) +

ātmānaṁ (of the self); sādhu – proper; yuktaḥ - proficient in yoga; prapaśyati – definitely identifies

As a person after seeing someone in a dream, recognises that one and exclaims, "This is he," so one who has the proper proficiency in yoga definitely identifies the form of the self.

Analysis:

Neither Patanjali nor this perfected siddha who taught Kashyapa admitted a unity with everyone. Neither spoke of the mergence of the limited spirit (*ātma*) with the Supreme Spirit (*paramātma*). The word *rūpam* itself objects to the idea, since it means the form of the item, which happens to be the self (*ātmānaṁ*) in this case.

Here we discuss the status of a single entity, as to how that entity can be freed from the intrigues of material existence and become freed individually, just as this ascetic, who explained this to Kashyapa.

Application:

In the conditioned stage the core-self misidentifies itself as its adjuncts. It feels that it is the psyche; that it is the mind; that it is the emotions; that it is the urges; that it is the reasoning and memories. Thus it speaks about going within itself as if entering the psyche or focusing in the psyche is entry into itself.

Until the self clarifies itself and segregates itself from the other components of consciousness, no significant progress would be made. The self should settle down in the psyche and take steps to sort itself from the other components. Later when it makes progress in this venture of self-discovery, it should identify the kundalini life force which is outside of the head of the subtle body, outside of the immediate mind compartment.

Another achievement is the discovery of the causal body, the form from which the subtle one developed. Only clarity and very sensitive psychic perception can cause the self to get the distinction of these.

Verse 21

इषीकां वा यथा मुञ्जात्कश्चिन्निर्हृत्य दर्शयेत्

योगी निष्कृष्टमात्मानं तथा संपश्यते तनौ

iṣīkāṁ vā yathā muñjātkaścinnirhṛtya darśayet
yogī niṣkṛṣṭamātmānaṁ tathā saṁpaśyate tanau (4.21)

iṣīkāṁ - straw fibres; vā – or; yathā – as; muñjāt – from reeds, basketwork grass (saccharum sara); kaścin = kaścit = someone; nirhṛtya – extracted; darśayet – show; yogī - yogi; niṣkṛṣṭam – displaced; ātmānaṁ - person-psyche; tathā – so; saṁpaśyate – definitely perceives; tanau – from the body

As one may show straw fibres after extraction from reeds, so the yogi definitely perceives the person-psyche which is displaced from a physical body

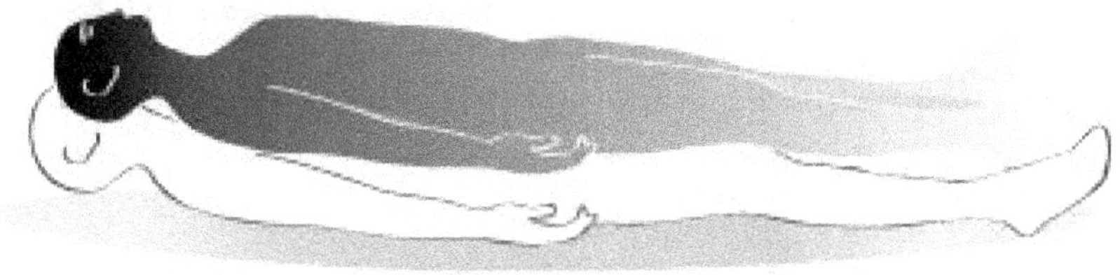

Analysis:

The person-psyche in this case is not the individual spirit alone. It is the individual spirit in its psyche along with other components like the sense of identity, the intellect, the memories, the sensual energies and the life force. These together move as one subtle being which transmigrates from one form to another. If anything, the psyche is a composite psychic organism which acquires material bodies in sequence.

Application:

The first step in understanding what the spirit is, involves only understanding the subtle body of the spirit. That subtle body is not the spirit but it is the container in which the spirit

is housed life after life. If a person cannot understand the subtle body and has not experienced astral projection, that person cannot have any deep insight into the spiritual truths.

Spiritual clarification begins with identifying the self as the subtle body. That is a misnomer but it is far better and it is a progression from the stage of identifying the self as the physical form. After understanding the self as the subtle body, one should then gain the insight to understand how the self is housed in that psychic form. As a basket-maker considers grass stalks to be forms from which fibers can be removed, the astral projector knows that the physical body is a form from which the astral body is displaced.

Verse 22

मुञ्जं शरीरं तस्याहुरिषीकामात्मनि श्रिताम्

एतन्निदर्शनं प्रोक्तं योगविद्भिरनुत्तमम्

muñjaṁ śarīraṁ tasyāhuriṣīkāmātmani śritām
etannidarśanaṁ proktaṁ yogavidbhiranuttamam (4.22)

muñjaṁ - basketwork grass (saccharum sara); śarīraṁ - body; tasyāhur = tasya (of this) + ahuh (announced, compared); iṣīkām – straw fibers; ātmani – person-psyche; śritām – referenced; etan = etat = this; nidarśanaṁ - illustration, analogy; proktaṁ - explained; yogavid = yogavitbhir = yogavitbhih = by expert yogis; anuttamam – best, ideal

The body is compared with the basketwork grass, and the person-psyche is referenced to the straw fibers. This is an ideal analogy explained by those who are expert yogis.

Analysis:

Astral projection is no small start in the journey of self-realization. Some persons do get stuck at the stage of astral travels and feel that this is spiritual life in full. Actually such persons should be appraised for realizing that the individual spirit does not have to be satisfied with material existence. Still, that is just the start of spiritual realization because the core-self is a resident of the astral body, just as it is a resident of the material form. Just as the material body will be finished in one hundred years or so, the astral body will be finished when the universe collapses. Of course that is very long span of time, but still it is not an eternity.

Application:

A yogi is a person who focuses day after day on the subject of the transcendental self. There is nothing more important than realizing what that self is, how it functions, and how it could be elevated away from material existence into a location which is comparably suitable to its transcendence. The search for these truths begins with objectively realizing the self in an astral projection.

Verse 23

यदा हि युक्तमात्मानं सम्यक्पश्यति देहभृत्

तदास्य नेशते कश्चित्त्रैलोक्यस्यापि यः प्रभुः

yadā hi yuktamātmānaṁ samyakpaśyati dehabhṛt
tadāsya neśate kaścittrailokyasyāpi yaḥ prabhuḥ (4.23)

yadā – when; hi – indeed; yuktam – having yogic insight; ātmānaṁ - of the self; samyakpaśyati – deeply perceives; dehabhṛt – body-supported soul; tadāsya = tadā (then) + asya (of this); neśate = na (not) + īśate (is master of); kaścit – anyone, anything; trailokyasyāpi = trailokyasya (of the three partitions of the universe) + api (also); yaḥ - who; prabhuḥ - liberated entity

When the body-supported soul deeply perceives the spiritual self through yogic-insight, then nothing is master of that self but it becomes a liberated entity in the three partitions of the universe.

Analysis:

The control over the self which material nature exercises, occurs due to massive ignorance in the self about its constitution and its relationship to the adjuncts in the psyche.

This is why Patanjali highlighted the segregation of the self from the perception equipments as being a mandatory accomplishment in yoga practice. He suggested that the yogi should shut down the thinking apparatus and develop a segregated presence from it, in order to come to terms with the false unity the self has with its perception technologies.

It is important for the self to realize that it is body-supported. Since the beginning of time, it transmigrated because of needing physical bodies. Can it remove its needs for such forms?

The self which solves the puzzle of its affiliation with a material body, a subtle body, and the adjuncts in the subtle form, gains relief from that massive dependence and becomes a person with controlled response to this situation.

Application:

The struggle between material nature and the spiritual self will continue until the self is liberated from material existence. That will not happen so long as the self cannot segregate itself from the perception equipments which it was awarded by material nature.

There is a technical verse about this in the **Bhagavad Gītā** ***where Krishna, the Supreme Being, described the condition of the limited selves in this creation:***

mamaivāṁśo jīvaloke jīvabhūtaḥ sanātanaḥ
manaḥṣaṣṭhānīndriyāṇi prakṛtisthāni karṣati (15.7)

My partner is in this world of individualized conditioned beings. He is an eternal individual soul but he draws to himself the mundane senses of which the mind is the sixth detection device. (Bhagavad Gītā 15.7)

Regardless of how the self became fused with the perception equipments, it has to destroy the adhesive force before it can realize itself without respect to those psychic technologies.

Verse 24

अन्योन्याश्चैव तनवो यथेष्टं प्रतिपद्यते

विनिवृत्य जरामृत्यू न हृष्यति न शोचति

anyonyāścaiva tanavo yatheṣṭaṁ pratipadyate
vinivṛtya jarāmṛtyū na hṛṣyati na śocati (4.24)

anyonyāś = anyonyāh = one after another; caiva – and so; tanavo = tanavah = bodies; yatheṣṭaṁ = yathā (as) + īṣṭaṁ (desired); pratipadyate – acquired; vinivṛtya – transcending; jarā – senility; mṛtyū – death; na – neither; hṛṣyati – is exhilarated; na – nor; śocati – is saddened

One after another, bodies are acquired as desired. Transcending senility and death, the self is neither exhilarated nor saddened.

Analysis:

Even though the bodies are acquired as desired, it is a desire in ignorance. It is not an informed opinion. The soul plays a game of blindman's buff with nature which is the governing principle in real terms. In one life, nature allows the soul to gain the upper hand and then in another or even in the same life, the soul is frustrated without fulfillments.

Where do desires originate? How can an eternal soul desire to prolong the life of a temporary body, unless that soul is confused about its duration?

Application:

In the conditioned stage the problems of the perishable material body are the problems of the soul, since the soul feels that it is the body. Then again after the soul learns to astral project and develops confidence in itself as a subtle body, it appears to suffer from the upsets which frustrate the subtle form.

Patanjali therefore advised all yogis to develop the segregation between the core-self and the perception technologies in the subtle body. This breach in the unity of the

psyche gives the self the realization that it does not have to be a recipient of the frailties of these forms.

Verse 25

देवानामपि देवत्वं युक्तः कारयते वशी

ब्रह्म चाव्ययमाप्नोति हित्वा देहमशाश्वतम्

devānāmapi devatvaṁ yuktaḥ kārayate vaśī
brahma cāvyayamāpnoti hitvā dehamaśāśvatam (4.25)

devānām – of the supernatural controllers; api – also; devatvaṁ - psychology like that of the gods; yuktaḥ - being proficient in yoga; kārayate – creates; vaśī – one who is a master of his nature; brahma – spiritual world; cāvyayam = ca (and) + avayayam (the imperishable); āpnoti – attains; hitvā – having abandoned; deham – body; aśāśvatam – not eternal, perishable

Being proficient in yoga, the person who is a master of his nature, creates for the self a divine psychology which is like that of the supernatural controllers. Having abandoned the perishable body, that person attains the imperishable spiritual world.

Analysis:

This is the most secret information about how the spiritual self which is in the material creation gets away from here and gains entry into the eternal world, the spiritual place. The spirit, using its bare spiritual self, creates for itself a spiritual form out of itself.

The spiritual form unlike the subtle body does not have adjuncts or psychic equipments which were given by a deity or by material nature or by both. It is out of the spirit itself that the senses of the spiritual body are developed. No additional material from anywhere is used. No fusion with any other anything is accomplished in the manifestation of the spiritual form.

If anything the spirit should take a hint from how a material body is created and used as well as how a subtle body is produced and used, to get the view about how a spiritual form with limbs and senses could develop from just the spiritual raw material of the core-self.

Application:

There are two sets of deities who preside over this creation. The lower set are the archangels (devas or devatas) in the astral heavens. These persons are permanent residents of the astral paradises. Their life-spans are incredible when compared to the lifetime of a human being. For all practical purposes, these entities are gods. Their creative power is so fantastic that compared to a human they are all-powerful and can create worlds. As an aborigine riding in a canoe can hardly understand the life of a shipping magnate in a developed country, so a human being cannot fathom the life of these lower deities who have personal realms in the astral paradises and vast creative powers.

And yet these persons are the lower deities. Apart from these there are the highest deities who may or may not have registry in the astral or material world. These beings are Krishna and His parallel divinities. They are permanent residents in the spiritual world which is beyond the astral existence.

As materialistic beings we are focused on this earthly life. As astral beings the lower deities are focused on the higher astral dimensions. As spiritual beings Krishna and his associates are focused on the spiritual dimensions. That is the varied situations.

We develop first as physical beings. When we suspect that condition we strive to become astral beings. Attaining the status of the astral people, we remain in that category for some time. When we suspect that, we aspire to be spiritual beings. Then we strive to attain the last and best of the categories.

It is a rare yogi who is translated directly from a material body to a spiritual one without first spending millions of years in the subtle world of the lower deities. Usually an entity moves from physical existence to subtle existence and then after millions of years gets an idea to move to the spiritual level which is the final frontier.

Mudgal whose history is described elsewhere in the Mahābhārata, is an example of a person who developed a spiritual body while using an earthly one and who then transited through the astral heavens and attained the spiritual dimensions. His situation is exceptional because even the Pandavas, Arjuna and his brothers, are reported to have gone to the Swarga heavenly places after departure from their bodies in the same life in which Krishna told this Anu Gītā *to Arjuna.*

Verse 26

विनश्यत्स्वपि लोकेषु न भयं तस्य जायते

क्लिश्यमानेषु भूतेषु न स क्लिश्यति केनचित्

vinaśyatsvapi lokeṣu na bhayaṁ tasya jāyate
kliśyamāneṣu bhūteṣu na sa kliśyati kenacit (4.26)

vinaśyatsv = vinaśyatsu = in the destruction; api – also; lokeṣu – in the world; na – no; bhayaṁ - fear; tasya – of him; jāyate – is developed; kliśyamāneṣu – in pain; bhūteṣu – in the beings; na – not; sa – he; kliśyati - afflicted; kenacit - anyone

If the world was destroyed, no fear would develop in him. If all beings were pained, he would not be afflicted by anyone.

Analysis:

If a spirit transfers its focus to the exclusive spiritual environment, it would be immune to the threats which ravish the material and astral worlds. When a person gains proficiency in astral projection, dangers to the physical body are not regarded as substantial threats, but the subtle body is also threatened by high frequency ravishes. It is based on light energy, just as the material body is based on material substances.

When the light frequencies of the cosmos are destroyed or violently transformed in cosmic explosions, some of the subtle bodies are either fatally affected or killed instantly. This means that even the astral body is perishable even though it is much more durable than a material form.

Advanced yogis are not fascinated by the astral bodies because those forms will face extinction in the far-away future just as these material bodies will definitely be destroyed in a short time-span.

Animals frolic and play and pay no attention to the fact that their bodies will only last for a few more orbits of the earth around the sun. Similarly those who are not aware of the potential for astral decay enjoy in their astral forms for the time being.

Application:

The idea of suffering relates only the type of body used. The soul is incapable of suffering by a direct physical means. This was explained by Krishna to Arjuna in this way:

nainaṁ chindanti śastrāṇi nainaṁ dahati pāvakaḥ
na cainaṁ kledayantyāpo na śoṣayati mārutaḥ (2.23)
acchedyo'yamadāhyo'yam akledyo'śoṣya eva ca
nityaḥ sarvagataḥ sthāṇur acalo'yaṁ sanātanaḥ (2.24)

Weapons do not pierce, fire does not burn, and water does not wet, nor does the wind dry that embodied soul.

This embodied soul cannot be pierced, cannot be burnt, cannot be moistened and cannot be dried. And indeed, this soul is eternal. It can penetrate all things. It is a permanent principle and is stable and primeval. (Bhagavad Gītā 2.23-24)

If the soul is not directly affected by physical means, it seems to be affected because it is linked to a supernatural mechanism which absorbs the subtle aspect of material activities. So long as the soul is linked with these psychic technologies, it will feel as if it is affected.

Hence it is important to take Patanjali's advice for the segregation of the spiritual self from the perceiving technologies.

Verse 27

दुःखशोकमयैर्घोरैः सङ्गस्नेहसमुद्भवैः

न विचाल्येत युक्तात्मा निःस्पृहः शान्तमानसः

duḥkhaśokamayairghoraiḥ saṅgasnehasamudbhavaiḥ
na vicālyeta yuktātmā niḥspṛhaḥ śāntamānasaḥ (4.27)

duḥkha – distress; śoka – distress; mayair – by psychosis; ghoraiḥ - by horrors; saṅga – attachment; sneha – affection; samudbhavaiḥ - feelings; na – not; vicālyeta – affected; yuktātmā – yogically-proficient person; niḥspṛhaḥ - free from attachment; śāntamānasaḥ - spiritually pacified mind

In regards to the horrors and psychosis of happiness and distress, the feelings of affection and attachment, the yogically proficient person is not affected by it. That one is free from attachment and has a mind which is spiritually-pacified.

Analysis:

The cultivation of detachment which is reinforced by sensual restraint and trance states in meditation results in a psyche which is spiritually-pacified. Many instances of harassment which are suffered by others, are endured by a mature yogi without stress.

The yogi trains the intellect not to respond to much of what the senses perceive. He infuses the kundalini with fresh breath energy which makes it change its sensitivity.

Application:

By internal investigation of how the core-self is linked to the perception equipments, a yogi from within the psyche learns how to disconnect or at least to reduce the feedback between the self and the psychic adjuncts. This gives an advantage whereby the yogi can select safe non-reactionary responses to circumstance.

A student should persist in practice, day after day, until the internal psyche becomes insightful and the various components of consciousness are sorted satisfactorily.

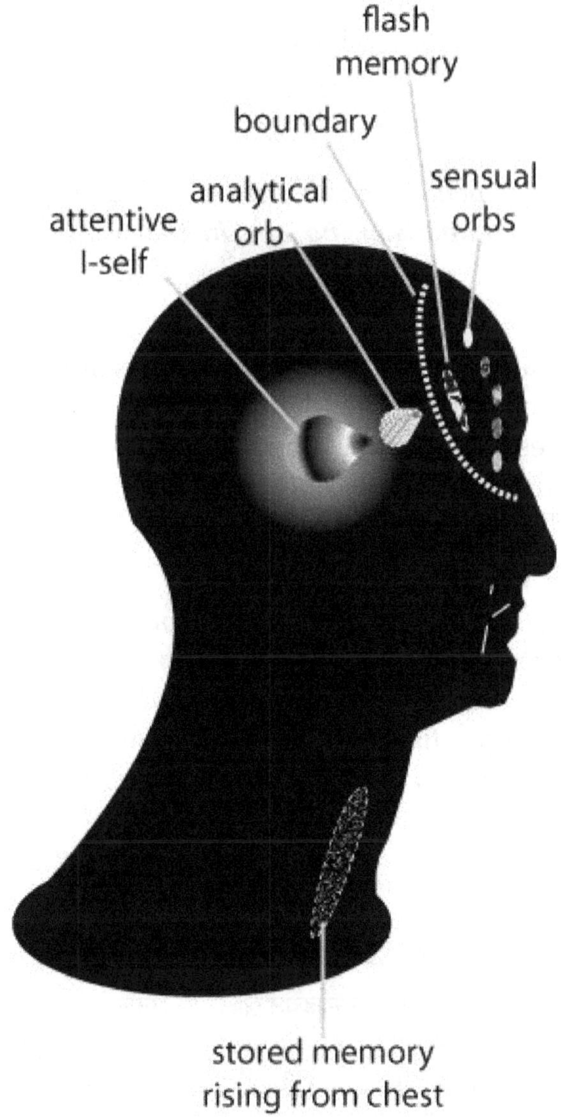

Verse 28

नैनं शस्त्राणि विध्यन्ते न मृत्युश्चास्य विद्यते

नातः सुखतरं किंचिल्लोके क्वचन विद्यते

nainaṁ śastrāṇi vidhyante na mṛtyuścāsya vidyate
nātaḥ sukhataraṁ kiṁcilloke kvacana vidyate (4.28)

nainaṁ = na (not) + enam (this); śastrāṇi – weapons; vidhyante – penetrate; na – not; mṛtyuś = mṛtyuh = death; cāsya = ca (and) + asya (of this); vidyate – affect; nātaḥ = na (not) + atah (hence); sukhataraṁ - happier than; kiṁcil = kiṁcit = anyone; loke – in the world; kvacana – where; vidyate – is existing

Weapons do not penetrate this person, nor does death affect this one. Hence in comparison, no one in the world is happier than this person.

Analysis:

Theoretically, we can accept that if the self is eternal, it need not be bothered with mortal dangers. However, the truth is that most creatures are affected drastically by wounds and fatality. An individual can transcend this by achieving the self-realization described by this great yogi.

Application:

The technique is to switch the focus of the self to the spiritual side of existence. One should retract one's interest in the material world and find a spiritual locale where it can be applied fittingly. In the meantime however, one should meditate regularly, identify the mental machinery and segregate the core-self from it.

Verse 29

सम्यग्युक्त्वा यदात्मानमात्मन्येव प्रपश्यति

तदैव न स्पृहयते साक्षादपि शतक्रतोः

samyagyuktvā yadātmānamātmanyeva prapaśyati
tadaiva na spṛhayate sākṣādapi śatakratoḥ (4.29)

samyag – full, adequate; yuktvā – being proficient in yoga practice; yadātmānam = yadā (when) + ātmānam (spiritual self); ātmany = ātmani = in the psyche; eva – even so; prapaśyati – perceives; tadaiva = tadā (then) + eva (so); na – no; spṛhayate – feels endearment; sākṣād – special, direct; api – also; śatakratoḥ - Indra who performed one hundred religious ceremonies

When being fully proficient in yoga practice, that person perceives the spiritual self in the psyche, then he feels no special endearment to Shatakratu Indra, the celestial king who did one hundred religious ceremonies.

Analysis:

If a yogi achieves partial proficiency in yoga, that person will reach the heavenly world of Indra, the celestial being who became famous for completing one hundred very special religious rites. Indra's paradise is fabulous but a visitor from the earth, can only remain in that place for as long as the effect-energy of the pious work on earth is not exhausted.

Whoever does what is desired by Indra, is recognized and rewarded by that deity in the afterlife but only for so long as the effect-energies are supportive. As soon as the piety effects are finished, the migrant experiences a fading away from that heavenly place and a presence in the lower astral regions which are adjacent to this earthly place.

Some neophytes who do not develop the full proficiency before death of the physical body, may avoid having to go to Indra's paradise, if those ascetics develop a resistance to heavenly pleasures and have a connection with the siddhas who practice yoga on the astral planes.

Application:

People who are dreaming about heaven, those who think that their pious social acts will be rewarded by God or by a deity, may after the death of the body, travel to an astral paradise where they would enjoy legendary pleasures and experience super-luxuries and unimaginable prosperity.

It is unfortunate that this elevation will come to an end as soon as the effect-energy of their pious activities on earth is dissipated. Then in disappointment, and with grief they will find themselves fading away from those heavenly places; their celestial bodies which elevated them to indescribable beauty with multicolors suitably mixed, turns grey and dusty.

Suddenly without warning they find themselves on the lower astral planes with people who are seeking to acquire physical bodies. In that plight they might cry in sorrow but they will begin looking for the next father and mother who will give the opportunity for them to become human babies.

A student yogi should in the astral projections go to the celestial heavens which are ruled by the Indra deity. The yogi does this to test his attraction to such places. This gives the student some idea of the areas of his psyche which need improvement. Attraction to the deity of the astral heavens, is a sure indication of a lack of proficiency in yoga practice. Resistance to Indra's influence or a natural indifference to the status of this Indra deity is a sure sign of yoga progress.

Verse 30

निर्वेदस्तु न गन्तव्यो युञ्जानेन कथंचन

योगमेकान्तशीलस्तु यथा युञ्जीत तच्छृणु

nirvedastu na gantavyo yuñjānena kathaṁcana
yogamekāntaśīlastu yathā yuñjīta tacchṛṇu (4.30)

nirvedas = nirvedah = discouraged; tu – but; na – not; gantavyo = gantavyah = attained; yuñjānena – with proficiency in yoga; kathaṁcana – anyway; yogam – yoga; ekānta = eka (one, primary) + anta (end, objective); śīlas = śīlah = behavior, lifestyle; tu – but; yathā – as; yuñjīta - proficiency in yogic trance; tac = tat = that; chṛṇu = śṛṇu = hear

But one who is attaining the proficiency in yoga practice, should not be discouraged. Hear about this how one whose primary objective in life is yoga, practices trance consistently.

Analysis:

A person who is partially trained in yoga should have no delusions about what will happen hereafter. One should abandon all desire to go to the astral heavens. Unknown to most persons on this earth, the yogi gets special treatment in the astral world, even better treatment than those who do national or global pious work.

As soon as a yogi leaves the body, he might be greeted by angelic women. If the yogi is female she might be greeted by attractive angelic males. Such celestial beings want to get the austerity energy of yogi because that energy is very pleasing and produces a bliss effect in the celestial bodies. If the yogi was adept at the practice of kundalini yoga, a pleasure energy will be travelling upward in the subtle body. This energy is much desired by the angelic hosts.

This is dangerous for a neophyte since he or she might become infatuated when greeted in that glorious way. In all respects, meeting with angelic people in the afterlife is a great danger to a yogi, for it can make the ascetic forget his or her hard-earned austerities. Yogis who make such mistakes do learn over time, that rendezvous with heavenly attendants is no advantage for a yogi.

Application:

Yoga is based on personal practice and assistance given by advanced ascetics and divine beings. A yogi should be confident that Krishna, Shiva or Balaram will by their grace show the way of successful austerities. However it is not that the course will be easy in every instance. Some of it will be completed with great difficulty. Still the yogi should persist.

Verse 31

दृष्टपूर्वां दिशं चिन्त्य यस्मिन्संनिवसेत्पुरे

पुरस्याभ्यन्तरे तस्य मनश्चार्यं न बाह्यतः

dṛṣṭapūrvāṁ diśaṁ cintya yasminsaṁnivasetpure
purasyābhyantare tasya manaścāryaṁ na bāhyataḥ (4.31)

dṛṣṭa – seen; pūrvāṁ - before; diśaṁ - place; cintya – thinking; yasmin – in which; saṁnivaset – should reside; pure – in the city; purasyābhyantare = purasya (of the city or psyche) + abhyantare (in the interior, inside); tasya – of his; manaś = manah = mind; cāryaṁ - behavior, operation; na – not; bāhyataḥ - outside

When thinking of a place which was seen before, one should reside in the city in which the incidence occurred. The mental operations are within the psyche, not outside of it.

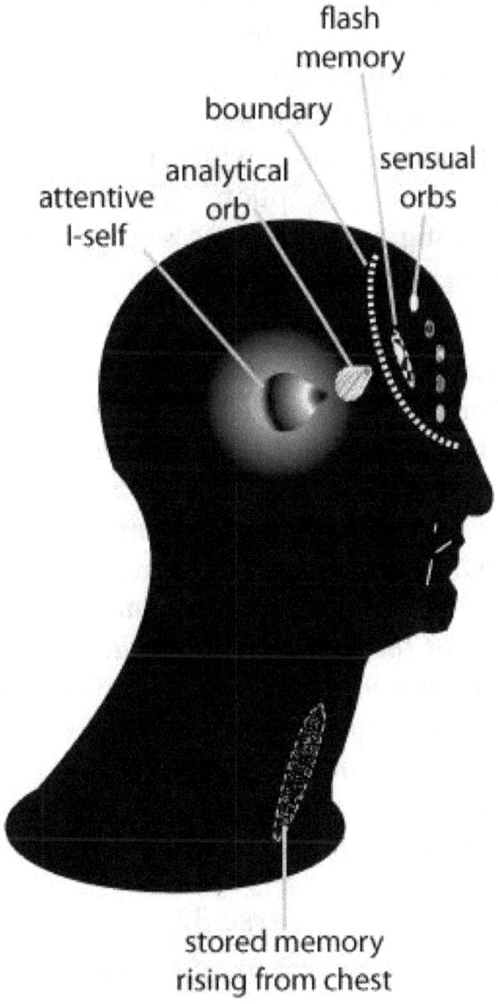

Analysis:

To study a city in detail one should go to that city and take a tour. Even if one has seen the city before, the memory of it is not as realistic as being in the actual place. The research of the psyche which one mistook for the self initially, deserves a very detailed tour. To so this one should go into the psyche to investigate.

Introspection means that the core-self which lives in the psyche, turns its attention to what is in the psyche and abandons the investigation of the external world.

Initially to go within, does not mean to go within the core-self. It means to go within the psyche to discover all the components of consciousness which combined with the core-self allow physical perception. The core-self cannot be successfully investigated until it is segregated from the other psychic accessories.

Application:

Kriya yoga is a lonely process because the core-self is required to abandon its extrovert pursuits. It is required to be introverted which means that it should withdraw the attention which flows through the senses into the external world. The self has to use its attention energy to investigate all locations within the mind space. It has to segregate the core-self from everything else in the psyche. It should analyze to determine the function of each of the components. It should also calculate its dependence on each psychic technology within the mind space.

There are gateways to other dimensions in the psyche. When the self stops the intellect from gyrations, these entries to other dimensions will manifest to the yogi. All transfers to other dimensions can be made from within the mind space.

Verse 32

पुरस्याभ्यन्तरे तिष्ठन्यस्मिन्नावसथे वसेत्

तस्मिन्नावसथे धार्यं सबाह्याभ्यन्तरं मनः

purasyābhyantare tiṣṭhanyasminnāvasathe vaset
tasminnāvasathe dhāryaṁ sabāhyābhyantaraṁ manaḥ (4.32)

purasyābhyantare = (purasya of the city) + abhyantare (inside); tiṣṭhany = tiṣṭhani = situated; asmin – in this; nāvasathe = na (not) + avasathe (city); vaset – should reside; tasmin – in this; nāvasathe = na (not) + avasathe (city); dhāryaṁ - absorbed in; sa – with; bāhyābhyantaraṁ = bāhya (exterior) + abhyantaram (interior); manaḥ - mind

Being situated inside the city, he should reside there with his mind absorbed in the exterior and interior features of that place.

Analysis:

This is the beginning of rāj yoga practice. This is also known as kriyā yoga, advanced ashtanga yoga, buddhi yoga, insight yoga and by many other names.

The psyche is sometimes called the self. Many persons mistake the psyche as the self. They say that by entering the mind, one enters the self. The lack of distinction within consciousness causes many persons to experience the connecting-consciousness of the various components as the self. That is not the self but it will suffice as that so long as one cannot distinguish the various components of consciousness.

The psyche is like a city. The self is like an inhabitant in that city. This city of the psyche is not the self but the self cannot understand that so long as it is not segregated from the other components. The psyche is a psychological environment in which there are psychic organs and a specific core-self.

The yoga-guru advised Kashyapa to go on a tour of the psyche. He did not say, 'You are the psyche. It is all one.' He wanted Kashyapa to distinguish between the self and the existential technologies in the psyche.

Application:

A yogi should crack the puzzle of how the mind operates on the inside, as well as how it relates to what occurs on the outside of the mind and also on the outside of the physical body.

The brain and spine are regulators of the actions of the body. The intellect and the kundalini are the regulators of the actions of the subtle body. The self should discover how these actions take place. Since it is liable for the activity of the mind and body, the self would serve itself a favor by directly comprehending how the mind operates.

Verse 33

प्रचिन्त्यावसथं कृत्स्नं यस्मिन्कायेऽवतिष्ठते

तस्मिन्काये मनश्चार्यं न कथंचन बाह्यतः

pracintyāvasathaṁ kṛtsnaṁ yasminkāye'vatiṣṭhate
tasminkāye manaścāryaṁ na kathaṁcana bāhyataḥ (4.33)

pracintyāvasathaṁ = pracintya = meditating; kṛtsnaṁ - whole reality; yasmin – in which; kāye – in the body; 'vatiṣṭhate = avatiṣṭhate = being situated; tasmin – in that; kāye – in the body; manaś = manah = whole; cāryaṁ - wander; na – not; kathaṁcana – any way; bāhyataḥ - outside

Meditating in that place, the self sees the whole reality being situated in the body. The mind should not in any way wander outside the body.

Analysis:

During meditation, the mind should not wander outside of the body. This means that the core-self should compel the adjuncts to cease procuring sensual objectives which are in the external physical world and in the external psychic world. The adjuncts are disinclined to this introversion but a student yogi has the task to make the self comply with this demand.

So long as the subtle body is fused into the physical one, meditation within the physical one could provide access to other dimensions. The subtle body is connected to the other dimensions in the subtle world. From within the subtle body one can reach any of the subtle existences.

Application:

Everything the self needs for clarity regarding what the psyche is, what its relationship to the physical, subtle and spiritual worlds is, as well as what the other components of the psyche should function as, is available in the psyche itself. However even though it is true that a person can locate everything needed in the psyche, just as Gautama Buddha did, some of the needed items become visible in the psyche after particular types of meditations. Some components in the psyche must go through alteration before these psychic gadgets can be of any use in locating higher worlds.

From within the psyche the core-self can go to other astral or spiritual environments which are outside the core self. In the mind chamber, the core-self should locate the intellect which is outside of the core-self but is in the mind, just as the core self is. There is a sense of identity which is distinct from the core self and which is in the mind as well. All of this becomes visible when the core-self learns how to distinguish itself from the other psychic components.

Verse 34

संनियम्येन्द्रियग्रामं निर्घोषे निर्जने वने

कायमभ्यन्तरं कृत्स्नमेकाग्रः परिचिन्तयेत्

saṁniyamyendriyagrāmaṁ nirghoṣe nirjane vane
kāyamabhyantaraṁ kṛtsnamekāgraḥ paricintayet (4.34)

saṁniyamyendriya = saṁniyamya (completely restraining) + indriya (sensual energies); grāmaṁ - aggregate; nirghoṣe – without noise; nirjane – without people; vane – in the forest; kāyam – body; abhyantaraṁ - inside; kṛtsnam – whole reality; ekāgraḥ - one object of focus; paricintayet – deeply meditate

In an uninhabited and noiseless forest, while completely restraining the aggregate sensual energies, he should deeply meditate within the body on the whole reality as one object of focus.

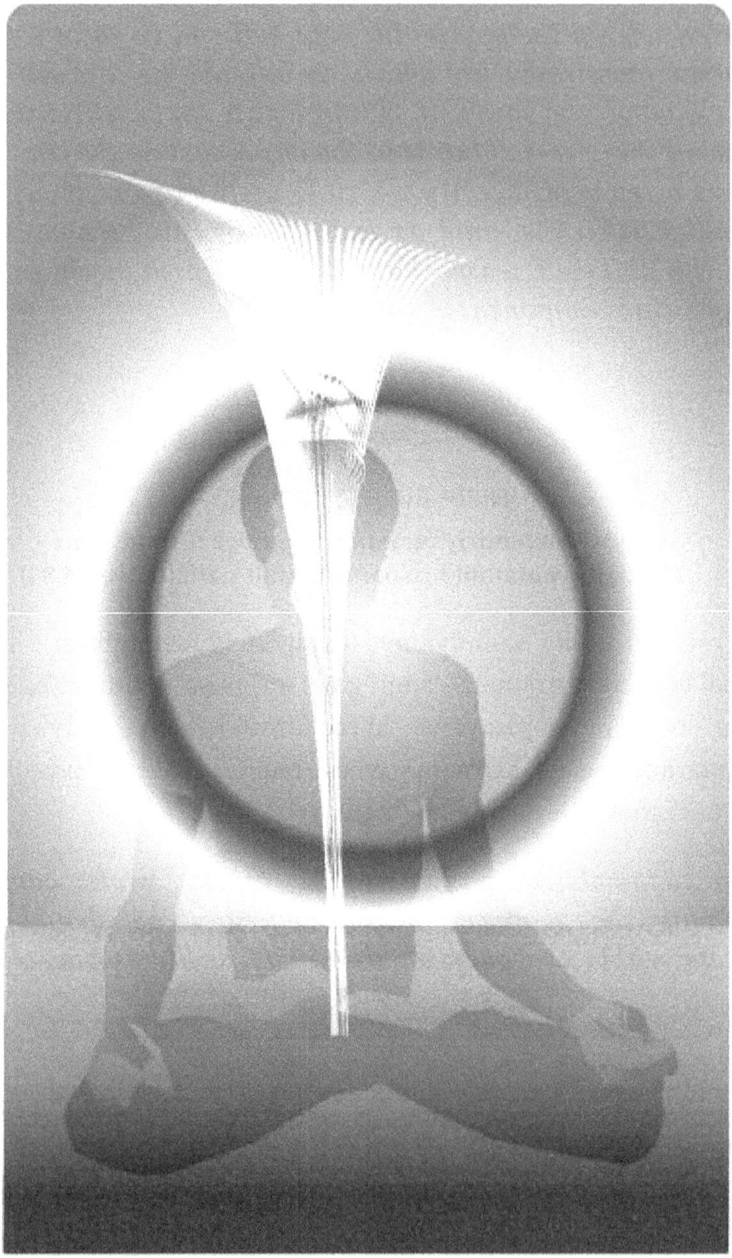

Analysis:

In meditation, it is possible for the yogi to see the vast array of dimensions as one reality. This becomes possible for a yogi who restrained the aggregate sensual energies. The advice of Patanjali on this practice is clear:

yogaḥcittavṛtti nirodhaḥ

The skill of yoga is demonstrated by the conscious non-operation of the vibrational modes of the mento-emotional energy. (Yoga Sūtras 1.2)

Application:

Even though the whole existence is one reality, still there is perpetual diversity in it. It is not one whole existence without differentiation within it. The diversity is just as perpetual as the oneness of it.

The requirement for a location in which to meditate to this advanced level is an uninhabited and noiseless forest, a place which is free of the humbug human civilizations. The mind is sensitive to external stimuli. Thus the yogi should deprive the mind of a place which is littered with much social activity. Then it will be easier to achieve advanced trance states.

Verse 35

दन्तांस्तालु च जिह्वां च गलं ग्रीवां तथैव च

हृदयं चिन्तयेच्चापि तथा हृदयबन्धनम्

dantāṁstālu ca jihvāṁ ca galaṁ grīvāṁ tathaiva ca
hṛdayaṁ cintayeccāpi tathā hṛdayabandhanam (4.35)

dantāṁ = dantān = teeth; stālu – palate; ca – and; jihvāṁ - tongue; ca – and; galaṁ - throat; grīvāṁ - neck; tathaiva – so even; ca – and; hṛdayaṁ - heart; cintayec = cintayet = should meditate; cāpi = ca (and) + api (also); tathā – as well; hṛdaya – heart; bandhanam – whatever blocks

The teeth, palate, tongue, throat as well as the neck and the heart; on these he should meditate and on what blocks the heart.

Analysis:

The yogi should research all parts of the psyche not just the components in the head. The psyche goes with the entity when it finally leaves the body at death. Thus meditation practice should not be restricted to the head only. Below the base of the brain is the spinal column which runs the length of the trunk of the body. This is the physical manifestation of the kundalini life force. A yogi should study this energy. Even though the kundalini does not use the head of the body as its default location, still it affects what occurs in the head. One should study how kundalini spreads its influence through the psyche.

Application:

Some defects in the physical body are mimicked in the subtle form. Even though a yogi's primary concern is the subtle body, he or she should pay attention to the gross form, at least in so far as there is feedback between the two systems. If oxygenated blood from the lungs does not reach the heart, there will be ill health in the body. And this is only a description of the physical effects.

Pranaiama yoga is for the efficient flow of energy in the subtle body. Wherever there is blockage there is inefficient use of the energy. This causes a dulling of the consciousness which is not in the interest of the yogi.

Verse 36

इत्युक्तः स मया शिष्यो मेधावी मधुसूदन

पप्रच्छ पुनरेवेमं मोक्षधर्मं सुदुर्वचम्

ityuktaḥ sa mayā śiṣyo medhāvī madhusūdana
papraccha punarevemaṁ mokṣadharmaṁ sudurvacam (4.36)

ity = iti = thus; uktaḥ - as heard; sa – that; mayā – by me; śiṣyo = śiṣyah = student; medhāvī – intelligent; madhusūdana – killer of Madhu; papraccha – inquired; punar = punah = again; evemaṁ = eva (so) + imam (this); mokṣadharmaṁ - lifestyle which facilitates liberation; sudurvacam – what is difficult to describe

Hear as it was heard by me, O Krishna, killer of Madhu, what that intelligent student, again inquired about the lifestyle which results in liberation, and which is so difficult to describe.

Analysis:

The greatest secret in the material world is the information about how to use a human being to attain complete liberation. When it gets right down to it, the living being does not want to continue in this perverse existence, especially if there is an alternative world which is trouble free and which is compatible to the spiritual self.

Application:

A student yogi must hear again and again, about the technique which causes a being to master the lifestyle which results in liberation. The details of the process are rife with complications. It is understood fully over time after hearing of it repeatedly and after practicing in many life-times.

Verse 37

भुक्तं भुक्तं कथमिदमन्नं कोष्ठे विपच्यते

कथं रसत्वं व्रजति शोणितं जायते कथम्

तथा मांसं च मेदश्च स्नाय्वस्थीनि च पोषति

bhuktaṁ bhuktaṁ kathamidamannaṁ koṣṭhe vipacyate
kathaṁ rasatvaṁ vrajati śoṇitaṁ jāyate katham
tathā māṁsaṁ ca medaśca snāyvasthīni ca poṣati (4.37)

bhuktaṁ bhuktaṁ = repeatedly tasting; katham – how; idam – this; annaṁ - food; koṣṭhe – in the stomach; vipacyate – is eaten; kathaṁ - how; rasatvaṁ - hormones; vrajati – produced; śoṇitaṁ - blood; jāyate – creator; katham – how; tathā - as for; māṁsaṁ - flesh; ca – and; medaś = medah = bone marrow; ca – and; snāyv = snāyu = tendon; asthīni – muscle; ca – and; poṣati - nourish

How after repeatedly tasting, does this food become digested in the stomach? How are hormones produced? How is blood

created? As for flesh, bone marrow, tendons and bones, how are these nourished?

Analysis:

Is it important for a soul to understand how it is connected to the material body. The connection is indirect. Some of it is through proximity only, by influence. One who understands exactly how a soul can acquire a material body and become responsible for the activities of that form, can approach the quest for liberation. Others do not have sufficient interest to urge them to seek freedom from these rebirths.

Application:

The spiritual influence of the individual spirit is the main power source for the subtle body and the gross form. The digestive operations of the material body, are in part sponsored by the spirit's diffused power which is used by the life force to complete survival functions.

Verse 38

कथमेतानि सर्वाणि शरीराणि शरीरिणाम्

वर्धन्ते वर्धमानस्य वर्धते च कथं बलम्

निरोजसां निष्क्रमणं मलानां च पृथक्पृथक्

kathametāni sarvāṇi śarīrāṇi śarīriṇām
vardhante vardhamānasya vardhate ca kathaṁ balam
nirojasāṁ niṣkramaṇaṁ malānāṁ ca pṛthakpṛthak (4.38)

katham – how; etāni – these; sarvāṇi – all; śarīrāṇi – bodies, śarīriṇām – in the body (of the mother); vardhante – they are growing; vardhamānasya – of the growing human being; vardhate – growing; ca – and; kathaṁ - how; balam – strength; nirojasāṁ - of the non-vitalizing substances, niṣkramaṇaṁ - what is expelled; malānāṁ - excrement; ca – and; pṛthakpṛthak - especially

How do these bodies develop in the body (of the mother)? How is strength produced out of the growing human being as the body increases in size? How are the pollutants and excrement removed from the body, being separated from the nutrients?

How are non-vitalizing substances and especially pollutants, expelled from the body?

Analysis:

It is really a miracle how a fetus develops in the womb of the mother. It is something we take for granted but from a scientific view, it is very amazing that nature can operate life forms and cause reproduction.

Once created how does an infant body grow into maturity? How is the body maintained within itself by itself even without the supervision of the self which is encased in the psyche.

Wherefrom has material nature derived such creative intelligence?

Application:

We experience that some retarded persons have healthy bodies which live for many years. Obviously the body maintains itself irrespective of the intelligence of the entity who is psychically encased in it. How is that possible?

Verse 39

कुतो वायं प्रश्वसिति उच्छ्वसित्यपि वा पुनः

कं च देशमधिष्ठाय तिष्ठत्यात्मायमात्मनि

kuto vāyaṁ praśvasiti ucchvasityapi vā punaḥ
kaṁ ca deśamadhiṣṭhāya tiṣṭhatyātmāyamātmani (4.39)

kuto = kutah = how; vāyaṁ - vital energy; praśvasiti - inhaling; ucchvasity = ucchvasiti = exhaling; api – also; vā – or; punaḥ - again; kaṁ - what; ca – and; deśam – location; adhiṣṭhāya – set place, default; tiṣṭhaty = tiṣṭhati = situates; ātmāyam – self; ātmani – in the psyche

How does one inhale and again exhale the vital energy? What is the default location of the self, which is situated in the personal psyche?

Analysis:

Everything which is automatically being done by material nature is a reminder that the self is not centralized but is only a useful side feature to nature. The self might be compared to the power supply which is used in a computer. It has value and the computer is inoperable without it, and still it is taken for granted by the consumer.

Application:

A person finds the process of yoga after becoming aware of the self as just a component in the psyche. Is it the one component which has full autonomy?

When the psyche turns in on itself, there is a discovery that there is a core-self which mistook itself for the psyche. Then it becomes essential to discover the default location of that core-self and to figure how it can gain leverage over the psychology.

Verse 40

जीवः कायं वहति चेच्चेष्टयानः कलेवरम्

किंवर्णं कीदृशं चैव निवेशयति वै मनः

याथातथ्येन भगवन्वक्तुमर्हसि मेऽनघ

jīvaḥ kāyaṁ vahati ceccesṭayānaḥ kalevaram
kiṁvarṇaṁ kīdṛśaṁ caiva niveśayati vai manaḥ
yāthātathyena bhagavanvaktumarhasi me'nagha (4.40)

jīvaḥ - individual spirit; kāyaṁ - body; vahati - tolerate; cec = cet = when; ceṣṭayānaḥ - exertion; kalevaram – of the body; kiṁ - what; varṇaṁ - color; kīdṛśaṁ - what kind, characteristic; caiva – and even; niveśayati - it leaves; vai – indeed; manaḥ - the human being; yāthātathyena - with complete details; bhagavan – person deserving of the highest honor; vaktum – explanation; arhasi – you speak; me – to me; 'nagha = anagha = purity personified

How, by exertion, does the individual spirit within the body, carry the body? What color and what characteristic does the mind have when it leaves the body? O purity personified, person deserving of the highest honor, you may explain this to me in as detailed a way as possible.

Analysis:

Does the self make a psychic exertion to mobilize the physical body? Is the mind colorless? Does it have characteristics? Can it be perceived objectively once it makes a permanent exit from the material body?

Application:

If the spirit is a perpetual energy source, how is its power distributed to the material body. When the material body dies where does the spirit focus itself for acting again as a power supply.

Can the mind chamber be seen visually? Can a spirit be perceived directly?

Verse 41

इति संपरिपृष्टोऽहं तेन विप्रेण माधव

प्रत्यब्रुवं महाबाहो यथाश्रुतमरिंदम

iti saṁpariprṣṭo'haṁ tena vipreṇa mādhava
pratyabruvaṁ mahābāho yathāśrutamariṁdama (4.41)

iti – thus; saṁpariprṣṭo = saṁpariprṣṭah = fittingly questioned; 'haṁ = aham = I; tena – by him; vipreṇa – by the learnt ritualist; mādhava – Madhava Krishna; pratyabruvaṁ - replied, answered; mahābāho – person with powerful arms; yathā – as; śrutam – heard; ariṁdama – chastiser of the rebellious souls

As fittingly questioned, O Madhava Krishna, that learnt ritualist answered him (Kashyapa). I replied just as I heard, O person with powerful arms, chastiser of rebels.

Analysis:

This information is valid for all time, for all persons who are serious about transcending material nature.

Application:

Today, the psyche of the human being is just as it was thousands of years ago. Despite the progression of civilization the configuration of the components of the psyche remain the same. The remedy which worked thousands of years ago can still be applied effectively.

Verse 42

यथा स्वकोष्ठे प्रक्षिप्य कोष्ठं भाण्डमना भवेत्

तथा स्वकाये प्रक्षिप्य मनो द्वारैरनिश्चलैः

आत्मानं तत्र मार्गेत प्रमादं परिवर्जयेत्

yathā svakoṣṭhe prakṣipya koṣṭhaṁ bhāṇḍamanā bhavet
tathā svakāye prakṣipya mano dvārairaniścalaiḥ
ātmānaṁ tatra mārgeta pramādaṁ parivarjayet (4.42)

yathā – as; svakoṣṭhe – in personal storage; prakṣipya – by placing; koṣṭhaṁ - storage room; bhāṇḍamanā – in possession; bhavet – becomes; tathā – so; svakāye – in a body; prakṣipya – by placing; mano = manah = mind; dvārair = dvāraih = by the orifices; aniścalaiḥ - restricting; ātmānaṁ - spiritual self; tatra – here; mārgeta – should research; pramādaṁ - delusion, distractions; parivarjayet – renounce, avoid

As placing property in storage, one becomes the possessor of it, so placing the mind in the body, and restricting the orifices, one should research the self and avoid distractions.

Analysis:

When someone puts something in storage, that person is liable for the property. The self is held responsible for the activities of the physical body as well as for the operations of the subtle form. Hence it makes sense that the self should regulate both systems.

The same psychic mechanism which pursues sense objects, must be used to discover the components of consciousness. To do this the intellect has to forego its thought-production and image-creation stunts. When the intellect ceases these psychic maneuvers, the core self will be empowered for self-research.

Application:

The freedom of the self to make itself available as a power supply is not in its interest. It was by seduction that material nature encouraged the self to give itself over for usage of its power at its expense. This is very unfortunate for the self, even though it is an advantage for material nature.

Verse 43

एवं सततमुद्युक्तः प्रीतात्मा नचिरादिव

आसादयति तद्ब्रह्म यद्दृष्ट्वा स्यात्प्रधानवित्

evaṁ satatamudyuktaḥ prītātmā nacirādiva
āsādayati tadbrahma yaddṛṣṭvā syātpradhānavit (4.43)

evaṁ - thus; satatam – always; udyuktaḥ - meditatively absorbed; prītātmā – pleased in the self; nacirād – soon; iva – as if; āsādayati – thrown, transited; tad = tat = that; brahma – spiritual level of existence; yad = yat = that; dṛṣṭvā – being perceptive; syāt – may, is; pradhānavit – knowing the life force energy potential

Thus, being always meditatively absorbed and being pleased in the self, one is soon transited to the spiritual level of existence after becoming perceptive of the life force energy potential.

Analysis:

Somehow the spiritual self became linked to an individual kundalini life force. This energy sponsors and maintains the struggle for existence. It is forever doing this and doing that which leads to the self having to follow that life force through numerous transmigrations.

One may get some ideas of how to become free from this life force. How was the entity connected to this energy in the first place? How can it now unlink itself from this psychic mechanism?

Application:

Without mysticism a self cannot become liberated. The self should review its history to see how it was fused with the psychic components. A slave who cannot remember how he was captured, can still design an effective escape. It requires knowledge of the slave-owner's habits and the methods used to keep the slave under control.

Verse 44

न त्वसौ चक्षुषा ग्राह्यो न च सर्वैरपीन्द्रियैः

मनसैव प्रदीपेन महानात्मनि दृश्यते

na tvasau cakṣuṣā grāhyo na ca sarvairapīndriyaiḥ
manasaiva pradīpena mahānātmani dṛśyate (4.44)

na – not; tv = tu = but; asau – by two; cakṣuṣā – by eyes; grāhyo = grāhyah = grasped, comprehended; na – not; ca – and; sarvair = sarvaih = all; apīndriyaiḥ = api (also) + indriyaiḥ (by the senses);

manasa – by the mind; iva – as if; pradīpena – by the vision; mahān – supreme; ātmani – self; dṛśyate – is perceived

It is not comprehended by the eyes, or by any of the senses. It is by the vision of the mind, that the supreme spiritual self can be perceived.

Analysis:

The physical senses do not have the range of perception required for personal investigation of the psyche. As modern civilization takes help from science, so the self must open its psychic perception if it wants to pry into the secrets of how it is fused into material nature.

Physical vision is itself evidence of psychic perception. Physical vision is here because a transcendent self is linked to psychic means of perception, which in turn are empowering the physical eyes. The task is to unlink the psychic perception equipments from the physical system. If a yogi accomplishes this, he or she can experience vision using the psyche when it is disconnected from the physical senses.

Application:

The first direct evidence which a spirit gets about its capacity for psychic vision comes when it daydreams or when it has a revelation in the frontal part of the head. The second piece of evidence is perception of the astral domains during an astral projection. Since these are subjective experiences, they are sometimes dismissed as hallucinations.

However a yogi should not be daunted by people who are doubtful about psychic perception. There is no need to argue with such people. The yogi should proceed with meditation practice, until he or she gains the required proficiency for consistent psychic perception.

Verse 45

सर्वतःपाणिपादं तं सर्वतोक्षिशिरोमुखम्

जीवो निष्क्रान्तमात्मानं शरीरात्संप्रपश्यति

sarvataḥpāṇipādaṁ taṁ sarvatokṣiśiromukham
jīvo niṣkrāntamātmānaṁ śarīrātsaṁprapaśyati (4.45)

sarvataḥ - everywhere; pāṇi – hand; pādaṁ - foot; taṁ - him; sarvato = sarvatah = in every direction; kṣi – eye; śiro = śirah = head; mukham – face; jīvo = jīvah = the individual spirit; niṣkrāntam – is displaced; ātmānaṁ - psyche; śarīrāt – from the body; saṁprapaśyati – perceives

It has hands and feet everywhere. It has eyes, heads and faces in every direction. The individual spirit perceives when the psyche is displaced from the body.

Analysis:

When the psyche is permanently displaced from a material body, people regard that as the death of the person. It is really the displacement of the person from the means of relating to the physical world. Having lost the physical means of sense perception, the individual spirit is left with its psychology only. This psyche has the form of a subtle body which resembles its last physical form.

Application:

The individual spirit has awesome powers, as if it had hands, feet, eyes, heads and faces in all direction. These energies are constrained and reduced when the spirit is linked to a physical body and to a low energy astral form.

The self can realize its glory if it segregates itself from the adjuncts like the intellect, memory and life force. Until it attains full liberation, its segregation from the psychic components occurs now and again. Thus it should improve the performance of the psychic components by energizing them with higher energy. This is done by pranaiama breath infusion techniques and by mystic mind shifting techniques.

Verse 46

स तदुत्सृज्य देहं स्वं धारयन्ब्रह्म केवलम्

आत्मानमालोकयति मनसा प्रहसन्निव

sa tadutsṛjya dehaṁ svaṁ dhārayanbrahma kevalam
ātmānamālokayati manasā prahasanniva (4.46)

sa – that one; tad = tat = that; utsṛjya – abandoning; dehaṁ - body; svaṁ - own; dhārayan – effortlessly linking through meditation; brahma – spiritual existence; kevalam – alone, segregated from contamination; ātmānam – self; ālokayati – perceives; manasā – by the mind; prahasan – smiling; niva = iva = as if

Abandoning the body, that one, using the mind, perceives the self, while effortlessly linking through meditation with only the spiritual existence, just as if the self were smiling at the accomplishment.

Analysis:

The release of the self from the fusion-oneness with material nature and with the psychic apparatus which links the self to nature, exposes the self to spiritual bliss consciousness which the ascetic compared to the self smiling to itself.

Application:

A great relief is felt by the self when it is freed from oneness with the psychic equipments which linked it forcibly to material nature. Its freedom from that is the instant realization of its spiritual status of sat-chit-ananda, reality-perception-bliss.

Verse 47

इदं सर्वरहस्यं ते मयोक्तं द्विजसत्तम

आपृच्छे साधयिष्यामि गच्छ शिष्य यथासुखम्

idaṁ sarvarahasyaṁ te mayoktaṁ dvijasattama
āpṛcche sādhayiṣyāmi gaccha śiṣya yathāsukham (4.47)

idaṁ - this; sarva – all, every bit; rahasyaṁ - confidential information; te – to you; mayoktaṁ = maya (by me) + uktam (was explained); dvijasattama - best of the trained ritualists; āpṛcche – obtaining permission; sādhayiṣyāmi – I will depart; gaccha – go; śiṣya – disciple; yathā – as; sukham - pleased

Every bit of this confidential information was explained by me to you, O best of the ritualists. Getting permission, I will depart. You too, my disciple, should go as you wish.

Analysis:

Kashyapa was fortunate to get this vital information from the advanced siddha. Now it was up to Kashyapa to put the disciplines into practice which would actuate in his psyche the sorting of the psychic components and assumption of freedom of the core-self.

Application:

The grace of the Supreme Being may come directly from Krishna or through an accomplished siddha. In either case, the reception of it is the initiation into the sensual disciplines and change in focus of the core self.

Verse 48

इत्युक्तः स तदा कृष्ण मया शिष्यो महातपाः

अगच्छत यथाकामं ब्राह्मणश्छिन्नसंशयः

ityuktaḥ sa tadā kṛṣṇa mayā śiṣyo mahātapāḥ
agacchata yathākāmaṁ brāhmaṇaśchinnasaṁśayaḥ (4.48)

ityuktaḥ = iti (thus) + uktah (was heard); sa – he, that one; tadā – then; kṛṣṇa – Krishna; mayā – by me; śiṣyo = śiṣyah = student; mahātapāḥ - performer of great penance; agacchata – went; yathā – as; kāmaṁ - desired; brāhmaṇaś = brāhmaṇah = ritual ascetic; chinnasaṁśayaḥ - one who removes uncertainty

Thus, it was heard by me, O Krishna, how that student who was a performer of great penance, went as he desired. He is a ritual ascetic who removes uncertainty.

Analysis:

Listening to stories of previous ascetics and their students gives a yogi faith in the process of attaining freedom from fusion with the psychic equipments which are the linchpin between the core self and the material world. These stories are very potent as a source of inspiration for those who want to escape the imprisonment of the core-self in the subtle body.

Application:

A yogi should develop confidence in divine grace. If he or she requires assistance or requires a special technique, that method will be shown either by a physical teacher or by someone in the astral existence. No yogi who is at the proper stage is left without a method of practice for advancement to the next stage.

Verse 49

वासुदेव उवाच

इत्युक्त्वा स तदा वाक्यं मां पार्थ द्विजपुंगवः

मोक्षधर्माश्रितः सम्यक्तत्रैवान्तरधीयत

vāsudeva uvāca
ityuktvā sa tadā vākyaṁ māṁ pārtha dvijapuṁgavaḥ
mokṣadharmāśritaḥ samyaktatraivāntaradhīyata (4.49)

vāsudeva – Krishna Vasudeva; uvāca – said; ityuktvā = iti (thus) + uktva (having lectured); sa – he; tadā – then; vākyaṁ - lecture; māṁ - to me; pārtha - son of Pṛthā; dvijapuṁgavaḥ - leader of the ritualists; mokṣa – liberation; dharma – righteous lifestyle; āśritaḥ - resorting to, assuming; samyak – perfectly; tatraivāntaradhīyata = tatra (there) + eva (so) + antaradhīyata - disappeared

Krishna Vasudeva said:

Then, O son of Pṛthā, that leader of the ritualists, having lectured to me perfectly about assuming the righteous lifestyle which yields liberation, disappeared right there.

Analysis:

When all is said and done, one must take up the austerities and meditation procedures which would yield segregation from the oneness the self is blighted with in a psyche which craves material bodies and the facilities such bodies enjoy in the gross cosmos. Until the self splits off from that fusion, it cannot realize itself all by itself. Thus it will never make the effort to change its predicament. It will continue with the conviction that its present psyche is itself and is a unity.

Application:

Divine grace is in a way, everything, and yet much is to be accomplished after a yogi is blessed with the assistance.

Verse 50

कच्चिदेतत्त्वया पार्थ श्रुतमेकाग्रचेतसा

तदापि हि रथस्थस्त्वं श्रुतवानेतदेव हि

kaccidetattvayā pārtha śrutamekāgracetasā
tadāpi hi rathasthastvaṁ śrutavānetadeva hi (4.50)

kaccid = I hope that; etat – this; tvayā – by you; pārtha - son of Pṛthā; śrutam – heard; ekāgra – singular focus; cetasā – mental focus; tadā - then; api – also; hi – indeed; ratha – chariot; sthas – sat; tvaṁ - you; śrutavān – heard; etad = etat = this; eva – so; hi - indeed

I hope that this was heard by you with singular mental focus, O son of Pṛthā. For while sitting on the chariot, you heard this just the same.

Analysis:

The information given by the advanced yogi to Kashyapa was the same instruction given to Arjuna just before the Battle of Kurukshetra under the title of buddhi yoga in chapter 2 and yoga in chapter 6 and elsewhere in the *Bhagavad Gītā*. The approach however is quite different.

Arjuna got the information as a prompt to cause him to complete duties as a member of a royal family, while Kashyapa got the knowledge upon request when he was ready to strive for complete freedom from mundane transmigrations.

Arjuna's condition of attachment to his family just before the war, seems to inhibit a serious quest for spiritual freedom. That vital impetus was imparted to him by Krishna on this occasion through the narration of the story of how Kashyapa came to be inspired with the knowledge and description of the process of liberation.

Application:

It is evident from this discourse that hearing about liberation alone is insufficient for causing a permanent change in the attitude of a living being. Speaking is the mission of the capable teacher but that is not everything. There should be a certain impetus for advancement in the nature of the disciple for the discourse to take full effect.

Prior to the battle of Kurukshetra, Arjuna was not in his right mind. He was attached to the relatives of his body and was biased in their corrupt interest. Even though Krishna snapped Arjuna out of that perplexity it still affected what Arjuna did with the information Krishna provided about yoga and liberation. This is serious. All yogis and devotees should take this discourse to heart and do some soul searching as to the why and wherefores of the desire for this spiritual information.

Arjuna's friendship with Krishna almost proved to be the hero's undoing. Arjuna was lucky that Krishna went to this extent to rescue him from laxness in the spiritual practice. Even a person as accomplished in karma yoga as Arjuna, came to this situation of losing touch with spiritual reality, so what can be said about others?

Those who feel that their devotion to Krishna will cover their defects in this regard should take a hard look at the situation Arjuna found himself in after the Battle of Kurukshetra. One should allow no teacher to fool one into thinking that a devotional relationship with Krishna is the guarantee of spiritual purity. After all how does one know if that devotion is really accepted by the divinity?

In the discourse to Uddhava, Krishna discussed the value of devotion to him as being reliant on its spiritedness (ūrjitā). Unless that impetus is operative in the life of the devotee to force the devotee to do what is necessary to implement these disciplines, the devotion will not serve the ultimate purpose of situating the devotee on the spiritual plane where Krishna and his parallel divinities reside.

na sādhayati māṁ yogo na sāṅkhyam dharma uddhava
na svādhyāyas tapas tyāgo yathā bhaktir mamorjitā

Neither yoga practice, nor Sāṅkhya philosophical analysis, nor righteous duty, nor Vedic study, nor austerity, nor giving up results, would attract Me, as much as spirited devotion. (Uddhava Gītā 9.20)

An austere attitude is relevant and it has to be intense (tīvra) or the devotee will not finish the required austerities, the result of which will be laxness and failure to attain the spiritual provinces.

evaṁ bṛhad-vrata-dharo brāhmaṇo 'gnir iva jvalan
mad-bhaktas tīvra-tapasā dagdha-karmāśayo 'malaḥ

Thus, the brahmin who maintains the celibate vow, is like a blazing fire. As a person who is freed from impurities, whose tendency for implicating activities is burnt by the intense austerities, he becomes devoted to Me. (Uddhava Gītā 12.36)

Verse 51

नैतत्पार्थ सुविज्ञेयं व्यामिश्रेणेति मे मतिः

नरेणाकृतसंज्ञेन विदग्धेनाकृतात्मना

naitatpārtha suvijñeyaṁ vyāmiśreṇeti me matiḥ
nareṇākṛtasaṁjñena vidagdhenākṛtātmanā (4.51)

naitat = na (not) + etat (this); pārtha - son of Pṛthā; suvijñeyaṁ - not easily integrated; vyāmiśreṇeti = vyāmiśreṇa (by singular mental focus) + iti (thus); me – me; matiḥ - dull-witted person; nareṇākṛtasaṁjñena = nareṇa (by a person) + ākṛta (did not accomplish) + saṁjñena = (with experience); vidagdhenākṛtātmanā = vidagdhenā (by corruption) + kṛt (habituated)+ ātmanā (psyche)

O son of Pṛthā, this is not easily integrated by one who is inattentive or dull-witted, or by a person who did not accomplish this experience, or by one whose psyche is habitually corrupted.

Analysis:

Certain people are exempt, even certain yogis or devotees.

Application:

Self critique is the way to analyze one's condition but it must be done in the kriya yoga practice when the self is able to turn its attention upon itself. This is the reverse of sensual life where one seeks to correct others and to convert others to spiritual practice.

The power of the self is not even sufficient to save itself. Hence the effort to convert others and to make others into spiritual stalwarts is ludicrous. When the ingredient of divine grace is added to the spiritual power of the self, then we get the sufficiency that could adjust the situation of the self.

Verse 52

सुरहस्यमिदं प्रोक्तं देवानां भरतर्षभ

कच्चिन्नेदं श्रुतं पार्थ मर्त्येनान्येन केनचित्

surahasyamidaṁ proktaṁ devānāṁ bharatarṣabha
kaccinnedaṁ śrutaṁ pārtha martyenānyena kenacit (4.52)

surahasyam – a secret; idaṁ - of this; proktaṁ - explained; devānāṁ - of the supernatural rulers in the celestial world; bharatarṣabha – best of the Bharatas; kaccin – O; nedaṁ = na (never) + idam (this); śrutaṁ - heard; pārtha - son of Pṛthā; martyenānyena = martyena (concerning the world of short life-span) + anyena (by any other); kenacit - anyone

O best of the Bharatas, this which I explained is a secret even among the supernatural rulers in the celestial world. Son of Pṛthā, this was never heard by any other person in this world of short life-span.

Analysis:

This discourse of the *Anu Gītā* is so special that it is even more concentrated, specialized and directed than the *Bhagavad*

Gītā. It is intended to provide the fuel for the fire of purification of the psyche which will result in migration to the exclusive spiritual places. Krishna said that even the deities in the higher astral regions consider this information to be secretive and very special. Before the siddha recited this discourse to Krishna, it was never mentioned to anyone on the earth.

Application:

The deities in the celestial world where earth-bound souls go for a sojourn in paradise, are distracted by their heavenly realms. They are aware of this information of the* Anu Gītā *but they cannot put it into practice because they lack the forceful impetus to complete the necessary austerities which would cause a severance of the cozy relationship between the core-self and the psychic components which allow them to perceive the celestial world.

Verse 53

न ह्येतच्छ्रोतुमर्होऽन्यो मनुष्यस्त्वामृतेऽनघ

नैतदद्य सुविज्ञेयं व्यामिश्रेणान्तरात्मना

na hyetacchrotumarho'nyo manuṣyastvāmṛte'nagha
naitadadya suvijñeyaṁ vyāmiśreṇāntarātmanā (4.53)

na – no; hyetacchrotum = hi (indeed) + etat (this) + śtrotum (to hear); arho'nyo = arhah (one who deserves) + anyah (other person); manuṣyas = manuṣyah = person; tvām – you; ṛte – besides, except; 'nagha= anagha (faultless one); naitad = na (no) + etad (this); adya – now; suvijñeyaṁ - integration; vyāmiśreṇāntar = vyāmiśreṇa (singular mental focus) + antar (internal); ātmanā - psyche

O faultless one, there is no person besides you who deserves to hear this. Nor is it easily integrated by one whose internal psyche has no singular mental focus.

Analysis:

Krishna began this discourse by condemning Arjuna's laxness with the information and revelation of the *Bhagavad*

Gītā. Then Krishna appraised Arjuna afresh, when Arjuna got seriously interested after hearing of Kashyapa and the perfected siddha.

Even if one is a devotee, if one does not have the internal singular mental focus, one cannot complete this practice. Stated in plain terms, one has to master purity-of-the-psyche yoga to subjugate the components of consciousness. There is no way around this. There was no way for Arjuna. And there is no way for anyone else either.

One may goof around as a devotee of Krishna for many millions of years, and still one will never reach the spiritual places if one does not break up the unity of the psyche to segregate the core-self and bring the accessory psychic organs to order. Each person must develop the required determination individually. There were others listening to this discourse between Arjuna and Krishna, and still Krishna singled out Arjuna as the person who qualified for this. Liberation is an individual attainment. Ideas of collective salvation are a fool's fantasy.

Application:

Even though Arjuna was the special person to hear this, it is by Krishna's arrangement that this writer translated this from the Sanskrit. This means that anyone who reads this might qualify, provided the singular mental focus and the affinity for Krishna is developed in that person.

It was by the grace of Rishi Singh Gherwal who is now long departed, that the writer translated and commented on this **Anu Gītā**. ***I read this text before but I did not see everything which was revealed to me when Rishi inspired this information into my mind. It is amazing how concentrated this discourse is. It is a wonder that many of the spiritual lineages from Krishna ignore this vital information. Michael Beloved (Madhvācārya dās) is honored to have his name affiliated with this special discourse.***

Verse 54

क्रियावद्भिर्हि कौन्तेय देवलोकः समावृतः

न चैतदिष्टं देवानां मर्त्यै रूपनिवर्तनम्

kriyāvadbhirhi kaunteya devalokaḥ samāvṛtaḥ
na caitadiṣṭaṁ devānāṁ martyai rūpanivartanam (4.54)

kriyāvadbhir = kriyāvadbhih = by those who perform approved social actions; hi – indeed; kaunteya - son of Kuntī; devalokaḥ - celestial world with its deities; samāvṛtaḥ - saturated; na – not; caitad = ca (and) + etad (this); iṣṭaṁ - desired; devānāṁ - of the deities, supernatural officials; martyai – short duration; rūpa – form, body; nivartanam - cessation

O son of Kuntī, the celestial world with its deities is saturated with persons who performed approved social actions. The cessation of these short-duration bodies is not desired by those supernatural officials.

Analysis:

The deities of the mundane paradises in the upper part of the astral world, are really against the progression of humanity. By this we mean the spiritual progression. They encourage pious activities which are social involvements which lubricate human society, but spiritual clarity is not their interest.

If one feels that any of these deities will sponsor a spiritual enlightenment, that person will be disappointed because it will never happen. One prisoner who cannot free himself cannot free any other. One who is addicted to a vice is disinclined in helping anyone to break the tendency.

Application:

From the deities of the astral paradises, human beings will get every assistance they need to perpetuate mundane social affairs, but they will never get the impetus to complete the spiritual practice which causes assumption of full spiritual existence. Association with the siddhas is the only way to get any hint of what we should do to segregate ourselves from the perception equipments which keep us time bound.

Krishna could well have shown Arjuna the Universal Form and the Four-Handed Divine Form again but instead he cited the instruction given by a person who achieved spiritual perfection in the failsafe way. Let us make a note of that!

Verse 55

परा हि सा गतिः पार्थ यत्तद्ब्रह्म सनातनम्

यत्रामृतत्वं प्राप्नोति त्यक्त्वा दुःखं सदा सुखी

parā hi sā gatiḥ pārtha yattadbrahma sanātanam
yatrāmṛtatvaṁ prāpnoti tyaktvā duḥkhaṁ sadā sukhī (4.55)

parā – highest; hi – indeed; sā – that; gatiḥ - objective; pārtha - son of Pṛthā; yat – which; tad = tat = that; brahma – spiritual existence; sanātanam – eternal; yatrāmṛtatvaṁ = yatra (where) + amṛtatvaṁ (immortality); prāpnoti – achieves; tyaktvā – abandoning; duḥkhaṁ - misery; sadā – always; sukhī – one who is happy

That objective is the highest, O son of Pṛthā, which concerns the eternal spiritual existence, whereby abandoning the miseries, one achieves immortality and is happy always.

Analysis:

It is simply a matter of requiring of the self, its freedom from oneness with the accessory psychic equipments which perpetually keep it time bound and hell-bent on continuing in the mundane transmigrations.

Application:

It takes a special person, one as perceptive as Arjuna, to understand our dire predicament in this material creation. Arjuna failed to keep in touch with the spiritual information and experience he was graced with before the battle. Nevertheless he knew that there was something terribly amiss with all phases, the good and the bad, of this material existence.

Verse 56

एवं हि धर्ममास्थाय येऽपि स्युः पापयोनयः

स्त्रियो वैश्यास्तथा शूद्रास्तेऽपि यान्ति परां गतिम्

evaṁ hi dharmamāsthāya ye'pi syuḥ pāpayonayaḥ
striyo vaiśyāstathā śūdrāste'pi yānti parāṁ gatim (4.56)

evaṁ - thus; hi – indeed; dharmam – ascetic righteous lifestyle; āsthāya – assuming; ye – the; 'pi = api = even so; syuḥ - are; pāpayonayaḥ - persons from faulty families; striyo = striyah = woman; vaiśyās – commercially-minded, money-hungry persons; tathā – as well; śūdrās – laborers; te – they; 'pi = api = also; yānti – achieve; parāṁ - supreme; gatim - destination

Assuming this ascetic righteous lifestyle, even persons from faulty families, women, as well as commercially-minded people, even laborers can achieve the supreme destination.

Analysis:

Generally, people from faulty families, females, persons who are obsessed with wealth and laborers, are so preoccupied with aspects of the material creation, that they have no time to think deeply of this world as a dead-end. The terminal conclusions which an ascetic may conceive of are far from their minds. They prefer to patch up the instances of inconvenience which are inflicted by material nature.

However Krishna declared that any of these persons could reach the supreme destination if somehow they were to turn about and assume this ascetic posture.

Application:

No deity stands in the way of a living entity's attainment of full spirituality. It is the entity's habits which prevent it from adopting a segregation from that which keeps it fused into this illusory existence. Thus at any stage, from any position, a living entity can strive for and attain freedom. There is no barrier except the fusion with a psychology which is glued to material nature.

Verse 57

किं पुनर्ब्राह्मणाः पार्थ क्षत्रिया वा बहुश्रुताः

स्वधर्मरतयो नित्यं ब्रह्मलोकपरायणाः

kiṁ punarbrāhmaṇāḥ pārtha kṣatriyā vā bahuśrutāḥ svadharmaratayo nityaṁ brahmalokaparāyaṇāḥ (4.57)

kiṁ - what; punar – again; brāhmaṇāḥ - trained ascetic ritualists; pārtha - son of Pṛthā; kṣatriyā – administrative rulers; vā – or; bahuśrutāḥ - one who read many texts; svadharma – one's approved duties; ratayo = ratayah = one who is committed; nityaṁ - eternal; brahma – spiritual; loka – world; parāyaṇāḥ - eagerly aspiring for

What of the trained ascetic ritualists, O son of Pṛthā, or the well-read administrative rulers who are committed to their approved duties, and who eagerly aspire for the eternal spiritual world?

Analysis:

If any spirit in any social or sexual category can attain freedom from material existence, then for certain the trained ritualists and the well-read administrators are capable of it. But of course they are mostly addicted to these transmigrations, which make them resistant to deeper insight.

These entities might be compared to condemned officials who were caught in a corruption scheme and who were sentenced to death. What can be said about them, except that they should have known better.

Application:

When one becomes a yogi, one becomes committed to abandon the social designations. A yogi has no use for social status which is just a nuisance affiliation. It is time consuming and adds up to zero in the end.

One should scale down the status, get humble by realizing that if anything, one is just a stooge of the senses. Then one should slowly but surely build up resistance and when it is sufficient declare a full revolt against material nature and the psychic adjuncts which are aligned against the core-self.

It is within the psyche that the war must take place between the self and its internal enemies. Only a crazy person would desire unity with enemies which are hell-bent on keeping the self bound as a slave of material nature.

Verse 58

हेतुमच्चैतदुद्दिष्टमुपायाश्चास्य साधने

सिद्धेः फलं च मोक्षश्च दुःखस्य च विनिर्णयः

अतः परं सुखं त्वन्यत्किं नु स्याद्भरतर्षभ

hetumaccaitaduddiṣṭamupāyāścāsya sādhane
siddheḥ phalaṁ ca mokṣaśca duḥkhasya ca vinirṇayaḥ
ataḥ paraṁ sukhaṁ tvanyatkiṁ nu syādbharatarṣabha (4.58)

hetumac = hetumat = due reason; caitad = ca (and) + etat (this); uddiṣṭam – stated; upāyāś = upāyāh = means, process; cāsya = ca (and) + asya (of this); sādhane – in the practice; siddheḥ - of the accomplishment; phalaṁ - result; ca – and; mokṣaś = mokṣah = liberation; ca – and; duḥkhasya – of misery; ca – and; vinirṇayaḥ - conclusion; ataḥ - therefore; paraṁ - superior; sukhaṁ - happiness; tvanyat = tu (but) + anyat (other besides); kiṁ - what; nu - for sure; syād = syat = it is; bharatarṣabha – leader of the Bharatas

This was stated with due reason as well as the process in the practice for attaining this, the results of the accomplishment, liberation and the conclusion about misery. Therefore, O leader of the Bharatas, there is no other happiness which is superior to this. That is for sure.

Verese 59

श्रुतवाञ्श्रद्दधानश्च पराक्रान्तश्च पाण्डव

यः परित्यजते मर्त्यो लोकतन्त्रमसारवत्

एतैरुपायैः स क्षिप्रं परां गतिमवाप्नुयात्

śrutavāñśraddadhānaśca parākrāntaśca pāṇḍava
yaḥ parityajate martyo lokatantramasāravat (4.59)
etairupāyaiḥ sa kṣipraṁ parāṁ gatimavāpnuyāt

śrutavāñ – one who is educated; śraddadhānaś = śraddadhānah = one who is confident; ca – and; parākrāntaś = parākrāntah = one who is energetic in the pursuit; ca – and; pāṇḍava – son of Paṇḍu; yaḥ - who; parityajate – discards; martyo = martyah = person with a short life-span; loka – world; tantram – course; asāravat – unsubstantial, meaningless; etair = etaih = by these; upāyaiḥ - by methods; sa – he; kṣipraṁ - soon; parāṁ - supreme; gatim – destination; avāpnuyāt - achieves

One who is educated, one who is confident, one who is energetic in the pursuit of this, that person with a short life-span, who discards as being meaningless the course of this world, O son of Paṇḍu, soon achieves by these methods, the supreme destination.

Verse 60

एतावदेव वक्तव्यं नातो भूयोऽस्ति किंचन

षण्मासान्नित्ययुक्तस्य योगः पार्थ प्रवर्तते

etāvadeva vaktavyaṁ nāto bhūyo'sti kiṁcana
ṣaṇmāsānnityayuktasya yogaḥ pārtha pravartate (4.60)

etāvad = etāvat = this; eva – so; vaktavyaṁ - what is said; nāto = na (not) + atah (thus); bhūyo = bhūyah = being; 'sti = asti = is; kiṁcana – anything; ṣaṇ - six; māsān – months; nitya – consistently, regularly; yuktasya – of proficiency; yogaḥ - yoga; pārtha – son of PÃhā; pravartate - accomplishing

This is all that is to be said. There is nothing beyond this. O son of Pṛthā, one who practices proficiently and consistently for six months accomplishes this yoga.

END

Index to Verses

D

E

F

U, V

W, X, Y, Z

Index to Analysis and Application

T

X,Y,Z

About the Author

Michael Beloved (Yogi *Madhvāchārya)* took his current body in 1951 in Guyana. In 1965, while living in Trinidad, he instinctively began doing yoga postures and tried to make sense of the supernatural side of life.

Later in 1970, in the Philippines, he approached a Martial Arts Master named Mr. Arthur Beverford. He explained to the teacher that he was seeking a yoga instructor. Mr. Beverford identified himself as an advanced disciple of Śrī Rishi Singh Gherwal, an astanga yoga master.

Beverford taught the traditional Astanga Yoga with stress on postures, attentive breathing and brow chakra centering meditation. In 1972, Michael entered the Denver Colorado Ashram of kuṇḍalinī yoga Master Śrī Harbhajan Singh. There he took instruction in bhastrika pranayama and its application to yoga postures. He was supervised mostly by Yogi Bhajan's disciple named Prem Kaur.

In 1979 Michael formally entered the disciplic succession of the Brahmā-Madhava-Gaudiya Sampradaya through Swāmī Kirtanananda, who was a prominent sannyasi disciple of the Great Vaishnava Authority Śrī Swāmī Bhaktivedanta Prabhupada, the exponent of devotion to Sri Krishna.

However, yoga has a mystic side to it, thus Michael took training and teaching empowerment from several spiritual masters of different aspects of spiritual development. This is consistent with Śrī Krishna's advice to Arjuna in the Bhagavad Gītā:

tad viddhi praṇipātena paripraśnena sevayā
upadekṣyanti te jñānaṁ jñāninas tattva darśinaḥ

This you ought to know. By submitting yourself as a student, by asking questions, by serving as requested, the perceptive, reality-conversant teachers will teach you the knowledge. (Bhagavad Gītā 4.34)

Most of the instructions Michael received were given in the astral world. On that side of existence, his most prominent teachers were Śrī Swāmī Shivananda of Rishikesh, Yogiraj Swāmī Vishnudevananda, Śrī Bābāji Mahasaya - the master of the masters of Kriyā Yoga, Śrīla Yogeshwarananda of Gangotri - the master of the masters of Rāj Yoga (spiritual clarity), and Siddha Swāmī Nityananda the Brahma Yoga authority.

Śrī Rishi Singh Gherwal inspired this translation, analysis and application of the Anu Gītā into the mind of the author. It is the compressed essence of the *Bhagavad Gītā* with no frills, no religious overtones, no Krishna magic to induce anyone to do as told by the divine will. This concerns the individual's progress from the material world into the spiritual atmosphere once and for all.

Publications

English Series

Bhagavad Gita English

Anu Gita English

Markandeya Samasya English

Yoga Sutras English

Uddhava Gita English

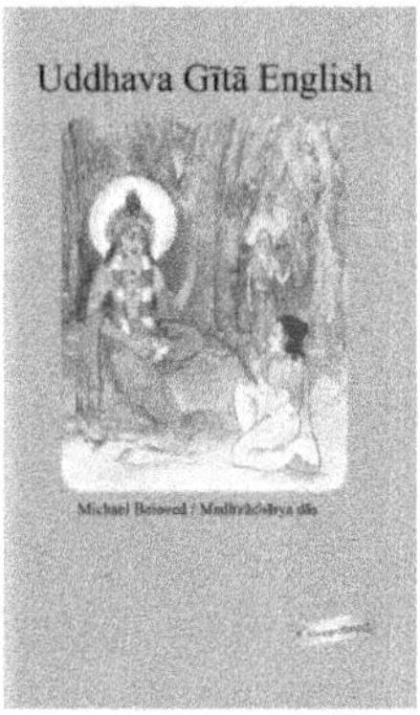

These are in 21st Century English, very precise and exacting. Many Sanskrit words which were considered untranslatable into a Western language are rendered in precise, expressive and modern English, due to the English language becoming the world's universal means of concept conveyance.

Three of these books are instructions from Krishna. ***In Bhagavad Gita English*** *and* ***Anu Gita English****, the instructions were for Arjuna. In the* ***Uddhava Gita English,*** *it was for Uddhava. Bhagavad Gita and Anu Gita are extracted from the Mahabharata. Uddhava Gita was extracted from the 11th Canto of the Srimad Bhagavatam (Bhagavata Purana). One of these books, the* ***Markandeya Samasya English*** *is about Krishna, as described by Yogi Markandeya, who survived the cosmic collapse and reached a divine child in whose transcendental body, the collapsed world was existing. Another of these books, the* ***Yoga Sutras English,*** *is the detailed syllabus about yoga practice.*

My suggestion is that you read ***Bhagavad Gita English****, the* ***Anu Gita English, the Markandeya Samasya English,*** *the* ***Yoga Sutras English*** *and lastly the* ***Uddhava Gita English****, which is much more complicated and detailed.*

For each of these books we have at least one commentary, which is published separately. Thus your particular interest can be researched further in the commentaries.

The smallest of these commentaries and perhaps the simplest is the one for the Anu Gita. We published its commentary as the Anu Gita Explained. The Bhagavad Gita explanations were published in three distinct targeted commentaries. The first is Bhagavad Gita Explained, which sheds lights on how people in the time of Krishna and Arjuna regarded the information and applied it. Bhagavad Gita is an exposition of the application of yoga practice to cultural activities, which is known in the Sanskrit language as karma yoga.

Interestingly, Bhagavad Gita was spoken on a battlefield just before one of the greatest battles in the ancient world. A warrior, Arjuna, lost his wits and had no idea that he could apply his training in yoga to political dealings. Krishna, his charioteer, lectured on the spur of the moment to give Arjuna the skill of using yoga proficiency in cultural dealings including how to deal with corrupt officials on a battlefield.

The second commentary is the Kriya Yoga Bhagavad Gita. This clears the air about Krishna's information on the science of kriya yoga, showing that its techniques are clearly described free of charge to anyone who takes the time to read Bhagavad Gita. Kriya yoga concerns the battlefield which is the psyche of the living being. The internal war and the mental and emotional forces which are hostile to self-realization are dealt with in the kriya yoga practice.

The third commentary is the Brahma Yoga Bhagavad Gita. This shows what Krishna had to say outright and what he hinted about which concerns the brahma yoga practice, a mystic process for those who mastered kriya yoga.

There is one commentary for the **Markandeya Samasya English**. *The title of that publication is Krishna Cosmic Body.*

There are two commentaries to the Yoga Sutras. One is the Yoga Sutras of Patanjali and the other is the Meditation Expertise. These give detailed explanations of the process of Yoga.

For the Uddhava Gita, we published the Uddhava Gita Explained. This is a large book and requires concentration and study for integration of the information. Of the books which deal with transcendental topics, my opinion is that the discourse between Krishna and Uddhava has the complete information about the realities in existence. This book is the one which removes massive existential ignorance.

Meditation Series

Meditation Pictorial
Meditation Expertise
Core-Self Discovery

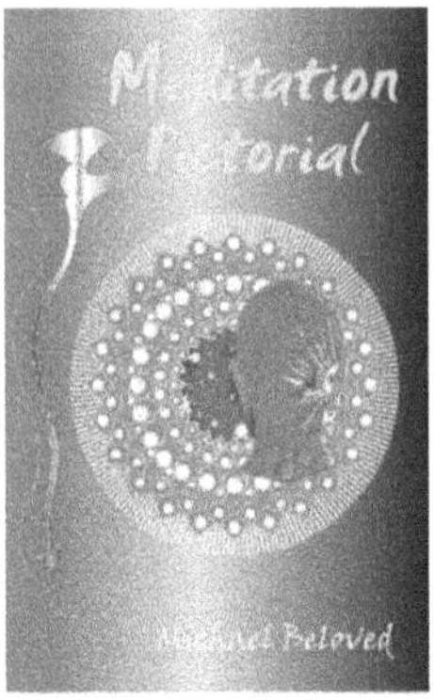

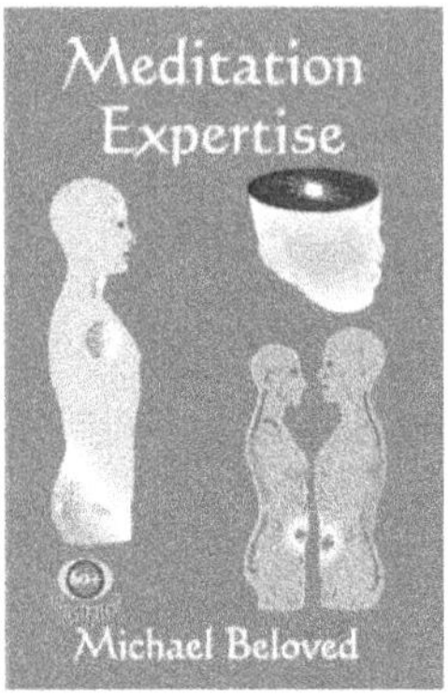

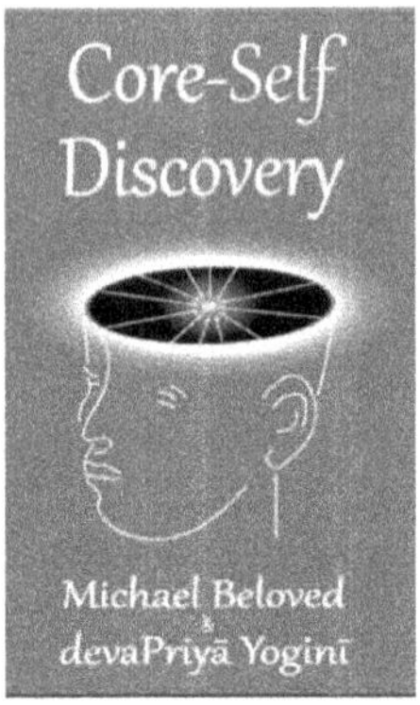

The specialty of these books is the mind diagrams which profusely illustrate what is written. This shows exactly what one has to do mentally to develop and then sustain a meditation practice.

In the **Meditation Pictorial**, one is shown how to develop psychic insight, a feature without which meditation is imagination and visualization, without any mystic experience per se.

In the **Meditation Expertise**, one is shown how to corral one's practice to bring it in line with the classic syllabus of yoga which Patanjali lays out as the ashtanga yoga eight-staged practice.

In **Core-Self Discovery**, one is taken though the course of pratyahar sensual energy withdrawal which is the 5th stage of yoga in the Patanjali ashtanga eight-process complete system of yoga practice. These events lead to the discovery of a core-self which is surrounded by psychic organs in the head of the subtle body. This product has a DVD component for teachers and self-teaching students.

These books are profusely illustrated with mind diagrams showing the components of psychic consciousness and the inner design of the subtle body.

Explained Series

Bhagavad Gita Explained
Uddhava Gita Explained
Anu Gita Explained

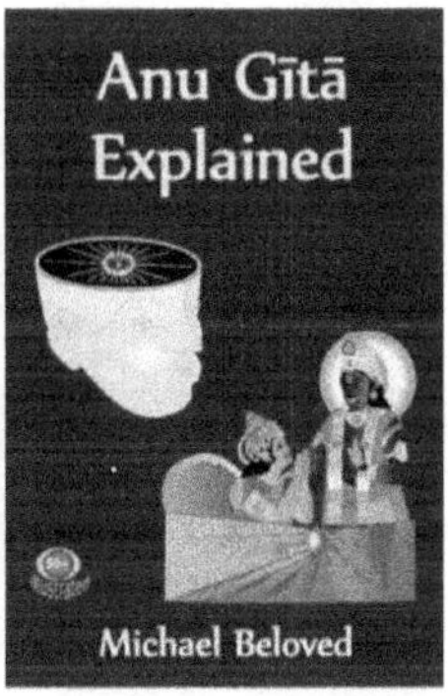

The specialty of these books is that they are free of missionary intentions, cult tactics and philosophical distortion. Instead of using these books to add credence to a philosophy, meditation process, belief or plea for followers, I spread the information out so that a reader can look through this literature and freely take or leave anything as desired.

When Krishna stressed himself as God, I stated that. When Krishna laid no claims for supremacy, I showed that. The reader is left to form an independent opinion about the validity of the information and the credibility of Krishna.

There is a difference in the discourse with Arjuna in the Bhagavad Gita and the one with Uddhava in the Uddhava Gita. In fact these two books may appear to contradict each other. In the Bhagavad Gita, Krishna pressured Arjuna to complete social duties. In the Uddhava Gita, Krishna insisted that Uddhava should abandon the same.

The Anu Gita is not as popular as the Bhagavad Gita but it is the conclusion of that text. Anu means what is to follow, what proceeds. In this discourse, an anxious Arjuna request that Krishna should repeat the Bhagavad Gita and again show His supernatural and divine forms.

However Krishna refuses to do so and chastises Arjuna for being a disappointment in forgetting what was revealed. Krishna then cites a celestial yogi, a near-perfected being, who explained the process of transmigration in vivid detail.

Commentaries

Yoga Sutras of Patanjali
Meditation Expertise
Krishna Cosmic Body
Anu Gita Explained
Bhagavad Gita Explained
Kriya Yoga Bhagavad Gita
Brahma Yoga Bhagavad Gita
Uddhava Gita Explained

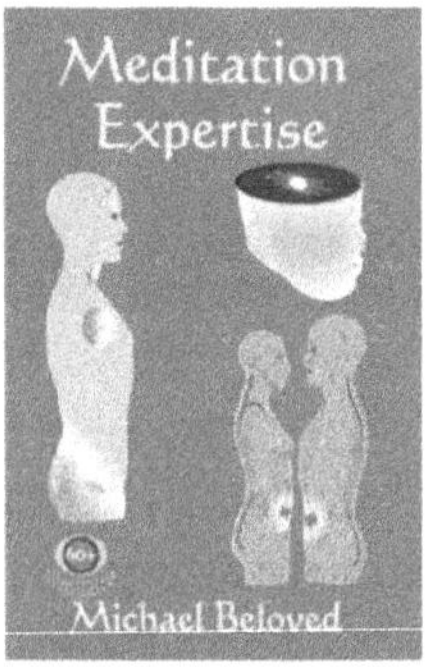

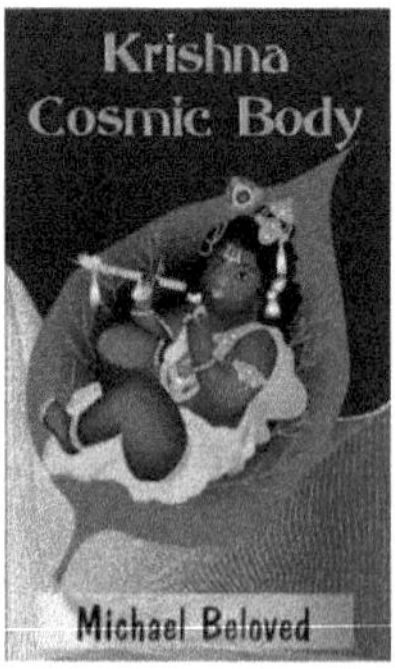

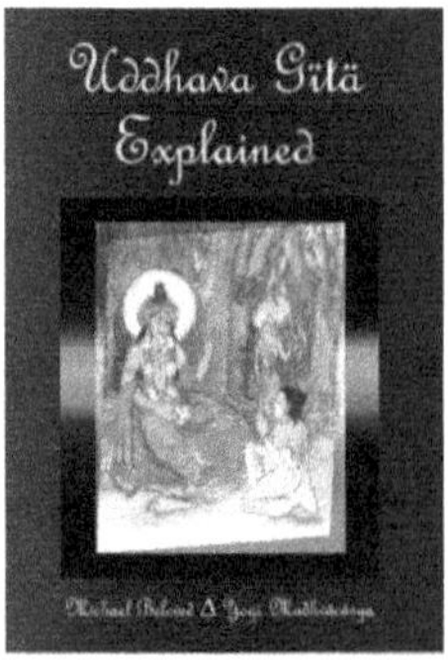

Yoga Sutras of Patanjali is the globally acclaimed text book of yoga. This has detailed expositions of yoga techniques. Many kriya techniques are vividly described in the commentary.

Meditation Expertise is an analysis and application of the Yoga Sutras. This book is loaded with illustrations and has detailed explanations of secretive advanced meditation techniques which are called kriyas in the Sanskrit language.

Krishna Cosmic Body is a narrative commentary on the Markandeya Samasya portion of the Aranyaka Parva of the Mahabharata. This is the detailed description of the dissolution of the world, as experienced by the great yogin Markandeya who transcended the cosmic deity, Brahma, and reached Brahma's source who is the divine infant, Krishna.

Anu Gita Explained is a detailed explanation of how we endure many material bodies in the course of transmigrating through various life-forms. This is a discourse between Krishna and Arjuna. Arjuna requested of Krishna a display of the Universal Form and a repeat narration of the Bhagavad Gita but Krishna declined and explained what a siddha perfected being told the Yadu family about the sequence of existences one endures and the systematic flow of those lives at the convenience of material nature.

Bhagavad Gita Explained shows what was said in the Gita without religious overtones and sectarian biases.

Kriya Yoga Bhagavad Gita shows the instructions for those who are doing kriya yoga.

Brahma Yoga Bhagavad Gita shows the instructions for those who are doing brahma yoga.

Uddhava Gita Explained shows the instructions to Uddhava which are more advanced than the ones given to Arjuna.

Bhagavad Gita is an instruction for applying the expertise of yoga in the cultural field. This is why the process taught to Arjuna is called karma yoga which means karma + yoga or cultural activities done with a yogic demeanor.

Uddhava Gita is an instruction for apply the expertise of yoga to attaining spiritual status. This is why it is explains jnana yoga and bhakti yoga in detail. Jnana yoga is using mystic skill for knowing the spiritual part of existence. Bhakti yoga is for developing affectionate relationships with divine beings.

Karma yoga is for negotiating the social concerns in the material world and therefore it is inferior to bhakti yoga which concerns negotiating the social concerns in the spiritual world.

This world has a social environment and the spiritual world has one too.

Right now Uddhava Gita is the most advanced informative spiritual book on the planet. There is nothing anywhere which is superior to it or which goes into so much detail as it. It verified that historically Krishna is the most advanced human being to ever have left literary instructions on this planet. Even Patanjali Yoga Sutras which I translated and gave an application for in my book, **Meditation Expertise**, does not go as far as the Uddhava Gita.

Some of the information of these two books is identical but while the Yoga Sutras are concerned with the personal spiritual emancipation (kaivalyam) of the individual spirits, the Uddhava Gita explains that and also explains the situations in the spiritual universes.

Bhagavad Gita is from the *Mahabharata* which is the history of the Pandavas. Arjuna, the student of the Gita, is one of the Pandavas brothers. He was in a social hassle and did not know how to apply yoga expertise to solve it. Krishna gave him a crash-course on the battlefield about that.

Uddhava Gita is from the *Srimad Bhagavatam (Bhagavata Purana),* which is a history of the incarnations of Krishna. Uddhava was a relative of Krishna. He was concerned about the situation of the deaths of many of his relatives but Krishna diverted Uddhava's attention to the practice of yoga for the purpose of successfully migrating to the spiritual environment.

Specialty

These books are based on the author's experiences in meditation, yoga practice and participation in spiritual groups:

Spiritual Master
sex you!
Sleep ***Paralysis***
Astral Projection
Masturbation Psychic Details

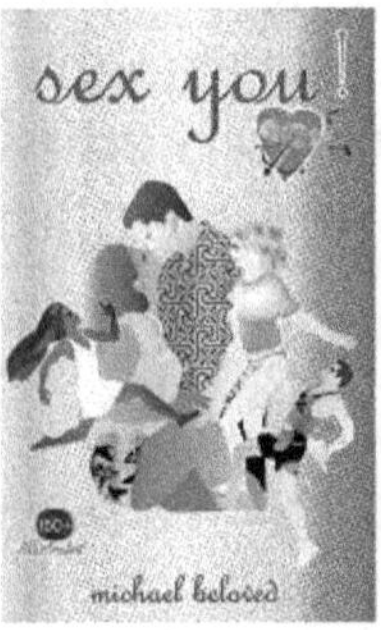

In **Spiritual Master**, Michael draws from experience with gurus or with their senior students. His contact with astral gurus is rated. He walks you through the avenue of gurus showing what you should do and what you should not do, so as to gain proficiency in whatever area of spirituality the guru has proficiency.

sex you! is a masterpiece about the adventures of an individual spirit's passage through the parents' psyches. The conversion of a departed soul into a sexual urge is described. The transit from the afterlife to residency in the emotions of the parents is detailed. This is about sex and you; learn about how much of you comprises the romantic energy of your would-be parents!

Sleep Paralysis clears misconceptions so that one can see what sleep paralysis is and what frightening astral experience occurs while the paralysis is being experienced. This disempowerment has great value in giving you confidence that you can and do exist even if you are unable to operate the physical body. The implication is that one can exist apart from and will survive the loss of the material body.

Astral Projection details experiences Michael had even in childhood, where he assumed incorrectly that everyone was astrally conversant. He discusses the life force psychic mechanism which operates the sleep-wake cycle of the physical form, and which budgets energy into the separated astral form which determines if the individual will have dream recall or no objective awareness during the projections. Astral travel happens on every occasion when the physical body sleeps. What is missing in awareness is the observer status while the astral body is separated.

Masturbation Psychic Details is a surprise presentation which relates what happens on the psychic plane during a masturbation event. This does not tackle moral issues or even addictions but shows the involvement of memory and the sure but hidden subconscious mind which operates many features of the psyche irrespective of the desire or approval of the self-conscious personality.

Online Resources

Visit The Website And Forum

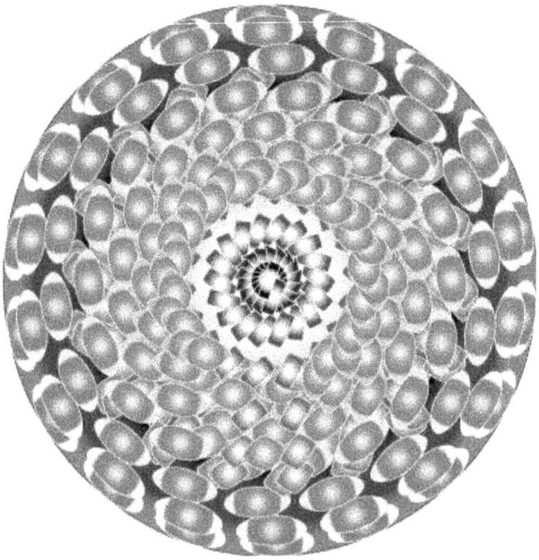

Email:	michaelbelovedbooks@gmail.com axisnexus@gmail.com
Website Forum:	michaelbeloved.com inselfyoga.com

www.ingramcontent.com/pod-product-compliance
Lightning Source LLC
Chambersburg PA
CBHW072338090426
42741CB00012B/2833
9780983381792